Keynes and Friedman on Laissez-Faire and Planning

The 2008 crisis has revived debates on the relevance of laissez-faire, and thus on the role of the State in a modern economy. This volume offers a new exploration of the writings of Keynes and Friedman on this topic, highlighting not only the clear points of opposition between them, but also the places in which their concerns were shared.

This volume argues that the parallel currently made with the 1929 financial crisis and the way the latter turned into the Great Depression sheds new light on the proper economic policy to be conducted in both the short and the long run in a monetary economy. In light of the recent revival in appreciation for Keynes' ideas, Rivot investigates what both Keynes and Friedman had to say on key issues, including their respective interpretations of both the 1929 crisis and the Great Depression, their advocacy of the proper employment policy and the theoretical underpinnings of the latter. The book asks which lessons should be learnt from the 1930s? And what is the relevance of Keynes' and Friedman's respective pleas for today? Through this exploration, we are able to see that, at the theoretical level, in some ways Keynes and Friedman shared a common approach to the functioning of a monetary economy. At the policy level too they seemed to have complementary lessons to offer us in regard to stabilisation policies, despite ideological backgrounds that seem at first sight to present an insurmountable barrier to any comparison between the two authors.

Sylvie Rivot is Assistant Professor at BETA-*Theme*, University of Strasbourg, France.

Routledge studies in the history of economics

Keynes and Friedman on Laissez-Faire and Planning

Where to draw the line?

Sylvie Rivot

Routledge
Taylor & Francis Group

LONDON AND NEW YORK

First published 2013
by Routledge
2 Park Square, Milton Park, Abingdon, Oxon OX14 4RN

Simultaneously published in the USA and Canada
by Routledge
711 Third Avenue, New York, NY 10017

Routledge is an imprint of the Taylor & Francis Group, an informa business

British Library Cataloguing in Publication Data
A catalogue record for this book is available from the British Library

Library of Congress Cataloging in Publication Data
A catalog record has been requested for this book

ISBN: 978-0-415-66676-3 (hbk)
ISBN: 978-0-203-76709-2 (ebk)

Typeset in Times New Roman
by Wearset Ltd, Boldon, Tyne and Wear

Printed and bound in the United States of America by Publishers Graphics, LLC on sustainably sourced paper.

L'avenir dure longtemps
[The future lasts forever]
Louis Althusser

Contents

Acknowledgements

My first thanks go to Bob Dimand and to Thomas Sutton, who has now joined the criminology department of Routledge. Without Bob Dimand's initial suggestion a long time ago to undertake this project and without Thomas Sutton's kind query, I would not have had the opportunity to write this book.

I also wish to thank Emily Kindleysides and Simon Holt at Routledge for their trust and their professional work.

Many ideas of this book have been presented to conferences of the European Society for the History of Economic Thought, the History of Economic Society as well as the French Association Charles Gide pour l'Étude de la Pensée Économique. I am grateful to the colleagues at those sessions who provided comments and critiques to the papers that originated the book project.

Over the past years, I have benefited from the strong support of Claude Diebolt (BETA, University of Strasbourg) and of Patrick Rondé (GRAICO, University of Mulhouse), the directors of the labs to which I belong. I am also indebted to my colleague and learned friend Laurent Grimal at the head of my department who carefully provided me with plenty of time and coped with all kind of difficulties, which allowed me to be kept fixed to my project during this time. Herrade Igersheim is the other colleague and learned friend, much more *micro* than me, to whom I am indebted.

I am deeply grateful to Pascal Bridel, Anna Carabelli and Ivo Maes who have devoted substantial amounts of their time to read extensively several drafts of the book and who have made many helpful critiques and suggestions. I remain solely responsible for errors and omissions.

My PhD supervisors Rodolphe Dos Santos Ferreira and Ragip Ege taught me a method to carefully elaborate a problematic, which requires the reading of texts and paying attention to the concepts, despite ideological dross and received ideas. I do not claim to live up to their expectations. Yet, I dedicate this book to them.

1   Introduction

Without denying what constitutes the specificities of their original findings about the functioning of economic macro-systems that led them at roughly 30 years of distance to launch the first two revolutions in macroeconomics of the twentieth century, our view is that significant similarities but also strong ties are at work in the logics that govern Keynes' and Friedman's respective approach to political economics. In particular, there is a problematic that is common to their two theoretical constructs, which is the issue of stability in a monetary economy. Truly, this shared concern for stabilisation is not founded upon identical theoretical principles and is not necessarily formulated in the same fashion (especially regarding the relevant time horizon to deal carefully with this fundamental issue). Strikingly, for both authors the main feature of the modern economies we live in is that they use monetary assets to facilitate exchanges. On this basis, through the lens of the stability issue a careful reading of their advocacies about the economic policy brings to light the convergent matters of concern at work in their political advices. In particular, for both of them the key task of policy guidelines they call for turns to anchor private agents' expectations. Hence, over and above the received ideas that might remain about their pioneering works, and even despite the professions of faith (hardly reconcilable) that these two authors themselves might have wanted to give, there are similar preoccupations that should deserve our attention.

It is with this perspective that another look could be taken at the way we currently grasp the issue of crises. To take but a few examples, Keynes should have for his part a lot to teach us about the necessity to implement new policy devices to stabilise both the real and the financial sides of the economy, which basically means the management of long-term expectations. On his side, Friedman should have a lot to warn us about the adverse consequences of erratic policies for the dynamics of private agents' expectations in the short run.

Let us first present the aims and scope of this book. We will then provide the reader with an outline of the following chapters.

1.1 Aims and scope

To which extent is State intervention able to stabilise a decentralised market economy and to improve its day-to-day functioning? Depending on the precise way one looks at the problem, on how one frames the terms of the debate at stake, the issue of the proper economic policy to be implemented is addressed in very different manners. But in any case, Keynes and Friedman are caricatured in the most stereotypical images as poles apart on almost everything.

The very first way one can address the issue is the way Hayek did, in particular in *The Road to Serfdom* (1944). Here, the alternative is set in terms of freedom versus planning. Worded this way, the issues that arise are the following. To what extent are freedom and efficiency deeply intertwined values to be pursued hand in hand? Once one allows the State to interfere with the daily functioning of markets, what should be the moral principles underlying its interventions? If the battlefield is formulated this way, the answer given by these caricatured figures would be for Keynes to give up to planning all that is necessary for the sake of efficiency and in the opposite a pure laissez-faire regime and not the smallest concession to freedom for Friedman.

The second basic way to address this basic problem is to gauge the self-adjusting capacity of a decentralised market economy, in the long run as well as in the short run. In case of a large and protracted shock, when the economy suffers a severe downturn, are discretionary actions of public authorities necessarily detrimental, so that the State should refrain from intervening and let the purge go on? On the contrary, if one considers that Say's law proves utterly irrelevant in our modern monetary economies, how are State authorities supposed to intervene so as to forestall the potential problems inhering in decentralised market economies? Once State intervention is acknowledged in the public's interest, how should these policy devices be designed and implemented? Besides, it can also be considered that a laissez-faire system is self-adjusting but only in a long-run perspective, so that it undergoes short-run departures from the growth path of the economy, which are costly in terms of collective welfare. If so, are State authorities supposed to intervene with the view to ensure the maintenance of full employment? And what is the best way to avoid those departures? Here again, Keynes and Friedman are said to be poles apart. Keynes would have made a radical case for big government, impotence of the monetary weapon, anti-cyclical discretionary policies, no care for public deficits and inflation and above all an insistence on short-term devices. As for Friedman, a dismissal of public spending and of short-term fine-tuning, anti-discretionary monetary policy and above all a strict kingly State, which means laissez-faire in every single area of State intervention.

As this book aims to show, the reality is a far cry from this oversimplified image. First and foremost, this book is an exercise of text reading. Through a careful analysis of what these two authors wrote concerning the functioning of a monetary economy, its ability to stabilise by itself at around full employment and also what they viewed as State duties regarding this fundamental goal, our aim is not merely to bring to light similarities and dissimilarities in their theoretical constructs. By the same token, we do not aim only to establish some parallels in their policy advice.

At the theoretical level, our ambition in this book is to investigate the logics that underlie these proximities in the way Keynes and Friedman respectively address the stability issue. An avenue of research will be to question their respective understanding of the 'individual versus collective' issue through the lens of institutions. By the latter we mean the ability of a collective body to behave more efficiently than an individual one, what is nowadays called the 'collective rationality' issue. Friedman's profound confidence in the individual leads him to advocate the return to the old principles of laissez-faire, i.e. the 'classical liberalism'. Hence Friedman's absolute distrust vis-à-vis centralised authority to behave according to collective welfare. By contrast, Keynes' confidence towards State authorities but also the opportunities he sees in the rise of the 'big company' for the collective interest is to be explained with regard to his mistrust towards the individual to behave rationally and, much more fundamentally, his claim that a collective body does much better than individuals, in particular on financial markets when decisions on long-term views are susceptible to be stifled by conventional judgements. Hence the 'new liberalism' Keynes calls for. Another line of approach will be to investigate the way our two authors envision the monetary character of a decentralised market economy and, from this, how they grasp the issue of uncertainty and expectations. We will see that, because of their dissimilar treatment of uncertainty and money, Keynes turns out to be concerned with the long-term real expectations (in particular the expectations held by investors and entrepreneurs), while Friedman focuses his attention on the short-term nominal expectations of every kind of agent.

At the policy level, we aim to show that a fresh look can be taken at Keynes' and Friedman's policy advice regarding State duties in a monetary economy once the perspective set above is adopted. This is the second dimension of our inquiry. Strikingly, both of them are true liberals in the political sense of the word, highly preoccupied by the preservation of our basic freedom. Both of them agree that untimely actions of public authorities might be detrimental for efficiency and both of them develop long-term views on the best way to stabilise the economy. In short, both of them agree that *some* degree of freedom has to be conceded for the ultimate purpose of preserving a laissez-faire system. It is on the extent of this concession towards planning and also on the practical definition of what has to be conceded that they part company. On the one hand, the need to achieve a compromise between a pure laissez-faire regime and planning (understood as collectivism and fully centralised activity) through the design and the careful implementation of a 'Middle Way' doctrine proves to be, so to speak, the cornerstone of Keynes' political writings. On the other, despite Friedman's own claims to be a true defender of a pure laissez-faire system and despite the inclination towards libertarianism he acknowledges, the implementation of a policy regime à la Friedman inevitably implies that *some* dose of State intervention has to be conceded to enforce the rules of the game, especially regarding monetary affairs. To put it differently, Friedman is definitely not a true anarchist, or a true libertarian. He could barely share the "libertarian goal of the shrinkage of the state" (De Long 2000a, p. 90) that is ascribed to him. So what appears for Keynes a crucial issue to be explicitly dealt with turns to be almost a blind spot for Friedman. Ultimately, it is on the issue of how to achieve this great compromise between freedom and efficiency rather than on the relevant compromise to be made (and in particular on the proper way to stabilise the economy) that they are poles apart.

Likewise, the specific logics that underlie their respective pleas can also provide the fundamental rationales of their advocacies regarding the way fiscal and monetary policies should be conducted. We will see that the contemporary perspective, which formulates the debate in terms of rules versus discretion, appears much too narrow to encompass the whole of the stakes of the debate between our two authors. On the one hand, what one now calls rules is much too discretionary to fit into a Friedmanian policy advice setting. On the other, what we now call discretion is merely alien to Keynes' overall policy principles. Keynes too advocates 'policy guidelines' although he parts company with Friedman about the ultimate goal of the rules and differs in the dose of leeway to be given to the authorities. Yet, we hasten to add that discretion is highly needed for Keynes when the system endures unforeseeable shocks despite the stabilising effect of the rules implemented. However, the fact remains that Keynes is quite alien to fine-tuning and to deficit spending.

Ultimately, with the help of Keynes and Friedman we should be able to rethink the critical issue of crises, which is at the centre of the debates today. Indeed, for both of them the basic tenets of the economic policy they call for are strongly embedded in their interpretation of the 1929 crisis and the way the latter turned into the Great Depression. Keynes and Friedman were both struck by the Great Depression. It is usually considered that the 1929 crisis and the way it turned into the most severe recession of the twentieth century fixed the whole of their respective intellectual background – as a contemporary for Keynes and much more as a historian for Friedman. As during the time of the Great Depression, one can now find again at the core of debates issues such as the self-regulating forces that a decentralised market system might possess (or not), the ability of financial markets to coordinate the inter-temporal plans of investors and savers, but also and strikingly the role played by public authorities in the sudden occurrence of economic crises.

First, what are the critical elements at the origin of the crisis? In particular, is it possible for State authorities and in particular for monetary authorities, to have *created* the crisis through misguided policies, as Friedman claims regarding the 1929 episode and as Taylor argues today in his *Getting off Track: How Government Actions and Interventions Caused, Prolonged and Worsened the Financial Crisis* (2009)? Or are the very causes of the current recession to be found in the financial side as well as in the real side of the economy, through financial markets' malfunctions and global imbalances, as Keynesians would argue?

On this basis, coming back to the policy devices Keynes and Friedman originally advocate should help us to *reframe* the terms of the debate surrounding the economic policy to be followed to escape the recession. What should be State priorities: the then-and-now diseases of a severely out of equilibrium economy? Or in a more long-run perspective the restoration of the self-stabilising forces that the system inherently possesses, having as its corollary a close attention paid to the growth-path tendency of the economy? Bearing in mind the overall advocacies of our two authors, no doubt policy-makers would argue that *something* has to be done, and that it does not make sense to simply and purely let the purge go on. As a reminder of Keynes' most important lesson, one should keep in mind that the State is the central player in the economy able precisely to influence the course of things. To this extent, the State authorities' duty is first and foremost to formulate a way ahead, to help private agents chart a course regarding the future 'states of the world'. In this perspective, one might seriously wonder whether a great recession is the right time for austerity in public finances. If the very duty of the State is to drive the investors' and the entrepreneurs' long-term real expectations, no doubt pessimistic expectations on behalf of centralised authorities can only be harmful for the already depressed private agents' expectations. By contrast, it might be the perfect time to design and to implement new institutional settings with the view to launch public-private partnerships, with the double goal of 'pump priming' in a short-term and demand-side perspective and the combined aim to make the economy more competitive in a long-term and supply-side perspective. And as a reminder of Friedman's deepest matter of concern, one should consider seriously the stickiness of private agents' nominal expectations. That is, people do take time to revise their inflationary expectations, and uncertainty regarding the discretionary policies carried out in the future is very likely to destabilise the real side of the economy. Consequently, confidence both in the economic climate and in the ongoing policy regime is critical to stabilise the economy around full employment. Erratic policies are very likely to make matters worse. Friedman's claim appears to be a deep warning directed towards those who concentrate on the short-run diseases and urge for devices which are immediately visible at the expense of long-term stabilisation concerns, especially when this sort of short-termism means a significant reversal of priorities in a very short space of time.

Keynes published his first academic paper in 1909 in the *Economic Journal* (Keynes 1909, "Recent Economic Events in India", CW 11, pp. 1–22). And he had always been committed to public life: he began as a civil servant for the Indian Office, then worked for the Treasury during World War I and ended his career as a political adviser – Keynes' last plea dates from 1945. As for Friedman, he started what would become his 'counter-revolution' precisely at that time, until the last edition of *Capitalism and Freedom* (1962a) in 2002 as well as in his posthumous "Tradeoffs in Monetary Policy" (2010). Friedman, too, was fully engaged in the political and intellectual debate until his death in 2006. In between there was a lot of water under the bridge. One saw the rise of the 'Keynesian revolution', progressively superseded by the monetarist 'counter-revolution'. The worlds respectively faced by our two authors were in many extents radically different. Regarding the way Keynes and Friedman respectively deal with the 'real' world, suffice it to mention the place allowed to the State in the economy or the role played by the 'big company'. As far as theory is concerned we have learnt a lot: new tools are at our disposal, such as econometrics; new disciplines emerged, such as public economics. Undoubtedly, such a long time span might render any inquiry such as ours quite perilous. Accordingly, the first stumbling block to be avoided all along this study is anachronism. Moreover, Friedman did not battle with Keynes himself, but with his heirs. Here, our investigation runs the risk of being distorted by the presence of the Keynesians, or at least by the proponents of the income-expenditure Keynesian sub-current. Accordingly, the second rock on which an undertaking such as ours might come to grief is ventriloquism.

As for the first reef, as time obviously elapsed between Keynes' first advocacy to Friedman's last plea, we need to be particularly cautious in taking into account the specific historical circumstances of such or such a plea. As far as Keynes is concerned, we will concentrate our investigation each time it will be possible to the time of and after the *General Theory*. As for Friedman, our way to solve this difficulty will be to put as far as possible his critique of Keynesianism aside, and to concentrate on his own original analyses. Finally, we will adopt for both authors consistency as a working hypothesis. Indeed, as for all great authors we will consider that Keynes and Friedman meant exactly what they wrote when scrutinising their texts and that, despite local amendments, their thoughts should be considered as consistent bulks.

1.2 Synopsis

If one plans to compare Keynes and Friedman on the issue of the proper way to enforce stability of macroeconomic systems, there is a prerequisite to be fulfilled, that is to put the Keynesians of the neo-classical synthesis off-stage. Chapter 2 deals with these preliminaries. Indeed, Friedman was definitely not a contemporary of Keynes. He did not battle with Keynes himself, but with his heirs, especially with those of the (Walrasian) neo-classical synthesis. The scope, scale and intensity of the quarrel varied as time elapsed. He is even said to have shown more flexibility towards Keynes in comparison to the Keynesians. This chapter aims to clarify the issues of the debate at stake, on both the theoretical and the methodological level, by specifying the context and especially by attempting to disentangle Friedman's critique towards the Keynesians from his own original arguments. We will see that Friedman's critiques of functional finance, of inflationary gap analysis as well as the Keynesian consumption function hardly apply to Keynes. Besides, since our main concern refers to political economy, the so-called 'Keynesian' Phillips curve will be at the core of our investigation in this chapter. The main issue of this chapter is to assess the relevance of Friedman's assault on the Phillips curve for the economics of Keynes himself. Again, we will see that Keynes' construct stands quite immune to Friedman's critique, whether in respect to the call for short-term devices, inflationary remedies to unemployment or the employment-wages dynamics underlying the 'Phillips curve exercises'.

Chapter 3 probes into Keynes and Friedman's respective views on institutions, either private, 'semi-public' or public. We know well that neither Keynes nor Friedman were directly and explicitly interested in institutions as such. Yet, both of them developed original thinking regarding the individualistic competitive body, the 'big company' or the 'State' understood as centralised authorities. Through this particular lens, we aim to bring to light some of the rationales behind their respective views on the self-adjusting capacity of a laissez-faire economy – which are hardly reconcilable. Here, we focus on the salient features of a modern economy with regard to the old type of laissez-faire: Keynes' ambitions to take advantage of the natural tendency of the system towards concentration while Friedman calls for the return to a purely competitive system. We also show that Keynes' and Friedman's appraisal of the 'State' as an institution ensues from their respective confidence towards the 'collective', a deep confidence in collective bodies regarding Keynes and a basic distrust towards anything which is not individualistic regarding Friedman. Finally, these findings are applied to their respective interpretation of the 1929 financial collapse. Their analyses of the main features of the US economy during the 1920s as well as their severe assessment of the Fed's inept monetary policy at the end of the period are not so distant. But a careful reading of their positions regarding the way the 1929 crash turned into the Great Depression brings to light the type of mechanisms at work in a monetary economy on which they respectively insist to sustain their opposite appraisals of the ability of collective institutions to behave efficiently: Keynes insists on the second-round real effects of a financial collapse while Friedman focuses solely on monetary disturbances. This comparison allows us to learn lessons regarding Keynes' and Friedman's policy philosophies: Keynes' new liberalism basically consists in the set-up of new institutions to cope with the inability of a laissez-faire regime to absorb by itself large and protracted shocks while Friedman calls for the return to the principles of the 'old liberalism', which means power as dispersed as possible in both the political and the economic markets.

Our concern in Chapter 4 is for the practical policy devices they call for to enforce stability in decentralised market economies. Here, we will focus on the employment policy along its two main fronts, the fiscal and the monetary policies. First, how to define and how to measure full employment? And what are the proper policy guidelines to ensure full employment? Keynes' and Friedman's respective pleas are mixes of true points of agreement, not so distant positions and hardly irreconcilable advocacies. Basically, what they share is a long-run concern – for both monetary and fiscal policy – the distrust of short-run devices to 'fine-tune' the economy as well as the rejection of inflationary remedies for unemployment. In particular, both of them take structural unemployment into account and are concerned about supply-side policies. Now, this is not to say that they are in perfect agreement on the efficiency of fiscal policy or on the proper target of monetary policy; far from it. On the side of budgetary policy, Keynes reminds us that the true purpose of a budgetary weapon is to drive private long-term *real* expectations in a world of uncertainty. Regarding Friedman, the analysis is complicated by the fact that Friedman moved from the acceptance of an 'automatic stabiliser' argument toward a crude acceptance of the crowding-effect. On the side of monetary policy, both Keynes and Friedman remind us that monetary policy implies much more complex issues than the management of overnight interest rates. All in all, Keynes and Friedman cannot be basically opposed, as is too often argued in a simplistic manner.

Do their shared visions that come out in our inquiry regarding the proper stabilising devices to be implemented in our modern economies correspond to fundamental points of agreement, or are they merely outward similarities? Chapter 5 aims to find the answer to this riddle. We divide this issue into two main parts. In the first step, we investigate their respective understanding of the functioning of a monetary economy, through especially the analysis of their respective demand function for money. We show that Friedman sticks to a 'real' determination of the interest rate whereas Keynes' monetary theory gives rise to a monetary determination of the interest rate. What is at stake here is Friedman's appraisal of Keynes' liquidity-preference concept. Even if for both Keynes and Friedman 'money matters' they hold contrasted views on the dynamics at work in a monetary economy, and from that contrasted understandings of coordination and stabilisation. It is not surprising that their views on uncertainty and their ensuing treatment of expectations are at the core of this ultimate explanation. In comparison with our contemporary rational expectations approach, Keynes' and Friedman's respective treatment of uncertainty is worth telling. While Keynes' concern for 'true' uncertainty (i.e. when the entire set of the 'states of the world' is not fully known) requires a genuine treatment of the liquidity issue, Friedman insists that private agents do take time to revise their nominal forecasts so that inflationary expectations should be considered adaptive rather than rational. Coordination failures appear as the rationale behind Keynes' overall economic guidelines. For him, it is a key role for the State to drive the long-term *real* expectations, which means to provide the indispensable stable policy regime without which individuals would not coordinate themselves towards full employment. In sharp contrast, the way Friedman grasps the issue of the 'transmission mechanism' leads him to argue that State stimulus is fatally flawed since a decentralised market economy possesses, at least in the long run, the endogenous mechanisms essential for its stability. For him, the State should content itself with providing a stable competitive framework, which means to provide a stable monetary background that anchors *nominal* expectations.

Finally, what kind of lessons should we learn from Keynes and Friedman for today? First and foremost, it seems to us that our two authors should help us to reframe the terms of the debate at stake regarding policy devices. The very lesson is that *some* policy devices have to be implemented, that *some* State intervention is needed. Beyond that, both Keynes and Friedman compel us to bypass and to move beyond the terms of the debate as it is framed today in terms of rules versus discretion. Viewed this way, Keynes' and Friedman's respective lessons are far-reaching but yet for completely opposed reasons. To say it quite plainly, on the one hand one might need to resort to certain institutional settings and policy devices that Keynes outlined at his time. This is true regarding the true purpose of monetary and fiscal policies in the long run. This is also true regarding almost forgotten devices such as the private-public partnerships that 'pump-prime' in the short run but have also the great advantage of improving the economy competitiveness in the long run. On the other hand, we should take seriously Friedman's warning against optimal control devices that lead to erratic reversals of priorities in our policy guidelines in a very short space of time. Yet, there is another way to shape the debate, almost forgotten today, which is our ultimate questioning. As Hayek would ask in the *Road to Serfdom* (1944): how and where should the line be drawn between laissez-faire and planning? On the one hand, Keynes' 'Middle Way' doctrine, his 'new liberalism', relies on pragmatism – despite his elitism. Keynes freely concedes that the world has changed and that State duties ought to change accordingly: *some* planning is to be conceded if we want ultimately to preserve our basic freedom. Yet, regarding the practical issue of *where* to draw the line, Keynes leaves us almost down-and-out. On the other hand, Friedman's plea for a return to the 'old liberalism', his libertarian posture can be qualified as more 'normative' – not to say dogmatic. As is the case for Hayek, Friedman's 'radical liberalism' concedes here and there that the logical extreme is not possible and that some compromise has to be recognised. It is 'as if' Friedman refused to draw the slightest line. But Friedman is not so much concerned with the practicality issue but rather with the evolutionary tendency, the long-term dynamics at work in our modern market societies: ultimately, are we following the right track?

2 Keeping the Keynesians off-stage

2.1 Introduction

There is a basic preliminary to be fulfilled in order to carry our investigation out, which is to separate the wheat from the chaff. In our view, a proper investigation on Keynes' and Friedman's analyses of stability requires clearly and strongly disentangling Keynes from the Keynesians. This means a two-step approach. First, there is the necessity to clearly disentangle Keynes from what Friedman considers his Keynesian opponents. Second, there is the necessity to disentangle in the statements, critiques and arguments put forward by Friedman the ones that fall within his critique of the Keynesians from original analyses he puts forward, in other words to disentangle his critique of Keynesianism from his contribution to the edification of the monetarist school of thought. But as Coddington (1976) acknowledges, there is a variety of Keynesianism, so that we have to be particularly careful in our disentanglement attempt. Here, we will be concerned mainly with the Keynesians of the neo-classical synthesis, the 'hydraulic' version of Keynesianism. Indeed, time elapsed between Keynes' revolution and Friedman's most influential papers. As a matter of fact, in almost all his writings Friedman battles with Keynes' heirs (and especially the ones of the neo-classical synthesis) instead of Keynes himself. That means that our investigation of Keynes' and Friedman's respective political economics runs the risk of being distorted by the presence of the Keynesians, or at least by the proponents of the neo-classical Keynesian synthesis. Things are rendered even more intractable if one remembers the appraisal of the Keynesian school by each of our authors, including Keynes himself. On the one hand, there is the famous "I am not a Keynesian" the late Keynes is supposed to have claimed at the time of 'functional finance' and 'inflationary gap' analysis. On the other, Friedman's own position is said to have moved. Friedman himself acknowledges in his memoirs that he began his career as a Keynesian.[1] It is commonly considered that in the end "we even find Friedman putting Keynes in his own camp, as against the Walrasian orthodoxy that raised to domination in the post World War era" (Dostaler 1998, p. 320). Between the two, one finds the monetarist counter-revolution. Avoiding ventriloquism and going back to the original theoretical and political writings of our two authors proves a true necessity.

At the theoretical level, Friedman criticises the Keynesians of the neo-classical synthesis for their treatment of the rate of interest, their neglect of long-run issues, and so on. At the policy level, he accuses them of shirking the practical issue. He also battles at length on the methodological ground: he claims to be a true Marshallian (just like Keynes, in Friedman's views) whereas the adversaries he targets belong to the Walrasian camp. Our major concern in this chapter can be stated as follows: to which extent is Friedman's critique against Keynesian economics relevant for the economics of Keynes himself? To put it another way, to which extent should the collapse of the Keynesian IS-LM synthesis be conflated with Keynes' theoretical constructs and, by the way, Keynes' advocacies regarding the proper economic policy to be carried out in both normal and special times?

Because of concerns we have with the question of how to stabilise a monetary economy the inflation-unemployment trade-off turns out to be the most critical issue at stake here. Indeed, this debate surrounding the Phillips curve takes place at both the theoretical and the policy grounds; it refers to nothing less than the self-adjusting capacity of a laissez-faire economy, and thus to the role State authorities are supposed to play in a decentralised market economy.

Here below, we will investigate Friedman's assessment of Keynesian economics (including both Keynes and the Keynesians of the neo-classical synthesis with whom Friedman battled directly) with exclusively the view to disentangle the Keynesians from Keynes himself. This narrow purpose will lead us to stress the developments and alterations in Friedman's critique of the Keynesian school. That is the reason why Friedman's original propositions in terms both of economic theory and of economic policy will be roughly left aside. This disentanglement attempt will also lead us to provide only an insight into the nature of Keynes' analyses.

We will proceed in two steps. First, we will analyse Friedman's appraisal of Keynesian economics with the view to shed light on this evolving process. We will see in particular that Friedman has not always been the monetarist he claims to be. The first papers on the part of the early Friedman show him as very close to the leading Keynesians of the day. Second, we will consider as a special issue Friedman's assault on the Phillips curve. We will show that Friedman's critiques targeted against the Keynesian use of the Phillips curve hardly apply to Keynes. Hence the necessity to clearly and sharply disentangle Keynes from his heirs if Keynes and Friedman are to be compared at the theoretical as well as the policy level.

2.2 Friedman's assessment of Keynesian economics

Following Hirsch and de Marchi's (1990) and Dostaler's (1998) studies, it is commonly considered relevant to break Friedman's appraisal of both Keynes' economics and Keynesian economics into two phases. The first period would go from Friedman's beginnings in the 1940s to the middle 1960s, circa 1963. During this first period Friedman's critiques are mainly based on the empirical level and Keynes' theory is conflated with standard Keynesianism, or at least with "bastard Keynesianism" – to borrow Robinson's famous words. At the time of and after the rise of the monetarist counter-revolution, in his appraisal of Keynes and the Keynesians Friedman is commonly said to distinguish more keenly Keynes from the Keynesians. It is as if the careful building of an alternative theoretical framework would have rendered Friedman more confident in his own position and hence would have allowed him to soften his harsh appraisal of Keynes' initial revolution.

In our opinion, it remains doubtful that Friedman finally nuanced his initial views on Keynes and that he reconsidered ultimately his prior amalgam between Keynes and the Keynesians. To show this, three stages will be considered below instead of the two considered by previous commentators: first, the early criticisms towards the Keynesian school; second, the arguments put forward at the time of the monetarist rise; and finally, Friedman's latest appraisal of Keynes' works. At each stage we will restrict ourselves to a disentanglement attempt between Keynes and the Keynesians from a political economics perspective.[2]

We will see that, regarding the early Friedman, it is the Keynesian flavour of his analyses that is noticeable. At the apex of the monetarist counter-revolution, Friedman's assault on the Keynesians might be well founded but it can be hardly seen as relevant regarding Keynes himself. Last, the late Friedman is far from disentangling Keynes from the Keynesians as is commonly acknowledged.

The inflationary gap issue in the early 1940s: the young Friedman as a dubious Keynesian

Undoubtedly, a contemporary reader gets mixed feelings when he comes back to Friedman's first writings. Hirsch and de Marchi (1990) consider the 1942–43 writings as "the early origins of Friedman's anti-Keynesianism" (Hirsch and de Marchi 1990, p. 187). In our view such a contention should be moderated. To a certain extent it is the 'Keynesian flavour' of these writings that is striking – especially if the Keynes of *How Pay for the War* (1940, CW 9) is kept in mind. As we will see below, it is not merely by chance that among the three papers written in 1942–43 the first piece was later included in Friedman's *Essays in Positive Economics* (1953a) and that in contrast the two others have been later overlooked.

Let us first consider Friedman's "Discussion of the Inflationary Gap" (1942). This paper is easily interpreted as a clear-cut denial of the 'inflationary gap', both at the theoretical level and as a basis for policy. It is true that, as a forerunner of later arguments, the main point Friedman raises is that the 'inflationary gap' is hardly measurable because of its *ex ante* character: "Inflationary Gap is never of the past or the present; it is always in the future" (Friedman [1942] 1953a, p. 251). Yet, Friedman's paper is quite nuanced so that its interpretation is more complex than it appears at first sight. To show this, let us quote extensively Friedman's (1942) paper:

An analysis directed towards policy should not, therefore, stop with an estimate of the primary expenditure gap. It should take as its function the evaluation of the quantitative aspects of the alternative measures that might be taken to close the gap. *Such an evaluation is essential to an intelligent choice among measures or an intelligent combination of measures.* It is not enough to list the various measures that might be employed ... The ideal would be a series of indifference surfaces, so to speak; that is, a list of the alternative combinations of policies that would serve to close gaps, however defined, of alternative sizes.

The analyses that have so far been made fall far short of this ideal.

(Friedman [1942] 1953a, p. 260; emphasis added)

As a matter of strict exegesis the precise point Friedman makes above cannot be interpreted as a clear-cut denial of Keynesian inflationary gap exercises. Indeed, the attention is drawn on the necessity for more empirical investigation, more knowledge on the economic structure and more careful analysis. In short Friedman claims here for improvements in both theoretical and empirical analysis; he does not purely and simply deny the relevance of the 'inflationary gap' analysis. Now, it is true that the end of the 1942 paper reinforces the anti-Keynesian flavour of Friedman's plea. One can see Friedman there arguing:

The present state of gap analysis is unsatisfactory not only because it does not go far enough but also because the estimates that are made are subject to such wide margins of errors. At the present stage of our knowledge of the functioning of the economic system, estimating the gap is a *presumptuous undertaking.*

(Friedman [1942] 1953a, p. 261; emphasis added)

Friedman appears here quite doubtful about the usefulness of inflationary gap analysis but, again, this statement can still be interpreted as a strong plea for further and clever investigations. Things are rendered even more complicated when, as an insight of later inquiries, Friedman notices that at the same time as World War II "useful estimates are possible at all only because of the special circumstances of the moment" (Friedman [1942] 1953a, p. 262). Here, the inflationary gap analysis might lose most of its scope of relevance, limited as it is to the funding of the war in a State-managed economy that endures scarcity of the resources available for the civil needs.

All in all, as a matter of principle it can be considered that in 1942 the early Friedman does not call for the definitive dismissal of the Keynesian concept of inflationary gap but rather for more cautiousness in its treatment.

In 1943 World War II is still ongoing and so is Friedman's inquiry on this issue of gap closing with two other papers, "The Spendings Tax as a Wartime Fiscal Measure" (1943a) and "Methods of Predicting the Onset of 'Inflation'" in the *Taxing to Prevent Inflation* (1943b) booklet written with Shoup and Mack. These two 1943 papers don't reinforce the 'monetarist' strand of Friedman's thinking, quite the contrary. In his "Spendings Tax as a Wartime Fiscal Measure" (1943a) Friedman acknowledges the peculiar circumstances of war that might render more complicated the achievement both of efficiency and of "the equitable distribution of the short supply of consumer goods" (Friedman 1943a, p. 50). In sharp contrast with later claims, his "Methods of Predicting the Onset of 'Inflation'" (1943b) starts with the following statement:

> 'Inflation' has its genesis in an increased volume of spending by consumers, business and government. This increase of spending can ordinarily be matched only in part by an expansion in the volume of commodities and service offered for sale; the rest is absorbed by a rise in the prices at which these goods sell. During the early stage of an upswing, the large volume of unutilized resources available enables the bulk of the increase in spending to be absorbed by an increased output of goods.... As expansion proceeds and the volume of unutilized resources decreases, a larger and larger part of the increase in spending is absorbed by rising prices.
>
> (Friedman 1943b, p. 111)

In the eyes of the Friedman of 1943, prices rise as the result of a disequilibrium phenomenon in the goods market. The Keynes of 1940 in *How to Pay for the War* (CW 9) would not argue otherwise. For a reader accustomed to the later claims that "inflation is always and everywhere a monetary phenomenon" (Friedman 1970a, p. 16),[3] the analysis carried out here is highly surprising. Next, regarding practical devices needed to control inflationary boom Keynes would also agree that "there is no hard and fast line between fiscal and direct controls" (Friedman 1943a, p. 52). And just like Keynes at that time, the Friedman of 1943 is fully involved in detailed empirical investigations to evaluate precisely the inflationary gap. Friedman too acknowledges the overriding need for adequate expectations in order to go beyond "historical relations" (Friedman 1943b, p. 115). His claim for "the pressing nature of the immediate problem made some attempt at quantitative forecasts imperative" (Friedman 1943b, p. 116) strongly echoes Keynes' matters of concern at about the same time. Friedman also clearly shares Keynes' concern for transitory measures to a peacetime economy: how to release enough purchasing power in the short run to meet growing production capacities? The Keynesian flavour of Friedman's papers appears even more strikingly in the following quotation:

> This 'inflationary gap' analysis does not give any specific technique for determining the rise in income or in prices that will be associated with a given increase in government expenditures. *At the same time, it seems exceedingly valuable.* It furnishes a significant framework for interpreting government policy, and reveals the basic factors on which its effects depend. It combines the monetary and the 'real' aspects of the problem in a way that gives each its proper place.
>
> (Friedman 1943b, p. 140; emphasis added)

Here, Friedman takes sides with the Keynesians, at least as a matter of principle. The 'inflationary gap' analysis is seen as highly valuable. Now, while Keynes favours in his *How to Pay for the War* (1940) compulsory savings as the most efficient device to withdraw current private purchasing power from consumption markets Friedman favours spendings taxes. Friedman states that "compulsory saving *alone* is, in principle, impossible to enforce since income and expenditures are never definitely known until after the end of a period" (Friedman 1943a, p. 52; emphasis added). This reversal of priorities is due to the distinction he puts forward between *ex ante* and *ex post* magnitudes. But that leads him neither to reject any kind of State intervention in general nor to reject compulsory savings in particular. The point here is a matter of degree: Friedman favours spending tax as "peculiarly on the borderline between fiscal and direct controls" (Friedman 1943a, p. 52). This would avoid backlogs insofar as his main concern is for "current collection" (Friedman 1943a, p. 62) of tax proceeds.

Now, it is true that Friedman makes at the very same time other statements that strongly moderate the Keynesian flavour of these analyses. His plea for savings-inducement methods stops with the following claim: spendings tax will minimise post-war adjustment problems while "minimizing the rôle of government intervention into the details of the economic system" (Friedman 1943a, p. 62). Here, the young Friedman appears as the forerunner of the true opponent to State intervention he will later become.

All in all, one cannot but get mixed feelings when comparing the two 1943 papers. In the final analysis, our reading shows that no clear-cut and straightforward conclusion can be drawn: in 1943, Friedman could have possibly become an eminent member of the Keynesian school of thought, much more concerned with data-uncertainty and model-uncertainty arguments than some Keynesians, but no more worried about that than Keynes himself.

First criticisms in the late 1940s: the Keynesians accused of shirking the practical issue

It isn't until the early 1960s that harsh critiques rise towards the Keynesians. Yet, before this apex it is possible to find some interesting pieces of work on behalf of Friedman that foreshadow the monetarist counter-revolution to come.[4] Let us focus on a particular occasion on which Friedman makes his point in terms of criticism while not yet putting forward the original views that will come later on.

In 1947 Friedman reviews Lerner's *Economics of Control* (1944). His assessment is well synthesised by his emphasis on the "hortatory character of the proposals" (Friedman [1947] 1953a, p. 302). As is well known, the devil is sometimes in the details: Lerner's basic mistake is that he misses the practical issue. Friedman denies any relevance to a rule that "is a purely formal statement that conceals all the difficulties" (Friedman [1947] 1953a, pp. 306–7). Besides, Friedman criticises Lerner for giving us no criterion to judge the validity of any policy objective. In particular, why are we supposed to favour 'full' employment over inflation? Here is a critical argument that Friedman will put forward over and over against the Keynesians, especially after having elaborated the underpinnings of his method in positive economics: our theoretical inquiries ought to be value-free. Besides, Friedman also puts into question the means advocated to reach this basic goal. As Friedman does, let us focus on 'functional finance'.[5] His assessment is clear-cut:

> Lerner's discussion of functional finance is a brilliant exercise in logic.... But ... the relevant question is whether the discussion of 'functional finance,' besides being a logical exercise, is also a prescription for public policy. The answer, it seems to this reviewer, is clearly negative. Once again, what looks like a prescription evaporates into an expression of *good intentions*.
>
> (Friedman [1947] 1953a, pp. 306–7; emphasis added)

Arguments that will be put forward later on in Friedman's career are already present here. In particular, Friedman insists that on a practical level it is extremely difficult to disentangle a "temporary deficiency" from "drastic deflation" (Friedman [1947] 1953, pp. 313–14) and even to disentangle between upward and downward stages in the economic cycle. Lags are also acknowledged in a twofold way: first, it takes time for the State to collect information on time (what corresponds to a data-uncertainty argument) and, by the way, State intervention through the functional finance principle also takes time to be effective. All in all, "this prescription of Lerner's, like others, thus turns into an exhortation to do the right thing with no advice how to know what is the right thing to do" (Friedman [1947] 1953a, p. 316). In short, this amounts to "playing at capitalism" (Friedman [1981] 1987, p. 24).

It would lead us too far to assess exhaustively the relevance of Friedman's critique towards Lerner. Since our aim here is only to escape the mix-up between Keynes and the Keynesians, suffice it to mention a few points to emphasise how complicated this affair is. First, as a matter of fact "the need for current and up-to-date information about net investment in the private sector" (Keynes 1945, CW 27, p. 409) is actually a constant matter of concern for Keynes. To take but one example, one can be reminded that Keynes sometimes complains that "the present state of our information is particularly defective, and deliberate obscurantism has prevailed" (Keynes 1944, CW 27, p. 370).[6] So Friedman's claim that the Keynesians pass over the critical issue of accurate information barely applies to Keynes himself. As a second example, Lerner's functional finance corresponds to what Keynes calls "deficit budgeting", which as a matter of fact he strongly opposes. Keynes is very clear on this point: "The capital budgeting is a method of maintaining equilibrium; the deficit budgeting is a means of attempting to cure disequilibrium if and when it arises" (Keynes 1943, CW 27, pp. 352–3), the latter being considered as a "particular, rather desperate expedient" (Keynes 1943, CW 27, p. 354).[7] So Keynes' advocacy regarding the economic policy does not conflate with functional finance, far from it. As this short insight of Keynes' approach shows, Friedman is missing his target here, at least as far as Keynes is concerned.

From now on Friedman's critique towards the Keynesians will grow *crescendo*. But arguing that the Keynesians are muddying the waters is far from enough. In the late 1950s the real issue becomes: how to provide a compelling alternative?

The rise of the monetarist counter-revolution

During the 1950s, the monetarist counter-revolution is on the way. This time, Friedman doesn't confine himself with a critique of Keynesian propositions at the empirical level. He puts his own arguments forward, and in particular the permanent income hypothesis. With both his *Theory of the Consumption Function* (1957) and the paper "A Statistical Illusion in Judging Keynesian Models" (1957) co-authored with Becker, 1957 appears as a clear turning point in the evolution of Friedman's thought. Following up the work undertaken with Kuznets, Friedman's first contribution is to deny any relevance on the empirical level of the Keynesian consumption function. Indeed, "early contributors to 'Keynesian' theory generally presumed the long-run stability of the short-run relation" (Leijonhufvud 1968a, p. 187). At the theoretical level, the implications are straightforward. Indeed, current consumption is now considered as determined by long-term trend rather than by current investment through the multiplier mechanism. By the way, the economy is considered much more stable than supposed by the Keynesians. In Friedman's words:

> Acceptance of the permanent income hypothesis removes completely one of the pillars of the 'secular stagnation' thesis; there is no reason to expect the savings ratio to rise with a secular rise in real income. In addition, it destroys the case for one proposed remedy [i.e. reducing inequalities].
>
> (Friedman 1957, pp. 236–7)

Yet, Friedman acknowledges that in a long-run perspective the Keynesian thesis of a secular stagnation tendency is not completely dismissed by his permanent income hypothesis. Precisely, the Keynesian denial of a full employment position in the long run still holds true together with the hypothesis of a constant ratio of savings to income. That being said, the "secular stagnation" thesis is severely undermined:

> To put in other terms: it means that a much larger part of current consumption is interpreted as autonomous and a much smaller part as dependent on current income and hence, through the multiplier process, on investment. The result is a smaller investment multiplier, and an inherently cyclically more stable system.
>
> (Friedman 1957, p. 238)

As far as Keynes is concerned, what is the relevance of Friedman's critique towards this simple Keynesian consumption function, in other words his claim that "Keynes took it for granted that current consumption expenditure is a highly dependable and stable function of income" (Friedman 1957, p. 3)? Leijonhufvud (1968a) is probably the one who disentangles most sharply the crude version of the consumption function incorporated in income-expenditure models from Keynes' initial analyses. In brief, Keynes' relation between current consumption and current income should be considered as a rough approximation, which holds only in the short run. In bringing to light a "second psychological law" (Leijonhufvud 1968a, p. 190) that deals with the savings-wealth relation, Leijonhufvud proves that Keynes' analysis does take wealth-effect on spendings into account through changes in the real value of assets. Besides, Keynes himself opposes in his time mechanical and restrictive interpretation of his consumption function. In particular, he expresses strong reservations concerning Meade's social security scheme that are based on "devices for causing the volume of consumption to fluctuate in preferences to devices for varying the volume of investment" (Keynes 1943, CW 27, p. 319). Arguing from a position closed to that of Friedman's idea of a permanent income, Keynes' main point against Meade runs as follows:

> In the first place, one has not enough experience to say that short-term variations in consumption are in fact practicable. People have established standards of life. Nothing will upset them more than to be subject to pressure constantly to vary them up and down. A remission of taxation on which people could only rely for an indefinitely short period might have very limited effects in stimulating their consumption.
>
> (Keynes 1943, CW 27, p. 319)

Here again, Keynes' position stands in contrast to the Keynesian 'straw man' portrayed by post-World War II caricatures, including of course monetarist caricatures.[8] But this conflation can easily be avoided by a brief insight either in the *General Theory* or in Keynes' political papers.

To conclude, the analysis made above makes clear that if the first points of harsh criticism raised by Friedman until the late 1950s, which deal with the practicality of Keynesian policy measures or more specifically with the relevance of devices relying on consumption stimulus, are well directed at the first leading Keynesians of the post-World War II era, they hardly apply to Keynes himself. Anyway, it is then time for Friedman to take the next step, namely to prove that in the long run a market economy possesses the self-correcting mechanisms to ensure full employment. The remainder of this chapter is dedicated to this issue of the self-stabilisation properties of a decentralised market economy while focusing on the unemployment-inflation trade-off. Before that, let us here say a few words about Friedman's own appraisal of the 'Keynes and the Keynesians' issue. Precisely: at the end of his career (when the monetarist counter-revolution was well established), to what extent did Friedman himself disentangle Keynes from the Keynesians, as Hirsch and de Marchi (1990) or Dostaler (1998) argue?

Friedman on Keynes and the Keynesians: finally, was there any disentanglement?

According to Dostaler (1998), "in the second phase, which corresponds to the rise and triumph of monetarism, Friedman is less critical of Keynes, whom he even at times considers an ally rather than an adversary, as against his critical stance towards Keynes's disciples" (Dostaler 1998, p. 331). This seems to suggest a higher opinion of Keynes' theoretical contribution, or at least a better disentanglement between Keynes and his followers, a favourable judgement that the achievement of the monetarist counter-revolution would have rendered possible.[9]

We do not share the point made by Dostaler, for three distinct reasons: first, as a matter of fact one can find early disentanglement attempts on the part of Friedman in the very beginning of his career; second, the reason for claiming for a distinction between Keynes and the Keynesians at the apex of Friedman's influence should not in our view stand scrutiny; last, because in Friedman's last pieces of work there is less disentanglement than ever. So let us see how precisely Friedman has become or not less critical towards Keynes than towards the Keynesians.

As a matter of fact, Friedman praises Keynes for his Marshallian lineage as early as 1949. Notice that this praise occurs on the methodological ground:

> Of course, it would be an overstatement to characterise all modern economic theory as 'Walrasian' in this sense. For example, Keynes's theory of employment, whatever its merits or demerits, is Marshallian in method. It is a general equilibrium theory containing important empirical content and constructed to facilitate meaningful predictions.
>
> (Friedman [1949] 1953a, p. 9)

The recognition of a common background appears at the very beginning of Friedman's career. Accordingly, such an acknowledgement should not be interpreted as a far-reaching conceding that would occur later on at a time when Friedman's influence is significantly growing.

The second time Keynes is disentangled from the Keynesians is in 1959 when Friedman argues about Keynes:

> He shifted emphasis from the relation between the stock of money and the flow of income which was at the heart of the quantity theory to the relation between different flows, in particular between the flow of capital and the flow of income.... His disciples, as disciples will, went much farther than the master.
>
> (Friedman 1959, p. 137)

Here, Friedman is not only interested in method but also in economic analysis. What he has in mind roughly corresponds to the caricatured version of the income-expenditure model. And he takes sides with Keynes in the sense that he sees the distinction between autonomous and induced flows of expenditures as much more valuable than the one between consumption and investment. Again, the statement made above appears as a significant acknowledgement made to Keynes well in advance of the achievement of the monetarist counter-revolution.

Let us turn to our second point, which is the relevance of Friedman's disentanglement of Keynes from the Keynesians at the time when the monetarist counter-revolution is well achieved. In 1972 Friedman turns again to the issue of the contrasted methodology supposedly used respectively by Keynes and his followers and argues:

> But Keynes was no Walrasian seeking, like Patinkin, or to a lesser extent Tobin, a general and abstract system of all-embracing simultaneous equations. He was Marshallian, an empirical scientist seeking a simple, fruitful hypothesis. And his was a new, bold, and imaginative hypothesis, whose virtue was precisely how much it could say about major problems on the basis of so little. Of course, his assumptions were not in literal correspondence with reality. If they had been, he would have been condemned to pedestrian description; his whole theory would have lost its power. Of course, he could be wrong. There is no point to any scientific theory that cannot be. The greater range of evidence that, if observed, would contradict a theory, the more precise are its predictions and the better a theory it is *provided it is not, in fact, contradicted.*
>
> (Friedman [1972] 1974, p. 134)

This quotation above must be approached in two ways: first, is Friedman right in his claim to be Marshallian in that precise meaning? Second, to what extent is Friedman right in embracing Keynes in this Marshallian lineage, again in that precise meaning?

First, in Friedman's view Marshall's approach to economics is the kind of research that involves "a continuous process where theorizing and observation go hand in hand at every step of the investigation and the check of deduced against observed fact is 'ultimate', but only because it is logically the latter phase of a repeated sequence" (Hirsch and de Marchi 1990, p. 20). By contrast, Walrasian methodology is supposed to be merely interested in pure theory, that is "abstractness, generality, and mathematical elegance" (Friedman [1949] 1953a, p. 91). Bearing against this Marshall-Walras divide, Friedman then claims to belong to the Marshallian lineage. Now, as shown by Hirsch and de Marchi (1990) or by De Vroey (2009) this claim is quite doubtful. What Friedman actually does is to reject the 'realism of hypotheses' principle, which he wrongly conflates with Walras. The same is true for "Friedman's claim that the Marshall-Walras divide is not a matter of partial versus general equilibrium" (De Vroey 2009, p. 336).

As for the second claim, namely Friedman's claim to be Marshallian in the same way as Keynes is, this is also open to serious doubt. This second issue is more important for our overall purpose. Despite his own statement, Friedman would hardly share Keynes' conception of economics. Indeed, for the latter "economics is a branch of logic, a way of thinking" (Keynes 1938, CW 14, p. 296). Empirical criticism is far from satisfying as a critique of a theory. Ironically enough, Friedman claims to have rejected Keynes' theory, "not because [of] its simplicity, its concentration on a few magnitudes, its potential fruitfulness" but because "it has been contradicted by evidence" (Friedman [1972] 1974, p. 134). In Keynes' perspective a theory does not pass the test this way. For him, "the material, or the object of economics, were the beliefs, the opinions of economic agents" (Carabelli 2003, p. 218). That means that economics is definitely not comparable to natural sciences. Said differently, economics is for Keynes "a moral science insofar as it deals with ethical values and introspection" (Carabelli 2003, p. 218).[10] No doubt Friedman would utterly reject such a conception of our discipline.

The way Keynes is Marshallian stands in sharp contrast with the way Friedman claims to be. In short, Keynes belongs to the Marshallian lineage in the sense that his analysis is rooted in Marshall's price theory in the short period. To take but one example, Keynes the Marshallian clearly disentangles short-run from long-run expectations while the Modern Walrasians who stick to the rational expectations approach do not. Whereas Walrasian economics is merely timeless and considers equilibrium as consistency of individual plans, Keynes is interested in the study of the 'laws of motion' of society. Marshallians are concerned about motivation, Walrasians about realisations.[11] To be fair to Friedman, it must be noticed that Friedman too is Marshallian in a similar fashion as Keynes is, in the sense that Friedman too is interested in the 'laws of motion' of the system, time and dynamics; Friedman as well disentangles short-run from long-run expectations (but yet in a highly different manner to Keynes, as we will see in Chapter 5). What is sure is that this is *not* the way Friedman himself puts the issue.

It might be on the precise question of the distinction to be made between theory and model, and by the way on the issue of the place that should be dedicated to mathematics and macro-econometrics, that Friedman and Keynes come as close as possible in a Marshallian lineage.[12] The following argument put forward by Leijonhufvud (2006) about Keynes and Marshall against Walras applies easily to Friedman: "Today, 'to theorize' means to deduce the properties of a model from a given set of primitive postulates about tastes and technologies. 'Theory' and 'model' are understood as synonymous terms" (Leijonhufvud 2006, p. 72). No doubt Friedman would share this rejection of sophisticated and abstract model building. But the remaining of Leijonhufvud's quotation shows the sharp contrast between Friedman and Keynes if one tries to locate them in a Marshallian lineage: "Marshall and Keynes, in contrast, were philosophical realists. Theory to them meant a set of beliefs about the world and about how to understand it" (Leijonhufvud 2006, p. 72). It seems quite hard to rationalise

Friedman's 'as if' methodological stance within such a general methodological framework. Obviously, a common distrust towards sophisticated and purely abstract models does not necessarily turn into a common appraisal of what economics should be dedicated to and it even less provides a common Marshallian background. That is, there are different ways to claim to be a 'true' Marshallian.

Finally, did Friedman really end his career by disentangling Keynes from the Keynesians, as Hirsch and de Marchi (1990) or Dostaler (1998) argue? Actually, the late Friedman had a paper published in 1997 simply entitled "John Maynard Keynes" in the Federal Reserve Bank *Economic Quarterly* (which is not to be considered as a journal of popular science) that completely undermines this interpretation. After having presented Keynes' life Friedman turns to the influence of the *General Theory*. Strikingly, Keynes' influence in terms of economic policy is confined to the 'political exploitation' of the Phillips curve.[13] No doubt that for Friedman "the widespread rejection of some of the key propositions that constituted the 'Keynesian revolution'" (Friedman 1997, p. 5) pertains to the Keynesians as well as to Keynes. And when he comes to the message delivered by the *General Theory*, Friedman mentions the supposed reversal of Marshallian quantity and price dynamics[14] as well as the distinction between consumption and investment instead of the one between autonomous and induced flows of expenditures that he previously considered and praised. Moreover, what Friedman lastly presents as Keynes' theory is nothing but the IS-LM model in its crudest textbook version. One even finds there the 45-degree diagram, assigned to Keynes and considered with derision as "marvellously simple" (Friedman 1997, p. 11). Nowhere in this paper would the reader find any attempt to escape the mix-up between Keynes' economics and its IS-LM standardised version.

At the end, we are merely back to Friedman's initial crude appraisal of Keynes and the Keynesians: there is no genuine disentanglement. In Friedman's latest views, the collapse of the Phillips curve amounts to the collapse of the Keynesian revolution, and by the way the collapse of Keynes' economics itself.

2.3 The 'expectations critique' of the unemployment-inflation trade-off

Precisely, let us now direct our attention to the special issue of the Phillips curve. The most serious undermining of Keynesian economics comes with Friedman's assault on the Phillips curve and on the political exploitation of the supposed unemployment-inflation trade-off that ensues. As we have done above, we will stay focused on our disentanglement attempt. That is, is Friedman's expectations critique of the Phillips curve relevant for Keynes' system of thought? To do this, we will concentrate here below on the reading of two of Friedman's most influential papers, namely his "Role of the Monetary Policy" (1968a) and his "Nobel Lecture: Inflation and Unemployment" (1977a).[15] Our discussion of Friedman's own original key argument, namely the idea that the economy naturally gravitates around 'full employment' – defined as the natural rate of unemployment –

will be postponed to a later time. The same will apply to his analysis of the 'mechanism of adjustment'.

We will proceed in three steps. First, we will briefly outline Friedman's critique of the Phillips curve, which applies at both the theoretical and the empirical level. Second, we will assess the relevance of this critique for Keynes. We will show that Keynes' theoretical construct stands out quite immune of Friedman's critique. Third, even if this issue is not at the core of our matters of concern, we will take this opportunity to briefly assess the relevance of Friedman's point for the Keynesians of the neo-classical synthesis. With the benefit of hindsight, what appears is that Friedman's critique of the Keynesians is also open to doubt.

Friedman's appraisal of the Phillips curve

The Phillips curve is considered as both as an empirical relation and as a theoretical explanation of the labour market functioning. Initially, Phillips (1958) tried to evaluate a non-linear relation between the rate of unemployment and money-wage changes. Lipsey (1960) then took account of labour productivity and firms' mark-up to translate Phillips' relation into a decreasing function between the rate of unemployment and the rate of inflation. To put it very briefly, since the labour force bargains over the money wage and since its marginal productivity is decreasing, a rise of output and thus of employment entails cost inflation. While the money income is determined by aggregate demand, the labour force is able to share out the latter in price and in quantity effects. Shortly after Phillips' (1958) empirical findings Samuelson and Solow presented at the 1959 American Economic Association meeting a paper (published in 1960), which established the Phillips curve applying to the USA. Taking productivity and price mark-up into account allowed the Keynesians to transform the initial relation into a relation between price changes and unemployment. Despite its explicit title, namely "Problem of Achieving and Maintaining a Stable Price Level, Analytical Aspects of Anti-Inflation Policy", the message addressed to policy-makers was that government is able to 'purchase' lower unemployment through demand policy provided that ongoing inflation was tolerated. The Phillips curve was now interpreted as a static and stable function instead of a dynamic relation. What is more, the relationship was considered *reversible*: the bargaining between inflation and unemployment could be done either way. Reuber (1964) used the Phillips' curve to propose a "highly sophisticated analysis of the trade-off interpretation, completed with social indifference curves" (Leeson 1998b, p. 605). A political economics relying on the Phillips curve then emerged, thanks to social utility functions: a society was able to choose its own level of unemployment, to be exchanged for inflation. The macro-econometric exploitation of the Phillips curve was launched. Outstanding figures were involved in these debates and many of them were fully involved in advisory committees. To give just a few examples of the leading figures involved, one can cite Samuelson, Solow, Modigliani, Tobin and Klein.

This period was somewhat of a golden age for the economists of the Keynesian neo-classical synthesis. So the story runs.

Friedman's assault on the 'Keynesian' Phillips curve is twofold. First, the Keynesians are open to accusation of relying on a supposed decreasing relation between inflation and unemployment rates, which they wrongly consider as a stable relation in the long run. In Friedman's words: "the hypothesis that there is a stable relation between the level of unemployment and the rate of inflation was adopted by the economics profession with alacrity" (Friedman [1977a] 1987, p. 366).[16] Two distinct lines of criticism can be distinguished in Friedman's argument: the first one is theoretical while the second one applies on the policy level.

At the theoretical level, Friedman argues that the Phillips curve supposes short-sighted expectations. In his words: "Implicitly, Phillips wrote his article for a world in which everyone anticipated that nominal prices would be stable and in which that anticipation remained unshaken and immutable whatever happened to actual prices and wages" (Friedman 1968a, p. 8).

Friedman (1977a) referred to his own works (Friedman 1963, 1966a, 1966b and 1968a) to reject this stable relation on the basis of the weaknesses of its theoretical underpinnings: in no way should individual expectations be considered as short-sighted. What has been later called Friedman's expectations critique derived from this. As soon as private agents adapt their expectations to new rates of price rise, the trade-off vanishes. In other words, once inflationary expectations are viewed as endogenous the Phillips curve becomes vertical.

Friedman's second element of indictment against the Keynesians applies to their employment policy advocacies. Keynesians are open to accusation of using this stable Phillips curve with the view to lower unemployment beyond its 'natural' rate by bargaining inflation for unemployment. Yet, "only surprises matter" (Friedman [1977a] 1987, p. 352): as a direct outcome of the first critique stated above, as soon as inflationary expectations adapt to the new policy the trade-off vanishes. Such political exercises derived from the Phillips curve don't have any value as a basis for policy.

The relevance of Friedman's assault on the Phillips curve for Keynes

At first sight the Phillips curve produces results that are in line with Keynes' work, so that Friedman's critique could easily apply to Keynes. Indeed, for Phillips as for Keynes – and contrary to Friedman – price rise is a 'real' phenomenon, insofar as it results from rises in output and employment levels. Before full employment is attained, each increase in effective demand spreads itself into an increase of the employment level, and thus output, money wages and prices. Just after stating that, as a first approximation, the supply curve might be considered perfectly elastic during unemployment and perfectly inelastic once full employment is attained, Keynes specifies the "complications which will in fact influence events"[17] (Keynes 1936, CW 7, p. 296) so that prices rise *before* full employment is attained. In particular, Keynes takes account of the heterogeneity of both labour and supply curves in individual industries. Hence, for Phillips as for Keynes the price level rises because of the employment-level effect on the marginal cost – the industry mark-up can also be taken into account. There is no 'L-shaped' labour supply curve.[18]

Now, Phillips parts company from Keynes on the issue of the employment and money-wage dynamics. Indeed, in Phillips' dynamics the money-wage changes are a non-linear function of the unemployment level, that is of the gap between labour supply and demand:

> When the demand for a commodity or service is high relatively to the supply of it we expect the price to rise, the rate of rise being greater the greater the excess demand. Conversely when the demand is low relatively to the supply we expect the price to fall, the rate of fall being greater the greater the deficiency of demand.
>
> (Phillips 1958, p. 283)

But in Keynes' employment-wages dynamics money wages do not react to the labour-market disequilibrium. They are an increasing function of the demand for labour rather than a decreasing function of the gap between supply and demand for labour. This point is already dealt with in the *Treatise on Money* (1930) where Keynes distinguishes the "spontaneous" from the "induced" changes in efficiency wages (Keynes 1930, CW 5, p. 151). In the *General Theory* Keynes argues that during the expansion money wages rise as employment rises. Moreover, this function might be non-linear:

> For although the struggle for money-wages is … essentially a struggle to maintain a high *relative* wage, this struggle is likely, as employment increases, to be intensified in each individual case both because the bargaining position of the worker is improved and because the diminished marginal utility of his wage and his improved financial margin make him readier to run risks.
>
> (Keynes 1936, CW 7, pp. 252–3)

The reverse is also true, since "labour [is] readier to accept wage-cuts when employment is falling off" (Keynes 1936, CW 7, p. 10).[19] Hence, the initial Phillips curve that links together variations in unemployment rate and variations in money-wage rates does not take the specificities of Keynes' dynamics between employment and wages into account. The different labour-market dynamics at work in Keynes' and Phillips' respective frameworks constitutes a first reason for disentangling Keynes' theoretical apparatus from the standard Keynesian one.

To say it quite plainly, in spite of what was sometimes argued at the beginning of the 'Keynesian Revolution' Keynes' argument in no way relies on money illusion: the real-wage fall that follows the aggregate demand rise brings the labour force closer to its labour supply curve. That is, increases in the employment level are not – temporarily – obtained because the labour force confuses – again, temporarily – money wages and real wages. To properly under-stand this point, it must be kept in mind that in Keynes' system and in sharp contrast to Friedman's conception of the labour-market functioning it is the employment level that determines the real wage and not the reverse: "the volume of employment is uniquely related to a given level of real wages – *not the other way round*" (Keynes 1936, CW 7, p. 30; emphasis added). This will prove a highly critical characteristic to be investigated in our study of Keynes' and Friedman's respective appraisal of the monetary economies' functioning. Then, why do workers oppose money-wage cuts when they do not oppose real-wage cuts obtained through a rise in the price level – a fact that Keynes does not deny? The answer comes precisely from the monetary character of the economy. First, there is no way to directly bargain over the real wage but only monetary salaries: "for there may be *no* method available to labour as a whole whereby it can bring the wage-goods equivalent of the general level of money-wages into accordance with the marginal disutility of the current volume of employment" (Keynes 1936, CW 7, p. 13). Second, a proportionate money-wage cut would hardly be obtained in a decentralised economy: money-wage changes are progressive, sluggish and obtained through extrapolation.[20] Accordingly, money-wage bar-gains determine the *relative* real wage rather than the general level of real wage. Strikingly the lack of money illusion is even an argument put forward by Keynes to prevent inflationary spirals: "Everyone, including the trade unions, has become index number conscious. Wages will pursue prices with not so lame a foot. And this new fact means that the old-type *laissez-faire* inflation is no longer to be relied upon" (Keynes 1940, CW 22, p. 120).

Thus, on the one hand Keynes does rely on a short-run positive relation between the employment level and the price level – until full employment is attained. But regarding the labour market functioning it can hardly be argued that in Keynes' monetary framework increases in the employment level are obtained *through* misperceptions of real wages. Friedman's expectations critique hardly applies to Keynes' theoretical construct.

Let us get to the heart of the matter, namely the issue of inflationary policy. Does Keynes advocate inflation as a necessary means to obtain full employment? In other words, is Keynes an inflationist?

The first point to be brought to light is that, as a matter of fact, Keynes has always been a strong opponent of inflation. It is worth recalling that the pam-phlet *How to Pay for the War* (1940) is precisely written with the view to con-vince the opinion to finance the war effort while avoiding inflation. Keynes views his "compulsory savings" scheme as less unfair than the "inflation tax". He even talks about the "poison of inflation" (Keynes 1941, CW 22, p. 320). As Leeson (1999) states, Keynes is a "reflationist". But in no way is he an "infla-tionist". To understand this point one needs to distinguish on the one hand price increases which go hand in hand with the recovery at the end of the slump, i.e. '*reflationism*', and on the other "true inflation". The following statement under-lines very clearly the distinction at stake:

What do we mean by 'inflation'? If we mean by the term a state of affairs which is dangerous and ought to be avoided, – and, since the term carries to most people an opprobrious implication, this is the convenient usage – then we must not mean by it merely that prices and wages are rising. For a rising tendency of prices and wages inevitably, and for obvious reasons, accompanies any revival of activity. ... It is when increased demand is no longer capable of materially raising output and employment that it is properly called inflation.

(Keynes 1937, CW 21, pp. 404–5)

When inflationary pressures are in sight, such as for example in 1937, Keynes is led to discuss the opportunity of a further increase of aggregate demand due to the war effort. He is well aware of market rigidities as well as bottlenecks. Much more importantly he has the firm will to oppose these inflationary pressures:

So long as surplus resources were widely diffused between industries and localities it was no great matter at what point in the economic structure the impulse of an increase demand was applied. But ... the economic structure is unfortunately rigid, and ... (for example) building activity in the home counties is less effective than one might have hope in decreasing unemployment in the distressed areas. It follows that the later stages of recovery require a different technique. To remedy the condition of the distressed areas, ad hoc measures are necessary.

(Keynes 1937, CW 21, p. 385)

The second main point to be emphasised, which directly ensues from his fear of "true inflation", is that Keynes also opposes inflationary remedies to unemployment. That means that for him rising prices must be viewed as the *consequence* of the recovery: they are a "symptom of rising output and employment" (Keynes 1934, CW 21, p. 299). One cannot hope to increase output *through* inflationary remedies. During the recovery, price rises are interpreted as a signal of future profits. As such, this 'profit-inflation' renders the recovery easier. But "there is much less to be said in favour of rising prices if they are brought about at the expense of rising output" (Keynes 1933, CW 21, p. 292). Indeed:

Too much emphasis on the remedial value of a higher price level as an object in itself may lead to serious misapprehension of the part price can play in the technique to recovery. The stimulation of output by increasing aggregate purchasing power is the right way to get prices up; *and not the other way round.*

(Keynes 1933, CW 21, pp. 292–3; emphasis added)

So Keynes would not 'ride on' the steeper part of the Phillips curve to 'purchase' increases in the employment level. He would neither try to obtain the recovery *through* a direct policy aiming at price rises. In short, Keynes would not barter inflation for unemployment. How to achieve full employment without "true inflation"? The stress is led in Keynes' analyses on the necessity of planning and organisation:

> It is easy to employ 80 to 90 per cent of the national resources without taking much thought as to how to fit things in. For there is a margin to play with, almost all round. But to employ 95 to 100 per cent of the national resources is a different task together. It cannot be done without *care* and *management*.
>
> (Keynes 1937, CW 21, p. 409)[21]

What has been gained through this return to Keynes' original analyses? What has been established is that, as far as Keynes is concerned, Friedman misses the mark. To say it another way, the collapse of the Phillips curve should definitely not be conflated with the collapse of Keynes' construct at both the theoretical and the policy level.

The relevance of Friedman's assault for the Keynesians

What about the Keynesians? Although this is not central to our work we think it useful to briefly discuss Friedman's indictment of the Phillips curve for the Keynesians themselves, and in particular for the IS-LM proponents.[22] Recall that Friedman's dismissal of 'Keynesian economics' is that, first, a downward Phillips curve is nothing but an artefact and that, second, there is no point in relying on a trade-off between inflation and unemployment as a basis for economic policy. Let us consider the relevance of these two distinct claims for both Phillips and his Keynesian followers.

First, there is Phillips (1958)'s initial work. As is well known, this paper is exclusively empirical: from his data covering three periods (1861–1913, 1913–48 and 1948–53) Phillips draws "scatter diagrams" (Leeson 1997a, p. 162) that link together unemployment rates with rates of changes of money wages. What he argues is that the relation is stable in the long run. One problem is that Phillips' data actually hardly fit in what will later become the 'Phillips curve'. Precisely, the relation roughly holds only for the 1861–1913 period.[23] As shown by Leeson (1997a) Phillips' results didn't convince his colleagues, in particular those of the LSE Methodology, Measurement and Testing (M²T) Staff seminar group in which the reception of his findings was quite cold.

Much more importantly, there is the theoretical context of Phillips' inquiry, that is Phillips' matters of concern at that time. Here, a careful reading of his "Stabilisation Policy in a Closed Economy" (1954) is particularly enlightening. Phillips' concern in that paper is for the dynamics of macroeconomic disequilibrium. He is well aware of time lags that might affect a stabilising policy. Worse, it cannot be excluded that a "certain type of policy may give rise to undesired fluctuations, or even cause a previously stable system to become unstable" (Phillips 1954, p. 290). One cannot help noting the Friedmanian flavour of such a statement. In this 1954 paper, the matter at hand is the relationship between the level of output and the rate of change in prices. Clearly, the analysis is dynamic: each relationship stands for a particular growth path. Hence, the stabilised output targeted by stabilisation policy necessarily implies a constant level of prices. One cannot find any stable and decreasing relationship between inflation and output in Phillips' (1954) theoretical paper. Besides, one can see Phillips arguing:

> We may conclude that the self-regulating properties of the system will be considerably improved if there is confidence that any movement of prices away from the level ruling in the recent past will soon be reversed, and that if such confidence is sufficiently great the self-regulating properties will also be better, the higher the degree of price flexibility in the system.
>
> (Phillips 1954, p. 314)

It clearly appears that Phillips himself takes inflationary expectations into account. He anticipates Friedman's expectations critique when he argues that current price rises accompanied by the anticipation of enduring inflation will worsen the self-regulating properties of this dynamic system. Friedman's (1977a) twofold claim that, first, the acceptance of the hypothesis of stable relation between inflation and unemployment rates was associated with Phillips and that, second, "this relation was widely interpreted as a causal relation that offered a stable trade-off to policymakers" (Friedman [1977a] 1987, p. 350) is thus severely undermined, at least regarding Phillips himself. As a matter of fact, Phillips can be seen as "one of the most belonging insightful critics towards the Keynesians Phillips curve estimation industry" (Leeson 1998a, p. 79).[24]

At this stage, we have already taken issue with the idea that Friedman's expectations critique would be well targeted against both Keynes and Phillips. There remains the possibility that Friedman also misses his points when he targets the leading Keynesians of the neo-classical synthesis, a possibility overlooked by Leeson's overall work. That is, is it possible for the Keynesians of the 1950s and 1960s to have admitted without caution Phillips' 'scatter diagrams'? And did they view this relation as 'politically exploitable'?

Following the empirical work undertaken by Phillips, the very first paper that launched the policy exploitation of the Phillips curve is the famous paper by Samuelson and Solow in 1960, in which the reader does find the well-known transformed Phillips curve linking together the unemployment and the inflation rates. But Samuelson and Solow clearly acknowledge that the relevance of their relation is limited to the short run: the curve is very likely to shift in the next few years, because of changes in expectations and because of the policies undergone. Their basic matter of concern is this: how to shift the Phillips curve so as to obtain at once and at the same time low unemployment and zero inflation? Friedman would hardly deny the supply-side policies they advocate. Finally, what seems to have been overlooked concerning this founding paper is the lesson Samuelson and Solow draw regarding the possible existence of a Phillips curve (linking unemployment rate and increase in money wages) for the USA. Given their empirical findings, "there might be no such relation for this country" (Samuelson and Solow 1960, p. 187). If so, the remaining reasoning simply vanishes.

Another good example of the debates that occurred during the 1960s is the 1968 special issue of the *Journal of Political Economy* that opens with Brechling's paper. No doubt Brechling (1968) presents the Phillips curve within a sophisticated framework of collective indifference curves. But he acknowledges that, once the expectations hypothesis is considered as correct, the practical issue becomes an intractable problem: "the choice of optimal price and unemployment paths is likely to be extremely difficult in practice" (Brechling 1968, p. 720). So regarding Brechling, he might appear guilty of Friedman's first critique (i.e. he adopted the Phillips curve "with alacrity") but he is clearly not guilty of the second one: the practical issue remained for him fully open.

With the two examples above (Samuelson and Solow 1960 and Brechling 1968), one can see that the Phillips curve as well as its political exploitation were not necessarily "adopted by the economics profession with alacrity" (Friedman [1977a] 1987, p. 366). More severely, Forder (2010a, 2010b) makes a strong case against this story of the Phillips curve. What Forder claims is that, first, the 'expectations critique' was far from new at the time of Friedman's point and that this critique can be traced as early as in Fisher (1926). Next, Forder argues that no one conflated real and nominal values as Friedman claims was the case. Worse, inflationary advocacies were very rare.[25] All in all, in Forder's view Friedman's account of the Phillips curve turns out to be merely "the Phillips curve myth" (2010a).

Does it mean that Friedman's argument against the post-World War II Keynesian policies turns out to be almost ineffective? Wasn't there any subject of dispute at stake here for an economist concerned with data and model uncertainty in the short run as Friedman was? In this heated quarrel between Friedman and the Keynesians, there was probably another debate at stake than the political exploitation of the Phillips curve, namely the feasibility of short-term optimal control devices to implement counter-cyclical policies, which have been commonly referred to as 'stop-and-go' policies. To be convinced of this, let us quote Leijonhufvud's (1968b) comment of Brechling's (1968) paper (to be found in the same issue of the *Journal of Political Economy*). At the very end of his comment, Leijonhufvud (1968b) incidentally raises a slightly different issue than the political exploitation of the Phillips curve:

> To the policy maker who believes that this [Phillips curve] regression line represents the steady-state trade-off that he actually faces, the urge to *go* would be nearly irrepressible – the costs in terms of inflation of bringing unemployment to a fraction of 1 per cent are apparently negligible. Yet, he is being misled in more ways than one: Not only does the regression line not tell him of the 'stops' that will lie ahead if he succumbs to temptation, it probably gives much too rosy a picture of the trade-off open to him in the go-phase considered separately.
>
> (Leijonhufvud 1968b, p. 743)

Economists as a whole might have been well aware and for a long time that people are not myopic and that expectations cannot be treated as short-sighted; no one in the Keynesian school might have seriously conflated real and nominal values or rely on collective indifference curves tracing a trade-off between inflation and unemployment to call for such or such policy guidelines; and as a matter of fact inflationary policies might have been very rarely called for. However, a sharp divide remains between the Keynesian *counter*-cyclical policies (a concern that is merely alien to Keynes) and Friedman's concern for *anti*-cyclical policy. The Keynesian plea for short-term devices to correct and to pre-empt recessionary as well as inflationary gaps, the call for the 'fine-tuning' to stabilise the economic system very smoothly, all these are the type of policies that concentrate on the short-run issue and that rely on the hypotheses that policy-makers are able to detect departures from equilibrium in both prices and employment, but also to act wisely (i.e. with perfect knowledge regarding the structure of the economy) and timely (i.e. without any delay in both the implementation of policy devices), and that private agents react instantaneously to these devices. Friedman's assault on the Phillips curve might be the assault on a "myth", as Forder (2010a) argues. However, there remains Friedman's distrust towards 'Keynesian' fine-tuning and counter-cyclical policies.

Friedman's success in his critique of the political exploitation of the Phillips curve is explained by the rise of 'stagflation' during the 1970s. At that time, it clearly appears that a succession of discretionary counter-cyclical policies, a succession of 'stop' and of 'go' is very likely to increase the instability of a decentralised market economy, an instability that is acknowledged by Friedman in his Nobel lecture. Hence his bias for long-term schemes that aim to foster anti-cyclical policies.

2.4 Conclusion: Keynes, Friedman, and (hydraulic) Keynesianism

What has been gained from our study above? With no surprise a great gap often crops up between the initial thinking of an author, his matters of concern at the time he was writing and what history made of them. Let us take the example of Phillips. His initial work at both the theoretical and the empirical grounds hardly corresponds to the argument later taken at face value. Yet, the so-called 'Phillips curve' had a life of its own, despite the strong reservations expressed by Phillips himself and despite the initial cold reception of his findings. We have highlighted the same trouble with Samuelson and Solow (1960): there is a wide gap between the major concern of their paper, namely inflation control together with the maintenance of full employment, and the only two isolated paragraphs that have been unfortunately taken out of their original context. In his assault of the Phillips curve, Friedman mixed up the issue of a politically exploitable trade-off between inflation and unemployment (which is doubtful, as we have seen) with the issue of short-term devices and counter-cyclical policies aiming at the fine-tuning of the economy that were designed and implemented until the mid-1970s.

The issue is even more critical for Keynes, because there has been a lot of water under the bridge since the publication of the *General Theory*, because Keynes' thought was quickly popularised, and lastly because Keynes' pleas enjoyed a very fast distribution as a basis of policy – yet without Keynes' authority. Most of the arguments studied above that were put forward as 'Keynesian' actually superseded Keynes' own constructs, whether his original views on the labour market dynamics, his strong concern for up-to-date information, his fear of inflation, his rejection of inflationary policies, and so on. At the theoretical level, the Phillips curve hardly fits in Keynes' analytical framework. At the policy level, deficit spendings, optimal control devices and counter-cyclical policies confined to a near-term prospect can hardly be put forward in his name. The first lesson to be learnt is that the return to the original text of the authors proves a true necessity.

Second, people's thinking evolves over time. Needless to say, this is true for Keynes and his 'revolution'.[26] But this also applies to Friedman. At the very beginning of his career, Friedman was not so distant from the Keynesian advocators of functional finance and even closer to the Keynesian users of 'inflationary gap' analysis. During the 1940s and the 1950s, he basically argued that every precaution should be taken before any kind of State intervention. What he called for was basically more careful and in-depth analysis. As the time progressed and as the monetarist counter-revolution he contributed to launch rose, Friedman sharpened the arguments he put forward.

In the following chapter we will analyse Keynes' and Friedman's respective appraisal of the functioning of decentralised market economies like the one we currently live in. It is usually recalled that Keynes and Friedman are at odds on the self-adjusting capacity of a laissez-faire economy. Yet, the worlds faced by each of them stand in many respects in sharp contrast. Suffice it to mention the size of the State in the economy or the growing role played by socialised institutions such as the 'big company'. That is the reason why the stress will be placed on the theoretical underpinnings of their respective views, namely the salient features of a modern economy with regard to the old type of laissez-faire. Our aim is simple: to shed light on the way their policy prescriptions are embedded in their appraisal of the economic system functioning.

3 Private, public and semi-public institutions

3.1 Introduction

As a matter of fact, neither Keynes nor Friedman is directly interested in institutions as such but only to the extent that there is a problem to be solved, namely how to ensure full employment together with stable prices in a decentralised market economy. Our hypothesis in this chapter is that beyond their respective appraisal of a laissez-faire regime within a purely competitive system one can investigate their views on intermediate institutions situated halfway between an individualistic body and centralised authorities, such as the big company. This perspective should provide us with some clues regarding their respective understanding about the State as a collective body that might (or not) be able to help individuals to coordinate themselves. In other words, behind their specific pleas for the necessary implementation of new institutions, such as a Public Capital Budget for Keynes or a strictly passive monetary authority for Friedman, there are their specific diagnoses regarding the ability of the institutional arrangements they respectively face to stabilise a decentralised market economy around full employment. Our basic purpose here is to provide theoretical rationales to these diagnoses. Likewise, behind a critical look at State prerogatives there are questions such as: Is a 'modern' economy, characterised in particular by the separation of ownership and management, still able to function according to the 'invisible hand' principle? And are non-purely competitive firms such as semi-public bodies or a 'big' company necessarily detrimental for collective welfare? The study of Keynes' and Friedman's hardly reconcilable answers to these questions should allow us to better understand why the former calls for a 'new liberalism' while the latter advocates the return to the old principles of laissez-faire, i.e. the 'classical liberalism'.

We know well that their respective answers take place at years of distance and in a completely different institutional set-up: Keynes experiences the emergence of the welfare state without which market economies might not have escaped the worst depression ever known until then whereas Friedman faces the excesses of 'big government'. Hence the risk for our comparison to be anachronistic. Yet, our basic goal here is *conceptual*. It is not so much the relevance of their views on laissez-faire regarding the historical set-up they respectively face that interests us here, but rather how these analyses can give us some clues to their respective analytical constructs, especially regarding the issue of intertemporal coordination within uncertainty.

We will proceed as follows. We will first study Keynes' and Friedman's respective views on the efficiency of a laissez-faire regime within a purely individualistic system. With no surprise, their overall policy guidelines will appear as rooted in diametrically opposed stances towards laissez-faire and unfettered markets.

Second, we will turn to their respective way of broaching the subject of intermediate bodies that are halfway between the individual and the State. That is, we will investigate the confidence they place in the 'big company' or semi-public bodies (such as the Port of London for Keynes or the US postal service for Friedman) with regard to collective betterment. Here again, their respective understanding of the 'collective' issue is purely and simply symmetrical. As we see it, their hardly reconcilable appraisal of the 'State' as an institution must be apprehended in relation to these results. On the one hand, Keynes' distrust towards the ability of an individualistic body to behave according to collective welfare as well as his general confidence in collective bodies to cope with these inefficiencies well explain the encompassing duties he wishes to grant to centralised authorities. On the other, quite the reverse is true regarding Friedman because of his overall distrust towards anything which is not purely individualistic.

In the third section of this chapter, we will apply these results to shed light on Keynes' and Friedman's respective interpretation of the Great Depression. In some respect, close reasonings will be brought to light, especially regarding their similar explanation of the 1929 collapse with respect to the key features of the 1920s. In another sense Keynes' and Friedman's respective views will appear highly contrasted, especially regarding the way they grasp the interdependence at work between the real and the monetary spheres of the economy, and the way the 1929 financial collapse turned into the Great Depression. In our view, beyond their respective analyses of what happened in 1929 there is a clear clue as to their overall conception of public authorities' capacity to improve the functioning of our modern economies, i.e. to help private agents to coordinate themselves in a monetary economy.

We will conclude in drawing lessons about Keynes' and Friedman's relationships towards the 'real' through the appraisal of their 'policy philosophy'. As Vercelli (2010) does, "by policy philosophy, we mean more than the policy implications of economic analysis, as we want to capture their common rationale, but less than political philosophy as we focus exclusively on the economic policy side of the latter" (Vercelli 2010, p. 64). Neither Keynes nor Friedman conflates capitalism with unfettered markets. Both of them are well aware that a market economy needs a peculiar institutional setting mandatory for their own liberalism to operate well. Ultimately, what is gained with our investigation of Keynes' and Friedman's respective understanding of the 'individual versus collective' issue through the lens of institutions is a clear groundwork for the analysis of the employment policy (i.e. fiscal and monetary policy) that will be the subject matter of the next chapter.

3.2 The efficiency of unfettered competition

What should be thought of the ability of a laissez-faire regime within an unfettered competition system to sustain stability? Does this idealised image held by the old classical school prove irrelevant once one aims to assess the self-adjusting capacity of a decentralised market economy? If so, such a diagnosis would open the door for State intervention to substitute for the lack of self-stabilising mechanisms. But if on the contrary our economic system is viewed as possessing the self-correcting forces that ensure (at least after a transitory adjustment process) the stability of the economy around full employment (together with stable prices) and if temporary departures from the long-term equilibrium path are nothing more than excuses on the part of some pressure group for interfering in the free play of markets, this ideal of a laissez-faire regime does and will always correspond to the best policy guidelines we should conform to.

Let us see the arguments Keynes and Friedman put forward to motivate their (hardly reconcilable) respective policy philosophy.

Keynes and the decay of laissez-faire

Keynes' overall views about the efficiency of unfettered markets, and more generally about capitalism understood as both a political and an economic system, largely predate the publication of the *General Theory*. Keynes had always been doubtful about laissez-faire.[1] In this perspective, the Great Depression must be seen as a dramatic episode that strengthens Keynes' initial views rather than a radical turning point. Despite his own claim in the preface of the *General Theory*, there is no 'Keynes I' who would have been a true defender of laissez-faire – as well as there is no 'Keynes II' who would have promoted full employment at any price and would by the way agree to give up all the basic individual freedom necessary to this purpose.[2]

In his appraisal of the self-adjusting capacity of individualistic capitalism carried out in the *End of Laissez-Faire* (1926) Keynes distinguishes on the one hand the political economy of great 'classical thinkers' such as Smith, Bentham and Marshall from the dogma that became the "political economist's religion" (Keynes 1926, CW 9, p. 280) on the other. The former corresponds to what Vercelli (2010) calls "economic liberalism", namely "a set of descriptive and policy assertions on the properties of markets and their limits based on state-of-the-art economic theory" (Vercelli 2010, pp. 64–5). The latter corresponds to the crude principle of laissez-faire, which means "a general prescription in favour of unfettered markets lacking sound theoretical foundations" (Vercelli 2010, p. 64). Whereas great liberal economists were well aware of the shortcomings of unfettered competition, one of the best examples of this being Smith himself, Keynes complains that the caricature of individualistic laissez-faire now expresses a shared view by public opinion. Both and at the same time, his purpose is to fight the "old-fashioned individualism and *laissez-faire* in all their rigour" (Keynes 1925, CW 9, p. 280) while preserving the basic principles of the old liberalism, namely the basic individual freedom.

Keynes' denial of a laissez-faire system ability to reach efficiency has several layers. First, there is what we now call market imperfections that render unfettered competition inefficient. Second, the invisible-hand principle on which laissez-faire is based proves untrue: either individuals do not behave 'rationally' or rational behaviour on the part of individuals does not provide efficient outcomes at the collective level. Third, and most importantly, a monetary economy does not work like a 'real' one, which means that the system can stabilise itself far below full employment.

Let us start with market imperfections that exist in the economies in which we live and render unfettered competition irrelevant as an ideal type to rely on. These imperfections include market powers, economies of scale, time adjustments and delays. Smith himself was highly concerned by market powers and huge fixed costs that render public intervention inescapable, especially regarding transport infrastructures. There is also the case "when overhead costs or joint costs are present" (Keynes 1926, CW 9, p. 284) that we might conceive as including externalities in line with Pigou's definition of the latter in his *Economics of Welfare* (1932). From this standpoint, as a founding father of welfare economics Pigou would not disagree when Keynes states that "the important thing for government is not to do things which individuals are doing already, and to do them a little better or a little worse; but to *do things which at present are not done at all*" (Keynes 1926, CW 9, p. 291; emphasis added). Now, Keynes and liberal economists part company in the way they draw conclusions from the "unreal assumptions" (Keynes 1926, CW 9, p. 284) on which the model of free competition is based.

For Keynes, market imperfections cannot be considered only as second-order complications: they basically disqualify perfect competition as a relevant analytical framework.[3]

Keynes' second line of objection against a laissez-faire regime goes much beyond this insistence on market imperfections as a matter of fact that renders the competitive model based on unrealistic assumptions. It consists of denying any relevance to the basic principle of the 'invisible hand' on which laissez-faire is rooted. Let us quote extensively Keynes' clear-cut denial of this principle:

It is *not* true that individuals possess a prescriptive 'natural liberty' in their economic activities. There is *no* 'compact' conferring perpetual rights on those who Have or on those who Acquire. The world is *not* so governed from above that private and social interest always coincide. It is *not* so managed here below that in practice they coincide. It is *not* a correct deduction from the principles of economics that enlightened self-interest always operates in the public interest. Nor is it true that self-interest generally *is* enlightened; more often individuals acting separately to promote their own ends are too ignorant or too weak to attain even these. Experience does *not* show that individuals, when they make up a social unit, are always less clear-sighted than when they act separately.

(Keynes 1926, CW 9, pp. 287–8)

To point out the lack of rationality of individuals and the ability of collective bodies to behave more efficiently entails far-reaching implications. For Keynes, because of their ignorance, their irrationality and their lack of knowledge, individuals might not behave efficiently (i.e. they might not pursue their self-interest). It might be that, because they cannot develop long-term views, individuals are submitted to waves of irrationality as explained by crowd-psychology. This point is clearly made in the *General Theory* about the financial markets functioning: "a conventional valuation which is established as the outcome of the mass psychology of a large number of ignorant individuals is liable to change violently" (Keynes 1936, CW 7, p. 154). When human nature leads us to spontaneous optimistic action rather than inaction, what we observe is the result of what Keynes calls "animal spirits", namely "a spontaneous urge to action rather than inaction, and not as the outcome of quantitative benefits multiplied by quantitative probabilities" (Keynes 1936, CW 7, p. 161). It might be also that private businessmen do not possess the knowledge required to take efficient decisions or even that they are too ignorant to treat the information they get. Yet, in our view this line should not go too far. Keynes' main point against laissez-faire does not rest on the irrationality or cycling mood changes private individuals would suffer from.[4] Rather, one should insist here on the critical application of Keynes' theory of uncertainty: when full knowledge is lacking, when we do not know all the 'states of the world' and when we even don't know to which extent our knowledge is lacking, one can no more assume that rational behaviour, understood "in terms of reasoned pursuit of self-interest" (Sen 2008, p. 857) leads to efficient outcomes, at both the individual and the collective level. Here, the point is not so much that individuals adopt an irrational behaviour, but that the lack of information prevents the efficient outcomes that these rational individuals would have otherwise provided.[5]

Accordingly, it cannot be excluded that collective bodies may reach better results for the community than purely individualistic entities: they are less subject to waves of mass psychology, they can develop more easily long-term views and might be able to possess more knowledge about the economy behaviour. If so, individualistic capitalism clearly lacks firm roots and there is now room for public authority initiatives much more encompassing than the mere preservation of individual property rights and free trade.

The third argument that definitively disqualifies a laissez-faire regime is the harmful effects financial markets have on the functioning of a monetary economy. The rise of financial markets is not a peculiar matter of concern for Keynes at the time of the *End of Laissez-Faire* (1926) as it will become in the *General Theory* (1936); the 1929 financial collapse is a determining factor for the evolution of Keynes' system of thought. Here is to be found the most intractable paradox of our modern economies. On the one hand, the existence of organised markets for capital goods, which makes investment 'liquid' for the individual, can raise the demand price of newly produced capital assets. It might be true that the rise of financial markets is a crucial innovation that allows the development of a modern economy, which leads North to argue that "in the modern world, insurance and portfolio diversification are methods for converting uncertainty into risks and thereby reducing, through the provision of a hedge against variability, the costs of transacting" (North 1991, p. 106). In the language of the *General Theory*, the precautionary motive for liquidity preference is dampened. But on the other hand, private investors now use the best of their knowledge to forecast the market valuation of financial assets instead of trying to "defeat the dark forces of time and ignorance which envelop our future" (Keynes 1936, CW 7, p. 155). Hence a speculative motive for liquidity preference that invalidates the full employment postulate on which individual liberalism relies.[6] In a world in which, because of their distrust towards what the future might bring forth, private individuals are able to 'keep liquid' through the holding of monetary assets, the current product will not necessarily be bought back by the factors of production. In short, one cannot rely on Say's law to *postulate* full employment as a necessary outcome of free market competition in an individualistic competitive system.

Here is to be found the definitive objection to a laissez-faire regime: the lack of self-correcting forces in a market economy and the existence of involuntary unemployment as its corollary. As stated in the *General Theory*: "the weight of my criticism is directed against the inadequacy of the *theoretical* foundations of the *laissez-faire* doctrine …; – against the notion that the rate of interest and the volume of investment are self-adjusting at the optimum level" (Keynes 1936, CW 7, p. 339).

At this stage of our reasoning, one might consider that from Keynes' standpoint there is a dilemma to overcome in our current market economy. There might be *some* freedom to be conceded through State intervention in order to secure full employment in a market economy: "our problem is to work out a social organisation which shall be as efficient as possible without offending our notions of a satisfactory way of life" (Keynes 1926, CW9, p. 294). But once laissez-faire is seen as a disqualified principle for a monetary economy, another line of reasoning can be sustained. That is, when in a market economy full employment results as the outcome of free market operations merely by chance involuntary unemployment can be seen as "a restriction of the options set available to individuals" (Vercelli 2010, p. 72). Viewed this way, the liberal claim against State intervention is turned on its head. Public authorities' intervention proves a true necessity to restoring an unconstrained choice-set faced by any individual (and in particular by the unemployed workers): "any measure of macroeconomic policy that succeeds in relaxing the effective demand constraint, expands the liberty of economic agents at the same time" (Vercelli 2010, p. 72). When 20 per cent of the workforce is unemployed as was the case in Great Britain in 1933, there is no trade-off to be thought about. The very issue is to restore both and at the same time efficiency in a free market society and freedom for the unemployed individuals deprived of their basic rights[7] (freedom being there understood in the Marxian sense of 'real' freedom).[8]

Friedman on Adam Smith's 'flash of genius'

What about Friedman? As is well known, he "defended free markets indefatigably and in every forum" (Hetzel 2007, p. 22). This position at the policy level is firmly rooted in his methodological stance: his 'as if' principle leads Friedman to argue in his *Methodology of Positive Economics* that "the ideal types are not intended to be descriptive; they are designed to isolate the features that are crucial for a particular problem" (Friedman 1953c, p. 36). Accordingly, Friedman considers perfect competition as the only relevant background to understand both the behaviour of individuals and the free play of a decentralised market economy in which "firms can be treated *as if* they were perfect competitors" (Friedman 1953c, p. 38). Hence the case against Hotelling, for example: the denial of monopolistic competition as a relevant theoretical background despite the apparent 'realism' of its hypotheses ensues from this position of principle. To qualify the fact that prices provide both and at the same time the information and the incentive to react to this information, Friedman speaks of a "real beauty, and [he] use[s] the word 'beauty' advisedly" (Friedman [1981] 1987, p. 22).[9] In *Free to Choose* (1979) as well as elsewhere, a new distinct function of prices appears: "they determine who gets how much of the product – the distribution of income" (Friedman and Friedman [1979] 1990, p. 14). The point is that prices would no more operate their function of signalling if they were prevented from playing their other function, namely their distributive role.[10] As we will see below, to the exception of a "negative income tax" (1968b) to provide access to goods such as schooling or health care through the market (that would be otherwise considered as public goods if directly provided by centralised authorities) Friedman opposes any redistributive fiscal policy: as soon as one interferes with the free play of prices "the only alternative is command" (Friedman [1981] 1987, p. 23), that is authority.

This general confidence in the free play of markets leads quite logically for Friedman to praise Smith for his discovery of the 'invisible hand' principle:

> Adam Smith's flash of genius was his recognition that the prices that emerged from voluntary transactions between buyers and sellers – for short, in a free market – could coordinate the activity of millions of people, each seeking his own interest, in such a way as to make everyone better off. It was a startling idea then, and it remains one today, that economic order can emerge as the unintended consequence of the actions of many people, each seeking his own interest.
>
> (Friedman and Friedman [1979] 1990, pp. 13–14)

Efficiency is achieved through the coordination of millions of individual decisions without centralised authority. It is no surprise that Friedman has great admiration for Smith's principle – despite his critiques towards Smith investigated below. It is not only that everyone looking for his own interest nevertheless contributes to the achievement of collective welfare, the reaching out of a common purpose, but that any interference with this complex system that "looks like chaos to untutored eyes" (Friedman 1977b, p. 11), the introduction of the single 'command' element, would be detrimental for this "finely ordered and effectively tuned system" (Friedman 1977b, p. 11).

Last, his confidence in an unfettered markets system leads Friedman to deny the relevance of any trade-off between freedom and efficiency, but for highly different reasons than Keynes. For him, freedom and efficiency go hand in hand in the sense that the slightest measure detrimental for one of them is necessarily detrimental for the other, freedom being here considered as 'formal liberty' to borrow Marxian terminology.[11] Strikingly, the concept of freedom applies explicitly to both the economic and the political sides. Great thinkers of the nineteenth century like Bentham and the Philosophical Radicals considered at their time that political freedom was a means towards economic freedom. Yet, for Friedman the relation goes also the other way round. Considered from today's perspective: "The kind of economic organization that provides economic freedom directly, namely, competitive capitalism, also promotes political freedom because it separates economic power from political power and in this way enables the one to offset the other" (Friedman 1962a, p. 9).

Regarding our concern here for Friedman's appraisal of laissez-faire, four points are worth noticing. First, it should be recalled that one of Friedman's best achievements in the 'positive' side of his research programme has been to extend the free choice paradigm: since his pioneered work, we know that issues that seemed at first sight sociologically determined are also the result of rational arbitrage on the part of self-interested individuals maximising their own utility.[12] As a result, "if so this is useful, if negative, information to the would-be interventionist" (Hirsch and de Marchi 1990, p. 180). In Friedman's eyes, much more human activities involve market mechanisms than one could guess at first sight. Authoritative interventions to 'correct' what appear as market imperfections would do nothing but muddy the waters.

But how are these free choices made? This leads to our second remark about the individual decision-making process. According to Friedman, one does not need to investigate the way in which individuals make their decisions. As is well known, one of Friedman's most famous claims – and probably the most controversial – made in his *Methodology of Positive Economics* is that one should consider individual behaviours 'as if' they were rational. This specific point is the result of a more general claim that can be summarised as follows: "a theory should be tested by accuracy of its predictions independently of the realism of its assumptions" (Teira 2007, p. 511). With the help of two metaphors,[13] Friedman argues about firms:

> ...under a wide range of circumstances individual firms behave *as if* they were seeking rationally to maximize their expected returns ... and had full

knowledge of the data needed to succeed in this attempt; *as if*, that is, they knew the relevant cost and demand functions, calculated marginal cost and marginal revenue from all actions open to them, and pushed each line of action to the point at which the relevant marginal cost and marginal revenue were equal.

(Friedman 1953c, pp. 21–2)

In Friedman's view rational behaviour is validated as a working hypothesis by its predictive power. There is a critical assessment at stake here. For Friedman, there is no need to investigate individual rationality: one has the market outcomes to deal with that issue. To put it differently, through price devices within a perfectly competitive background (assumed as an 'as if' theoretical relevant ideal type) the market is par excellence the institution that provides us with collective rationality. We do not need cooperation since the market process is but the only way to put this issue of collective rationality.

Third, Friedman's manner of highlighting market process and free choices that operate through price incentives is easily applied to undermine Keynesian economics. Here, it suffices to mention Friedman and Becker's (1957) paper dedicated to the "Statistical Illusion in Judging Keynesian Models" and Friedman's *Theory of The Consumption Function* (1957). Where the Keynesians see the aggregate consumption function as sociologically determined (with the claim for underconsumption as its corollary to sustain the secular stagnation thesis) what is actually at stake for Friedman is free choices on behalf of rationally optimising individuals. Again, there is no basic flaw in an unfettered markets system.

Last, one must keep in mind that Friedman's distrust towards the State applies to both the economic and the political sides. In his wording, power must be as dispersed as possible in both the economic and the political 'markets'. That is precisely the reason why competitive capitalism, that Friedman also calls a "*free private enterprise exchange economy*" (Friedman 1962a, p. 13) is the only type of social organisation able to preserve at once and at the same time individual freedom, the "ultimate goal in judging social arrangements" (Friedman 1962a, p. 12).

With no surprise, Keynes' and Friedman's respective appraisals of a laissez-faire regime within an unfettered competition system are purely and simply symmetrical. In Keynes' eyes, there is a principle of realism that invalidates the old type of laissez-faire. Accordingly, one has to rethink the theoretical principles underlying the functioning of monetary economies as well as the policy guidelines necessary to provide self-correction mechanisms to the system. Keynes' plea for a capitalism "wisely managed" (Keynes 1926, CW9, p. 294), which appears a long time before the *General Theory*, is explained by his long-standing distrust of laissez-faire. At the opposite end, Friedman claims that the point is not whether the economy we live in does *really* function or not along the lines of unfettered competition; it is whether a competitive individualistic system provides good predictions or not. And he replies in the affirmative: his overall policy guidelines compel us to come back to the principles of the old liberalism and to bring our policy philosophy closer to a laissez-faire regime; a regime of which we can be sure that it enforces stability, at least in a long-term prospect, if we are to conform our institutional settings.

3.3 Collective bodies: the 'big company' and the 'State' as an institution

Besides the ability of a laissez-faire regime to stabilise a purely individualistic system, it seems to us worthwhile to consider Keynes' and Friedman's appraisal of intermediate bodies, about halfway between the individual and centralised authority. Truly, Keynes' matter of concern in his writings on semi-intermediate bodies such as a big company or the Bank of England are quite different from Friedman's purpose in his discourses on the 'social responsibility of business'. Yet, in our views the dividing lines running through their political advocacies easily appear through their respective consideration for the 'collective' with regard to the 'individual' that underpins their writings about intermediate bodies. That is, their respective views on State authorities to provide significant improvements can be enlightened by a close look at the confidence they respectively place in a group ability to take more efficient decisions than an individual with regard to collective welfare.

As we will see, the encompassing duties Keynes wishes the State to take responsibility of is explained well by his general distrust towards the individual capacity to take decisions in line with collective welfare. Regarding Friedman, it is quite the opposite: his general distrust towards the 'collective', which he considers very likely to be the victim of a 'hold-up' on the part of some particular interest groups, sheds light on his call for the dispersion of both political and economic power.

Keynes, intermediate bodies and the 'degree of publicness'

At his time, Keynes is not the only one to observe the separation between ownership and management that results from the rise of the 'big company', "the trend of joint stock institutions, when they have reached a certain age and size, to approximate to the status of public corporations rather than of individualistic private enterprise" (Keynes 1926, CW 9, p. 289). Due to the expansion of heavy infrastructures and industries, due to also the rise of financial markets that results in big banks and insurance companies, the 1920s witness the questioning of the individualistic model of entrepreneurship. As the time progresses, big institutions are "socialising themselves" (Keynes 1926, CW 9, p. 290). What does this mean? Decision-makers are no longer driven by the sole profit-making motive: "the general stability and reputation of the institution are the more considered by the management than the maximum of profit for the shareholders" (Keynes 1926, CW 9, p. 289). It is striking that Keynes does not draw negative lessons regarding what we now call 'agency inefficiencies'. In contemporary wording, the stress is not on the agent's ability to maximise his own interests instead of the ones of the principal, a behaviour that might prove highly detrimental for the principal's surplus and by the way would prevent the 'invisible hand' principle from achieving efficiency when there is no transparency. In sharp contrast with those who today draw lessons in terms of market inefficiencies due to asymmetric information, the rise of the 'big company' is seen by Keynes rather as an opportunity to escape the basic troubles of an individualistic laissez-faire regime. Big institutions take into account other interests than the ones of their shareholders, what we now call the social interests of the firm's 'stakeholders' (i.e. its consumers, suppliers, the trade unions, in brief all the publics of the civil society the company faces). In Smithian terms, the distinction between 'selfish' and 'self-interested' behaviour returns to the forefront, but now this dividing line applies to collective bodies and not exclusively to individuals.

The 'big company' takes into account many more objectives than the shareholders value, which results in the disqualification of unfettered competition to maximise collective welfare. What Keynes suggests is to "take full advantage of the natural tendencies of the day" (Keynes 1926, CW 9, p. 290) in encouraging "semi-autonomous corporations" in the middle between the individual initiative and the State, these institutions being defined as:

> bodies whose criterion of action within their own field is solely the public good as they understand it, and from whose deliberations motives of private advantage are excluded, though some place it may still be necessary to leave, until the ambit of men's altruism grows wider, to the separate advantage of particular groups, classes, or faculties.
>
> (Keynes 1926, CW 9, pp. 288–9)

Such an advocacy echoes the pleas made at that time and after in favour of corporatist thinking, especially regarding the industrial policy. Keynes himself claims for "a return, it may be said, towards medieval conceptions of separate autonomies" (Keynes 1926, CW 9, p. 289).

Regarding industrial organisation, the purpose is to encourage technological change, location of firms and workforce, etc., following the initiative and with the agreement of all the stakeholders involved. In the *End of Laissez-Faire* Keynes enumerates "separate autonomies" (Keynes 1926, CW9, p. 289), such as the Bank of England or the Port of London Authority (that possess an obvious collective welfare dimension despite their strictly private legal status), but also big companies such as a railway or an insurance company. As emphasised by Phelps (2010), "the system's performance thus depends heavily on the established roles of established companies, helped by local and national banks" (Phelps 2010, p. 92). In the case of "big undertakings, particularly public utility enterprises and other business requiring a large fixed capital [that] need to be semi-socialised" (Keynes 1926, CW 9, p. 290) Keynes calls for what we now consider generally as public-private partnerships instead of purely public ownership. In his words, "we must probably prefer semi-autonomous corporations to organs of the central government" (Keynes 1926, CW 9, p. 290).

In our view, this plea for semi-autonomous bodies and for collective centres of decision instead of purely individualistic decision-makers is to be interpreted with regard to Keynes' distrust towards 'individual rationality', understood as the relevance of the invisible hand principle discussed above. To put it differently, corporatism is to be evaluated with respect to pluralism: "corporatism and pluralism are regarded as different ways of representing interests within capitalist democracies, and of solving the problem of how the public interest is to be reconciled with private interests in the contemporary industrial state" (Gamble 1991, p. 45). Pluralism means an institutional system in which individuals compete for the full recognition of their own interests, the forming and re-forming of coalitions depending on the issue at stake. In this way pluralism refers to the old type of individualist laissez-faire. By contrast, corporatism is supposed to transcend individual interests through the recognition of key interest groups that are fully involved in the definition and the implementation of State policies. Strikingly, in Keynes' system of thinking there is no room for detrimental effects of pressure groups or for lobbying; the possibility for a State agency to be 'captured' by its members with the purpose to get a 'rent' is simply set aside.

Let us now see how Keynes' appraisal of the 'State' can be inferred from his appraisal of collective bodies and semi-public institutions. We will leave for the next chapter the special issue of the employment policy.[14] Let us focus here on Keynes' views on the 'State' understood as an institution. His overall conception of State duties evolves as time elapses, depending on the private sector's ability to reach by itself efficient outcomes. With no surprise his policy advocacies on the role public authorities should play in a market economy became much more comprehensive after the 1929 episode. Yet, his conception of the State as "an agent of social rationality" (O'Donnell 1989, p. 301) comes from afar.

First, this implies in one way collection of information about the current state of the economy and in the other dissemination of knowledge about the economic structure to private actors:

> It must be the avowed and deliberate business of the Government to make itself responsible for the wholesale collection and dissemination of industrial knowledge. The first condition of successful control and usual interference of whatever kind from above is that it must be done with knowledge.
>
> (Keynes 1927, CW 19, p. 643)

In line with Keynes' *Treatise on Probability*, to take more rational decisions requires more reliable knowledge, a point that would not deny the proponents of an 'enlightened' liberalism.

Second, there is the issue of planning, to which we will return extensively in the next chapter. The role to be played by planning strengthened with the Great Depression. In the late 1920s Keynes considered that the erection of a National Investment Board (Keynes 1931, CW 20, p. 307),[15] roughly defined as a semi-autonomous body, would suffice to coordinate private initiative. At the time of

World War II when the employment policy in peacetime was widely discussed, Keynes came to change his mind and then advocated a "Capital Budget" (Keynes 1945, CW 27, p. 405) on behalf of the Chancellor of the Exchequer. This implies more centralisation and more direct impulse of government bodies. The difficulty to plan investment, "the practical difficulties of initiative and organisation" (Keynes 1931, CW 20, p. 305), is a recurrent concern in Keynes' policy writings, whether the economy is experiencing a high level of unemployment as in the early 1930s or on the contrary when it approaches what Keynes called "true inflation" at the end of the decade. But what does Keynes mean by "planning"? The most comprehensive definition of planning is probably offered in 1932, in the worst of the Great Depression:

> Let us make a useful distinction. Let us mean by planning, or national economy, the problem of the *general* organisation of resources as distinct from the *particular* problems of production and distribution which are the province of the individual business technician and engineer.... It is at the times of slump that the paradox of starving in the midst of potential plenty is most striking and outrageous. But I believe that we suffer a chronic failure to live up the opportunities of our technical capacity to produce material goods. To remedy this failure is the problem of planning.
>
> (Keynes 1932, CW 21, p. 87)

In line with his overall conception of semi-autonomous bodies that implies public-private partnerships and a growing tendency towards corporatism, central planning in Keynes' meaning of the term does not entail public ownership of the means of production. Indeed:

> It differs from Socialism and from Communism in that it does not seek to aggrandise the province of the State for its own sake. It does not aim at superseding the individual within the field of operations appropriate to the individual, or of transforming the wage system, or of abolishing the profit motive.
>
> (Keynes 1932, CW 21, p. 88)

This insistence on the necessity to make compromise, the need to take advantage of the money-making incentive of the individualistic capitalism while taking into account the need for coordination on behalf of public authorities leads Keynes to support what can be called a "Middle Way" (O'Donnell 1989, p. 325). As far as economic affairs are concerned, Keynes' Middle Way doctrine can be well summed up in "the particular amalgam of private capitalism and state socialism which is the only practicable recipe for present conditions" (Keynes 1939, CW 21, p. 492).[16]

Last, there are also the miscellaneous questions of labour and wages, family allowances, and so on. Indeed, as early as 1927 Keynes argues that the State must "treat the gradual betterment of the economic welfare of the workers as the first charge of the national wealth, and not leave it to the accident of private organisations and of private bargaining" (Keynes 1927, CW 19(2), p. 646). At a time when efficiency wages are considered as too high, one can see Keynes enumerating all sorts of alternatives to the demands of trade unions, such as "social insurance", "pensions" and even "a great increase of useful expenditure by the state on health, and recreation, and education, and the facilities for travel", "the housing of the working class" and "children's and family allowances" (Keynes 1927, CW 20, p. 14). Again, his appraisal of capitalism goes much beyond the issue of unfettered markets.

All in all, Keynes' conception of the public authorities' duty is highly comprehensive. And the proper institutional setting (including the role played by associations, guilds and combinations) able to support a market economy proves a matter of deep concern for him. Many actors are involved to achieve the updated liberalism he calls for: government bodies of course, but also trade unions, corporations such as semi-socialised companies and even "separate autonomies" (Keynes 1926, CW 9, p. 289) such as the Bank of England or the Port of London Authority, which are involved in the social interest despite their private legal status.[17] Actually, any body that is supposed to deal with the social interest and whose interests might go beyond the individualistic profit-making, whatever private law body or governed by public law, can be considered as belonging to the 'State' in Keynes' meaning of the word. This is precisely the position held by Skidelsky:

> Keynes's 'state' was defined, not by legal prerogative but what we might call 'degree of publicness'. By the 'state', he meant not the government and its servants, but that group of institutions, whether privately or publicly owned, which pursue public interest aims rather than short-term profits.
>
> (Skidelsky 2000, p. 273)

In our opinion, so a large and all-encompassing conception of State duties should come with no surprise to a reader who is reminded of both Keynes' denial of the invisible-hand principle to substantiate a laissez-faire regime within a purely competitive system and his bias towards 'collective' rationality. Ultimately, we should take advantage of the natural tendency of our modern economies towards concentration and socialisation to implement new policy guidelines.

Friedman as (not a true) libertarian

When Keynes argues that the role of his country should be "to preserve the liberty, the initiative and the idiosyncrasy of the individual in a framework serving the public good and seeking equality of contentment amongst all" (Keynes 1945, CW 27, p. 369), Friedman would hardly disagree in principle. Yet, what is implied by the development of this "middle way of economic life" (Keynes 1945, CW 27, p. 369) is merely alien to Friedman. There are plenty of statements that show Friedman as a libertarian, far from Keynes' 'new liberalism'. Indeed, Friedman would not bear the slightest concession to an individualistic system. As shown below, this is rooted in his overall distrust towards anything that is 'collective'.

Let us separate this big issue into three parts: first Friedman's appraisal of externalities and the way we should – or not – solve them; second his strong case against our contemporary concern for the 'social responsibility of business' together with the 'collective' bias which constitutes its rationale; last his conception of the State as an institution, which is embedded in his strong bias for the 'individual' at the opposite of Keynes' stance for the 'collective'.

Let us start with the issue of externalities, which Friedman calls "third-party effects" (Friedman and Friedman [1979] 1990, p. 31). In our view, his appraisal of externalities highlights his overall distrust towards State intervention. Friedman freely acknowledges that

> the market operates defectively in those cases in which an important part of the effects of any transaction – either benefits or costs – impinges on parties other than those directly involved in the transaction, parties whom it is difficult to identify.
>
> (Friedman [1981] 1987, p. 32)

Externalities open the door for public interventions but they "have typically turned out to do more harm than good" (Friedman [1981] 1987, p. 32). Friedman very rarely acknowledges a possible case for State intervention to cope with externalities.[18] His general position turns to deny any capacity of centralised authority for the improvement of market functioning, even in the case of externalities.

Consistently with this denial of State ability to mitigate externalities, Friedman utterly rejects Smith's famous third duty of State authorities, which he considers quite "mischievous" (Friedman 1977b, p. 11) insofar as it allows for a quite unlimited intervention of State authorities in the free play of markets. Let us remind ourselves that this third duty means:

> … the duty of erecting and maintaining certain public works and certain public institutions, which it can never be for the interest of any individual, or small number of individuals, to erect and maintain; because the profit could never repay the expense to any individual or small number, though it may frequently do much than repay it to a great society.
>
> (Smith [1776] 1930, in Friedman 1977b, pp. 10–11)

Friedman's critique is twofold. First, one should not forget that Smith considered only positive externalities; a negative externality such as the famous example of pollution is removed from Smith's analysis. Hence, we have gone too far in relying on this argument to support State intervention. Second, Smith's argument passes over further effects caused by the attempt to solve neighbourhood effects. This turns out to be a major element for Friedman's denial of State authorities' ability to improve market functioning: "governmental actions have further external effects, via their method of finance and via the danger to freedom from the expansion of government" (Friedman 1977b, p. 11). No doubt that in his views the best can easily be the enemy of the good. In this way, he shares Say's famous statement: "*A la tête d'un gouvernement, c'est déjà faire beaucoup de bien que de ne pas faire de mal* [At the head of a government, it is already doing a lot of good by not doing harm]" (Say [1803] 1841, p. 23).[19]

The next issue is Friedman's appraisal of collective bodies such as the 'big company' and in particular his harsh critiques towards our contemporary concern for the 'social responsibility of business'. As is well known, Friedman is a tough opponent of the latter. He offers several clear-cut statements against the ones who claim that 'businessmen' in a modern society should have strong concern for other interests than those of the shareholders. Much has been written about his paper in the *New York Times Magazine* entitled "The Social Responsibility of Business is to Increase Profits" (1970b). Indeed "with very few exceptions, every major article on or analysis of corporate social responsibility since ... has cited, mentioned, or challenged it" (Hood 1998, p. 682). Already in *Capitalism and Friedman* Friedman argued that:

> In such [a free economy], there is one and only one social responsibility of business – to use its resources and engage in activities designed to increase its profit so long as it stays within the rules of the game, which is to say, engages in open and free competition, without deception or fraud.
>
> (Friedman 1962a, p. 133)

In the 1970 paper, the following clarification is added: that responsibility of the corporate executive is generally "to make as money as possible *while conforming to the basic rules of the society, both those embodied in law and those embodied in ethical customs*" (Friedman [1970b] 1987, p. 37; emphasis added). In brief and adamantly opposed to Keynes' claim in the *End of Laissez-Faire* (1926), in no way should one consider the 'stakeholders' as an issue. Here again Smith is convened to remind us that regarding the individual:

> by pursuing his own interest, he frequently promotes that of the society more effectually than when he really intends to promote it. I have never known much good done by those who affected to trade for the public good.
>
> (Smith [1776] 1930, p. 133)

The crude and quite provocative tone of this plea set aside, Friedman's claim raises a number of ambiguous issues. First, the two major examples considered by Friedman are puzzling. Indeed, why only consider examples such as pollution or the hiring of hard-core unemployed? Truly, the corporate executive who takes into account this sort of 'social interests' penalises the firm he manages. But there is no reason to restrict the scope of the analysis to activities that prove undoubtedly detrimental for the owners of the firm, its wage earners or its consumers: "this is a starkly and profoundly zero-sum definition of what 'social responsibility' actually is" (Feldman 2007, p. 128). Further, once reminded that Friedman takes the 'basic laws of society' and the 'ethical customs' into account in his reasoning this clear-cut denial of 'social responsibility of business' becomes much more difficult to rationalise. Indeed, "in fact, pushed to an extreme, ethical custom could entail social democracy or a highly controlled form of mixed capitalism – things that Friedman would clearly abhor" (Feldman 2007, p. 129). Lastly, the reference to Smith's invisible hand to thwart this social matter of concern might appear as incongruous to a careful reader of Smith's political economy. Classical liberal thinkers in general, and Smith in particular, were quite alien to what appears here as a plea for a 'libertarian economy'.[20] To say the least, to take into account 'sympathy' or the imaginary (and internal) figure of the 'impartial spectator' – both concepts to be found in Smith's other magnus opus *The Theory of Moral Sentiments* (1759) – would render Friedman's line of argument much less easily defensible.[21]

But this is to forget that for Friedman "only people have responsibilities". Or to put it another way "a corporation is an artificial person" (Friedman [1970b] 1987, p. 36). Hence, there is no room for the 'collective' in a competitive economy, neither in terms of behaviour nor in terms of rationality and intention. Friedman is clear that "self-interest is not myopic selfishness" (Friedman and Friedman 1979, p. 27) so that private charity and ethical behaviour are not excluded in general but they ought to be removed from the economic sphere of the society. A society is, if not *should be*, a collection of individuals, all of them being selfish in the economic market and self-interested at a general level. So the issue is not only an issue of accountability, the fact that a manager *should be* nothing but the 'agent' of the shareholders. Friedman considers that, in taking 'social interests' into account the individuals who behave that way inevitably replace market mechanisms by political devices in an undemocratic fashion. In other words, they introduce a certain degree of collectivism in a free society. All in all, as Hayek claims in his *Road to Serfdom* (1944) such activities undertaken by individuals on behalf of a collective pave the way for Socialism.

Let us now see how this denial of any responsibility for collective bodies lead Friedman to confer to the State very restricted and narrow duties. Isn't he the author of the pamphlet *Why Government Is the Problem* (1993a)? Friedman is against the prohibition of drugs and the public management of schools, postal service, air traffic, highways, and so on. He also favours "An All-Volunteer Army" (1967a). Now, we know well that competitive capitalism can only be effective within a legal system that guarantees respect for the rules of the game: the return to the 'old type of liberalism' as advocated by Friedman in no way amounts to 'do-nothing' policies. That is, Friedman is not a true libertarian. The most comprehensive role attributed to State authorities by Friedman is to be found in *Capitalism and Freedom* (1962a):

A government which maintained law and order, defined property rights, served as a means whereby we could modify property rights and other rules of the economic game, adjudicated disputes about the interpretation of the rules, enforced contracts, promoted competition, provided a monetary framework, engaged in activities to counter technical monopolies and to overcome neighbourhood effects widely regarded as sufficiently important to justify government intervention, and which supplemented private charity and the private family in protecting the irresponsible whether madman or child – such a government would clearly have important functions to perform. The consistent liberal is not an anarchist.

(Friedman 1962a, p. 34)

There is first the care for the disabled and the needy, especially in a developed country. Friedman opposes the direct provision of public goods and public services. What he calls for is instead in a negative income tax.[22] A welfare programme based on a payment in money instead of a payment in kind would have two major advantages: first "it treats indigent as responsible individuals, not incompetent wards of the state"; second "it gives indigent an incentive to help themselves" (Friedman [1968b] 1987, p. 60). Better help people to have access to voluntary exchange through to the market rather than interfering with the functioning of a *"free private enterprise exchange economy"* (Friedman 1962a, p. 13). The same applies to his call for the abolition of the corporate tax.[23] Friedman's famous plea for a voucher plan for schooling should be interpreted along these lines: better to help households to finance the school of their choice rather than to provide the public furniture of schooling. The less interference with the free play of unfettered markets, the less loss of collective efficiency. We do not need other institutional settings than the perfect functioning of market process.

Second and most importantly, there is the issue of monetary affairs. Friedman does take seriously the monetary character of our economies. Accordingly, the field of money is beyond doubt Friedman's deepest matter of concern regarding the functioning of our current institutional set-up and the possible need to erect new public bodies and to design new policy regimes. The following quotation summarises well Friedman's overall goal:

The problem is to establish institutional arrangements that will enable government to exercise responsibility for money, yet will at the same time limit the power thereby given to government and prevent the power from being used in ways that will tend to weaken rather than strengthen a free society.

(Friedman 1962c, p. 220)

The very crucial duty of State authorities in a monetary economy should be to anchor nominal expectations. With a high degree of confidence in the institution setting, private agents can have a high degree of confidence in their ability to disentangle changes in relative prices from changes in the general price level. Hence the reinforced capacity of a monetary economy to stabilise by itself around full employment. Contrarily to other liberal economists that call for free banking (like the late Hayek) Friedman's political system noticeably makes room for a monetary authority. Yet, Friedman opposes an independent central bank since this would mean too much leeway and power for central bankers.

As the time progressed after 1962, it is striking that the extent of State responsibilities as envisioned by Friedman became narrower and narrower. In a way, on this issue Friedman travelled the path in the opposite direction with respect to Keynes who envisioned larger and larger State prerogatives. This is particularly true regarding the issue of monopolies and anti-trust law. Friedman's initial point was that monopolies obviously alter voluntary exchange in a free society, whether due to enterprise or labour market power. Accordingly, he called for "the elimination of those measures which directly support monopoly, whether enterprise monopoly or labor monopoly" (Friedman 1962a, p. 132). Friedman initially praised anti-trust laws, not basically because of their *ex post* effects for those caught defrauding but rather because of their *ex ante* effects in rendering collusion more expensive. He later changed his mind, becoming even distrustful towards State authorities in the field of the promotion of competition through anti-trust laws. This is also true regarding the regulation of the monetary side of the economy. From his initial position stated in terms of automatic stabiliser (monetisation of public deficits and demonetisation of surplus) Friedman moved to a highly passive monetary rule, what he called "legislated rules" (Friedman 1962c, p. 239). This means that this *passive* monetary authority would become a within-government body. This plea for a strictly governmental monetary authority appears as second best option with regard to our modern institutional framework: a day might come where purely free banking would be feasible.[24] All in all, to the critical exception of monetary affairs, what characterises Friedman's overall policy guidelines is an 'abstentionist' viewpoint:

> Speaking for myself, I do not believe that I have more faith in the equilibrating tendencies of market forces than most Keynesians, but I have far less faith than most economists, whether Keynesians or monetarists, in the ability of government to offset market failure without making matters worse.
>
> (Friedman's interview in Snowdon and Vane 1999, p. 138)

How to explain this growing distrust of State authorities? First, the government is under the pressure of lobbyists, the influence of special interests, which means that the costs of some State intervention (which are dispersed) largely exceed their benefits (which are concentrated). Noticeably, such a line of criticism is merely alien to Keynes' political system of thought. Second, Friedman claims that "the incentive of profit is stronger than the incentive of public service" (Friedman 1993a, p. 8) so that the bottom line is much stronger for private enterprises than for public bodies. Regarding schooling, for example, a voucher plan would enable "a private, for-profit industry ... that will provide a wide variety of learning opportunities and offer effective competition to public schools" (Friedman 1995, p. 1). There is no reason that the privatisation engaged in all the other industries (the 1990s witnessed the privatisation of almost all network-type industries) would not be successful within the education area. Again, in Friedman's eyes the market is the very institution that provides us with collective rationality. Thanks to the implementation of this new competitive market, education would no longer need to be considered as a pure collective good. And this point too is fully passed over by Keynes. Third, Friedman's growing distrust of State authorities is easily explained by the emergence of a new discipline, namely the new 'public choice' economics initiated by Buchanan – one of his colleagues in Chicago. Buchanan and Tullock (1962) argue that there is no benevolent State as such. Civil servants are viewed as bureaucrats maximising their own utility, which might depend on their discretionary power but also on their 'altruism' or whatever they consider the common good. That is the reason why an anti-trust body for example is very likely to be *captured* by its members.[25] Friedman is highly enthusiastic about this new discipline:

> The public choice perspective is extremely attractive intellectually because it aligns our interpretations of government and private activity. It has led to extensive research on the determinants of governmental behaviour as well as to renewed attention to the kinds of institutions and policies, if any, that can make each participant in government as in a free market operate as if, in Adam Smith's famous phrase, 'he were led by an invisible hand to promote an end that was no part of his intention', namely, the interest of the public.
>
> (Friedman and Schwartz 1986, p. 38)

In our view, we should go beyond these purely economic reasons for a narrow role dedicated to the State. Let us take the example of education. For Friedman, it is not only that the education institution has been *captured* by its members, as we would say in contemporary wordings, to secure an economic *rent* but also for political reasons: "one strong argument in favor of privatization has to do with the values instilled by our public education system" (Friedman 1999, p. 6). Here is to be found a critical interaction between 'economic' and 'political' markets that reminds us that in Friedman's eyes economic and political freedom form an indivisible whole. Friedman is vitriolic when he states that "our public education system is a socialist institution. A socialist institution will teach socialist values, not the principles of private enterprise" (Friedman 1999, p. 6). Hence the plea for schools administrated at the local level, where they are more easily controlled by citizens: economic freedom necessarily goes hand in hand with political freedom.

Let us take stock of Keynes' and Friedman's respective appraisal of the institutional settings they face while focusing on the principles that underlie the latter. Both of them claim to be liberals. Yet, Keynes aims to take advantage of the natural tendency in his days towards concentration and socialisation with the view to implement a 'new liberalism' whereas Friedman sees the injurious rise of the 'big government' and calls for a return to the old 'classical liberalism'. Their respective policy philosophies appear hardly reconcilable: both on the efficiency of a laissez-faire economy and on the ability of semi-autonomous bodies or of big companies to improve collective welfare, their respective appraisals are simply and completely symmetrical.

In our view, their respective understanding of the ability of a group to achieve better results than a purely atomistic body provides a cogent rationale to their hardly reconcilable stances regarding the ability of centralised authorities to improve the functioning of a market economy. On the one hand, Keynes would fully agree with Sen when the latter argues:

> It is by no means clear that individual self-interest-maximizers will typically do relatively better in a group of people with diverse motivations. More importantly, when it comes to comparison of survivals of different groups, it can easily be the case that groups that emphasize values other than pure self-interest maximization might actually do better ...
>
> (Sen 2008, p. 860)

On the other hand, this sort of reasoning is merely alien for Friedman: from his standpoint, one has nothing but the market process (i.e. price devices within perfect competition) to provide collective rationality.

From now on, we have taken issue with Keynes' and Friedman's respective ways of grasping the self-stabilising properties of an unfettered competitive system. We also have tried to find some rationales to their respective assessment of a laissez-faire regime in the confidence they place in the 'collective' by contrast to the 'individual'. Let us now apply these results to their peculiar analysis of the 1929 financial crisis and in particular to the way it turned into the Great Depression.

3.4 The Great Depression as a case study

Nowhere else was the depression as severe as in the USA. Between 1929 and 1933, output fell there more than 38 per cent. In particular, business investment fell by nearly 80 per cent. Total employment (including government workers) fell about 24 per cent so that the unemployment rate rose to 25 per cent.[26] During the same period the unemployment rate rose 'only' to 20 per cent in Britain. Depending on how they are measured, wages and prices cuts followed contrasted paths during this period. What is certain is that money-wage cuts (which were about one-third) were lower than in wholesale prices (which were cut by about half) so that as a matter of fact real wages *increased*. Besides, from 29 October 1929, known as Black Tuesday, to early 1930 asset prices at the New York Stock Exchange lost 30 per cent of their value. Now, as reminded by Gazier (2011) the characteristic features of the Great Depression "do not lie either in its magnitude or in the roughness of the collapse" (Gazier 2011, p. 92). Indeed, the 1987 crash in the New York Stock Exchange was similar to that of 1929 but it didn't give rise to any collapse in the economic activity of the United States. The same applies to the collapse of the 'new technologies bubble' in 2000–02. Instead of that, it is the whole period between 1929 and 1939 that appears as specific "with the deflationary pressures and the difficulties of restarting once the minimum is attained" (Gazier 2011, p. 92). The role played by the Gold Standard is unclear. Britain came back to the Gold Standard but yet abandoned it again in 1931. He United States did the same in 1933, which signifies the definitive collapse of the Gold Standard system.[27] What is sure is that "the 1929 crisis is thus the first to cause a point of disruption in trajectory on a global scale" (Gazier 2011, p. 93).

On the one hand, Keynes experiences the Great Depression as a contemporary. At his time, to understand what is happening and to offer proper remedies is a matter of economic and political emergency. On the other hand, Friedman faces this episode rather as a historian and his *Monetary History of the United States* (1963) co-written with Schwartz is still considered as a landmark.[28] In terms of comparison between our two authors, the issue here is complicated in that hardly reconcilable views coexist with similar analyses of the salient features of the economy *before* the financial collapse – especially as far as the banking sector behaviour in United States is concerned. For our purpose, two issues should be disentangled. First, what was the very cause of the 1929 collapse? Second, how did the financial crash turn into the Great Depression? There has been a huge literature on both these issues and the debate is unlikely ever to be resolved: the full and definitive explanation of the Great Depression turns to be the 'Holy Grail' of macroeconomics – to borrow the words of Bernanke (1995). In what follows, the stress is laid on the rationales behind Keynes' and Friedman's respective appraisals. That is, how did the real and the monetary spheres of the economy interact during that period? And what are the lessons to be learnt from the Great Depression regarding the self-adjusting capacity of a monetary economy? On the policy side of the debate, does this dramatic episode prove a definitive case for the State intervention to stabilise the economy in case of severe and protracted shock? Or at the opposite end is the Great Depression the best example of a deep recession 'created' by State authorities? What will be brought to light by this case study is that, in sharp contrast with the Austrians and despite Friedman's own claim for laissez-faire, both Keynes and Friedman belong to the interventionist wing of economists who favour 'reflationism', although the precise policy devices entailed by their own interventionist stance are not to be denied.

As shown below, Keynes' appraisal of the Great Depression can be rationalised as an extension, a development upon Friedman's one, which focuses on the monetary side of the economy. For this reason, we will start with Friedman. We will then study the case made by Keynes. We will then conclude in drawing some parallels with the current 'Great Recession'.

Friedman and the case for a State-induced recession

At the theoretical level, Friedman makes a strong case against the Austrian interpretation of the Great Depression, through his analysis in terms of aggregate and his denying of any detrimental role played by nominal rigidities. At the policy level too, Friedman and the Austrians, and in particular Hayek and Robbins, are poles apart. Friedman even points out their responsibility on the way the financial bust turned into the Great Depression:

> I think the Austrian business-cycle theory has done the world a great deal of harm. If you go back to the 1930s, which is a key point, here you had the Austrians sitting in London, Hayek and Lionel Robbins, and saying you just have to let the bottom drop out of the world. You've just got to let it cure itself. You can't do anything about it. You will only make it worse.... I think by encouraging that kind of do-nothing policy both in Britain and in the United States, they did harm.
>
> (Friedman in Epstein 1999)[29]

Let us first provide an outline of Friedman's explanation of the Great Depression. We will then see the lessons he draws regarding the role State authorities should play to sustain the self-stabilising capacity of a monetary economy.

First, Friedman and Schwartz situate the 1929 episode in a long-run perspective that portrays the late 1920s as a very special period, "a period of high prosperity and stable economic growth" (Friedman and Schwartz 1963, p. 296). In their eyes, the monetary policy carried out during that period was highly efficient: "the close synchronism produced much confidence within and without the System that the new monetary machinery offered a delicate yet effective means of smoothing economic fluctuations" (Friedman and Schwartz 1963, p. 296). Strikingly, the diagnosis offered by Friedman and Schwartz is simply the opposite of the 'relative inflation' considered by the Austrians,[30] despite the inflating bubble in the Stock Exchange index:

> The economic collapse from 1929 to 1933 has produced much misunderstanding of the twenties.... Far from being an inflationary decade, the twenties were the reverse. And the Reserve System, far from being an engine of inflation, very likely kept the money stock from rising as much as it would have if gold movements had been allowed to exert their full influence.
>
> (Friedman and Schwartz 1963, p. 298)

In the eyes of Friedman (and at the opposite end of the view held by Hayek, for example) the 1920s appear as a 'Golden Age' for the conduct of monetary policy, despite the lack of clear theoretical foundations for the latter. From 1922 to 1928, the Reserve System was greatly influenced by the banker Strong (governor of the Federal Reserve Bank of New York). As reminded by Timberlake (2008) Strong was well aware that as a matter of practice the Gold Standard had not been operational since 1917. As a consequence, the monetary policy he promoted rests on a modified quantitative theory of money that aims at the stability of the price level. At the very end of the 1920s, the implicit reliance (or worse the explicit reliance in the case of the influential Miller, a senior member of the Board of Governors) upon the real bills doctrine proved tragic.

This leads us to the second stage, i.e. the 1929 financial collapse. The tightening of monetary policy implemented to discourage the use of credit for speculating in Wall Street discouraged too the use of credit for 'productive' reasons. The decline in the total money stock and wholesale prices appeared *before* the 1929 financial collapse. No doubt a restrictive monetary policy precipitated the collapse: the Fed "followed a policy which was too easy to break the speculative boom, yet too tight to promote healthy economic growth" (Friedman and Schwartz 1963, p. 298).

Third, how did the 1929 financial collapse which could have given rise to a standard recession turn into the Great Depression? Again, the Fed played in this episode a critical (and dramatic role). Indeed, *before* the creation of the *Federal Reserve Board*, banking panics (such the 1907 one) were mainly managed at the local level by the banking system itself thanks to clearinghouses erected by the banks involved, through 'bank holidays' and suspension of withdrawals (that is, a restriction of convertibility of deposits into currency for the public) but not necessarily through suspension of payments. The Fed was created in 1913 with the precise intention of improving the management of banking panics. The Great Depression is for Friedman and Schwartz a direct outcome of the – unfortunate – tightening in monetary policy conducted by the Fed that turned an ordinary recession into a dramatic contraction. The money stock (i.e. currency held by the public, demand and time deposits) fell by one-third between 1929 and 1933 – a fact unique in the monetary history of the United States. Even if money stock, money income and price level roughly fell together, Friedman and Schwartz's basic claim is that causality goes from the former to the latter two. The point is that the Fed refused to provide relief to member banks of the system. By showing themselves unconcerned by bank failures, by considering the latter as "regrettable consequences of bad management and bad banking principles" (Friedman and Schwartz 1963, p. 358), that is by doing nothing, the members of the Fed precipitated the Great Depression in that they passively tolerated the "Great Contraction".[31] It must be noticed that this interpretation supposes that the Fed *did* have a good grasp both of the severe risks of recession and of monetary channels of transmission at work in the economy.[32] The picture Friedman and Schwartz offered of the 1933 ultimate banking panic corresponds to the almost complete discomfiture of a disqualified authority. The lack of coordination within the monetary system, the incapacity to prevent money stock contraction through the lending to banks in vital need of liquidity, all the counter-productive decisions undertaken by the Fed clearly show its direct responsibility in the monetary collapse from 1929 to 1933. All in all, "the contraction is in fact a tragic testimonial to the importance of monetary forces" (Friedman and Schwartz 1963, p. 300). At a minimum, the Fed should have provided support to the member banks. But how to explain so many mischiefs in the conduct of the monetary policy? To put it in a nutshell, the members of the Board wrongly applied the false principles of the real bills doctrine, a doctrine that states that banks should invest in the short-term bills which represent a production already realised. As is well known, without the illness and later the death of Strong Friedman and Schwartz consider that most of the mischiefs in the conduct of monetary policy would have been avoided. We might have had a financial crash, but it would not have turned into the Great Contraction. Yet, the case made by Friedman and Schwartz does not merely apply to individuals but to institutions. That is, their point is not that the right person (i.e. Strong) was not present when needed – the personalisation of power might be a curable disease.[33] Rather, what they point out is that we cannot trust the discretionary power of authorities.

Last, how then to explain the revival of 1933? Interest of policy-makers shifted to 'the view that money does not matter' that rose under Keynes' influence and henceforth from monetary to fiscal policy. But nothing positive came from fiscal stimulus. Paradoxically, in basically ignoring the potency of monetary policy the Fed at least refrained from causing monetary disorders: the Fed did not attempt to alter the high-powered money, either by open-market operations or by rediscounting. As a matter of principle, it cannot be excluded that the rise in money stock was a loan-demand-induced phenomena. That is the reason why, again, Friedman and Schwartz take pains to show that recovery came *after* the money stock started to rise, and not the other way round as an (endogenous) result of the recovery. In their analysis, the stress is led on the new monetary arrangements and in particular the large institutional reforms that occurred, although monetary policy (i.e. monetary loosening) was considered as rather impotent by policy-makers.

Let us take stock of the argument made above. What Friedman holds is a purely monetary explanation of the Great Depression. And the lesson Friedman draws from this dramatic episode is this: if the Fed had not existed, the recession would have probably been not so deep because second-tier banks would have provided the type of relief they did in 1907. So better no centralised authority at all than ill-behaved institutions: suffice it to have monetary order, i.e. to provide a stable monetary background, to avoid real disorders. Here, the confidence one can place in State authorities' ability to behave efficiently, and in particular the ability of monetary authorities to anchor nominal expectations, proves a true necessity in a monetary economy.

In our view, the rationale behind this plea is to guarantee that price devices are able to play their coordinating role in a decentralised market economy. Serious troubles come to the forefront when private agents cannot disentangle movements in relative prices from movements in the general price level. Strikingly, the issue of nominal rigidities that was a fully-fledged explanation of the duration of the Great Depression for Hayek is completely passed over in Friedman's reasoning. Nominal rigidities are clearly not an issue for him.[34] This should not be considered as too surprising, especially regarding the labour market functioning: in Friedman's eyes, nominal rigidities are a "catch-all excuse for all failures to provide a satisfactory explanation of observed phenomena" (Friedman [1962b] 2007, p. 12).[35]

What happened in 1929–33 is that the Fed imposed on the economy a large-scale and more importantly a long-lasting monetary shock (the opposite of a 'once-for-all' one). Private agents needed time to adapt their inflationary expectations to the contracting money supply and thus to the falling aggregate price level. If private agents had been in a capacity to disentangle cuts in relative prices from the fall in the general price level, aggregate output would not have shrunk. While for the young Hayek (1933b) economic recovery requires the 'liquidation' of malinvestments and the reallocation of resources according to consumer preferences and resources availabilities (i.e. correction in the distorted relative prices), Friedman is a reflationist who calls for a constant money supply so as to ensure a stable level of aggregate nominal demand.

Regarding Keynes' interpretation analysed below, it must be noticed that Friedman and Schwartz's purely monetary case rests on two strong assumptions. First, the monetary multiplier is supposed to be kept constant for monetary policy to operate rightly. As a matter of fact, the monetary base *increased* by 21 per cent from 1929 to 1933, which means that the policy followed by the Fed was not fully and deliberately restrictive. But second-tier banks just like the public accumulated excess reserves. As formulated by Samuelson (1948), the central bank can hardly compel the banking system to increase the total stock of money, so that the monetary multiplier might break down.[36] To put it clearly, the Fed might have lost control on the total stock of money (i.e. M2). In times of banking panics when the confidence has vanished, open market operations do not produce the expected results because second-tier banks no longer play their intermediary role. In Keynesian terms, commercial banks have their own liquidity preference.[37] The economy can easily be precipitated in a liquidity trap when second-tier banks refuse to part with liquidity, preferring to stockpile excess reserves instead of offering loans to private actors. Regarding the excess reserves held by banks, this is precisely what might have happened.[38] If so, Friedman and Schwartz's argument should be reshaped as follows: the Fed should have implemented a much more aggressive monetary loosening, in the hope that second-tier banks would have ultimately come to escape their liquidity trap, what the Keynes of the *Treatise on Money* calls open-market operations "*à outrance*" (Keynes 1930, CW 6, p. 331). Besides, one can also find the possibility of non-monetary effects of bank failures that partly undermine the purely monetary interpretation of the Great Depression put forward by Friedman. This is the case if, as shown by Bernanke (1983, 2004), banking panics in 1929–32 impeded the financial sector from playing its normal function of credit to the real side of the economy. Bernanke sees his own results as an extension of Friedman and Schwartz's work, i.e. a strictly monetary explanation of the Great Depression. Actually, Bernanke's work opens the door for a Keynesian interpretation, i.e. a real (and not only monetary) explanation.

In comparison with Keynes' interpretation of the Great Depression, the second strong assumption made by Friedman is that monetary loosening would have been efficient to escape so severe a slump. That is, the entire argument breaks down if monetary policy proves inefficient (if aggregate spendings do not react by one way or the other to monetary loosening). As we will see below, this is precisely the case made by Keynes regarding Great Britain: monetary loosening might prove inefficient when the long-term state of *real* expectations is too depressed.

Keynes and the case for State interference in the free play of markets

Let it be said at once, we face a methodological problem here. When he deals explicitly with the 1929 financial collapse or with the way this crash turned into the Great Depression, the theoretical framework underlying Keynes' assessment is the *Treatise on Money* (1930). Strikingly, the *General Theory* does not address directly the issue of a systematic explanation of 1929. What Keynes aims at there is offering a general theory of market economies subject to the risk of protracted slump; he would have missed the point if he had contented himself with an analysis restricted to the most severe deflation ever known. In what follows we won't try to offer an exhaustive analysis of Keynes' explanation of 1929 with regard to his *Treatise*. Similarly, we won't retrace the move towards the *General Theory* through a careful reading of the progressive construction of its analytical building block. Instead, we will focus on a few analytical points that show both points of agreement with and definitive departures from Friedman's purely monetary case.

Let us start with the points of agreement. Regarding the 1929 episode, Keynes' diagnosis is very close to Friedman's. Contrary to many commentators at that time who see in the surge on stock markets the seeds for upward pressures on prices, Keynes does not consider this period as inflationary. He acknowledges the downward pressure on wholesale prices that started in 1928. While Great Britain endured stagnation, in United States "the investment activity ... was something prodigious and incredible" (Keynes 1931, CW 13, p. 345). Investments in fixed capital rose significantly from 1923 to 1928–29 and then started to decline. But Keynes denies the inevitability of the slump as the 'liquidationists' claim.[39] At the very beginning, Keynes is far from discerning the depth of the depression. The problem comes from the public being in "an extravagant rather than in a saving mood", an extravagance allowed by "the great expansion of corporate saving" (Keynes 1930, CW 6, p. 174), i.e. wastage of savings and not overinvestment. On the causes of the crash on the New York stock exchange, Keynes holds the same interpretation as Friedman: for him, the dear money policy carried out by the Fed with the purpose of curbing speculation on financial markets drained the credit necessary for productive investment. The starting point of the recession was due to the decline in business profits and the following decline in investment (that predate the financial collapse). The preliminary conclusion he draws is in all respects consistent with Friedman's: "Thus I attribute the slump of 1930 primarily to the deterrent effects on investment on the long period of dear money which preceded the stock-market collapse, and only secondarily to the collapse itself" (Keynes 1930, CW 6, p. 176).[40] It takes time for Keynes to grasp the magnitude of the recession. At its very beginning, he considers that the recession will be quite short and probably less severe in

Britain. In case of "the obstinate persistence of a slump" (Keynes 1930, CW, p. 332), the Keynes of the *Treatise* advocates "the purchase of securities by the central bank until the long-term market rate of interest has been brought down to the limiting point" (Keynes 1930, CW 6, p. 332), which corresponds to open-market operations "*à outrance*" (Keynes 1930, CW 6, p. 331). To the extent that Keynes considers that monetary loosening should be operative, and more easily implemented in the United States, his analysis appears as similar to Friedman's. Yet, regarding Keynes first doubts are raised at the beginning of 1930. And it is only in December 1930 that he acknowledges "the extreme violence of the slump" (Keynes 1930, CW 9, p. 127).

Accordingly, let us now turn to the analytical points on which Keynes and Friedman part company, i.e. the way how the 1929 financial collapse turned into the Great Depression. What appear in Keynes' reasoning are the real mechanisms of secondary deflation that worsen the initial recession. Let us quote Keynes extensively on this point:

> But the collapse having occurred, it greatly aggravated matters, especially in the United States, by causing a disinvestment in working capital. Moreover, it also promoted the development of a profit deflation in two other ways – both by discouraging investment and by encouraging saving. The pessimism and the atmosphere of disappointment which the stock-market collapse engendered reduced enterprise and lowered the natural rate of interest; whilst the 'psychological' poverty which the collapse of paper values brought with it probably increased saving.
>
> (Keynes 1930, CW 6, p. 176)

Here are to be found the first elements that provide non-monetary transmission mechanisms of the financial collapse to the real side of the economy – preliminary elements that lead to the elaboration of the *General Theory*.[41] If "the stimulating effect of cheap money and abundant credit on the new issue market is exceedingly rapid" (Keynes 1930, CW 20, p. 346) in normal circumstances, such a policy would be inefficient in the special circumstances that the United States, and above all Great Britain, experienced at that time: "when enterprise and confidence have collapsed to the extent that they have today, the response to what would have been in other circumstances a strong stimulus may be very reluctant" (Keynes 1930, CW 20, p. 346). Worse, this deflationary contraction is self-feeding. Such a diagnosis about the impotency of monetary policy in 'special' circumstances opens the door for 'unconventional' remedies, i.e. aggressive monetary policy (that Friedman supports) but also public works.

Let us take stock. In our view, Keynes' recommendations must be viewed as complementary to the case made by Friedman, who restricts his advocacy to monetary reflation. In direct opposition to Hayek the crucial issue is for Keynes to boost investment. Keynes too calls for monetary loosening. Like Friedman, he favours open-market policies over operations through the discount rate. Yet, the first difference with Friedman at the theoretical level is that Keynes reasons in terms of interest rate and does not refer to the total stock of money: he advocates a fall in the long-term rate of interest (but acknowledges that the banking sector has direct control only on short rates).

The second difference is that Keynes is well aware that private banks possess their own liquidity preference and might not follow suit if the Fed aims to increase the total stock of money through an increase of the monetary base. That is, private banks might face a liquidity trap.[42]

Third, for Keynes too the recovery of confidence turns out to be a matter of huge concern. But the recovery of confidence he is concerned with does not only apply to the monetary and financial side of the economy, but also at a more general level to "a return of confidence to the business world" (Keynes 1931, CW 13, p. 358). The wording used in his Chicago talk is highly significant:

> That morbid psychology, though quite intelligible and natural, is a tremendous obstacle to right development of affairs when it exists. There is an element of that morbid psychology present today; there are financial institutions and individuals who want to safeguard themselves against any possibility of future loss, and are therefore unwilling to run sound risks.
>
> (Keynes 1931, CW 20, p. 537)

Fourth, what about nominal rigidities in Keynes' explanation of the Great Depression – an issue that is directly dismissed by Friedman? Keynes' position towards nominal rigidities evolved as the Great Depression developed.[43] In the very beginning Keynes took stock of nominal wage rigidity, "the almost complete rigidity of our wage rates" (Keynes 1930, CW 20, p. 377) and thus advocated a reform of the dole. As time elapsed Keynes recognised that, as a matter of principle, money-wage cuts would be helpful but are not worth thinking about from a practical point of view: to obtain the cut of 20 per cent in the real wages needed in Great Britain, money-wage cuts would have to be cut by about 40 per cent. At the time of the *General Theory*, Keynes' argument against money-wage cuts relies on much firmer theoretical underpinnings: because in a monetary economy money-wage adjustments are necessarily progressive they give rise to deflationary expectations that are very likely to worsen the initial disequilibrium. That is the reason why all in all "the maintenance of a stable general level of money-wages is, on balance of considerations, the most advisable policy for a closed system" (Keynes 1936, CW 7, p. 270). To say it quite plainly: contrary to the view held by Hayek, Keynes argues that nominal rigidities are a necessary condition for the stability of a decentralised market economy.

Last, Keynes, the Englishman, disentangles the situations faced respectively by Great Britain and the United States. Truly, Keynes shares Friedman's diagnosis regarding the United States when he makes his strong case in favour of an expansionary monetary policy for this side of the Atlantic:

> I think the argument for public works in this country is much weaker than it is in Great Britain.... Here you can function as though you were in a closed

system, and ... for such a system I would use as my first method operating on the long rate of interest.

I think in this country deliberate public works should be regarded much more as a tonic to change of business conditions, but the means of getting back to a state of equilibrium should be concentrated on the rate of interest. That condition not being so in Great Britain, one had to lay great stress on public programs but in this country I should operate on the rate of interest.

(Keynes, summer 1931, Harris Foundation meeting, quoted in Moggridge and Howson 1974, pp. 458–9)

But in Great Britain, the situation is really different: the country endured a protracted slump throughout the 1920s. Monetary expansion might be not sufficient to escape so severe a slump. Hence the need of public works made in "The Means to Prosperity" (1933) with the view to 'pump-prime', a case already made *before* the *Treatise on Money*. The capital market is so depressed, in the language of the *General Theory* the marginal efficiency of capital is so low, that State intervention is needed to raise *directly* the demand price of newly produced capital assets.

What comes out of our comparison between Keynes' and Friedman's interpretations of the Great Depression is both and at the same time strong similarities and definite points of divergence, which raises the question of the theoretical underpinnings behind the case they respectively make. While they share the same diagnosis regarding the causes of the 1929 crisis, they hold very different analyses on the way the depression developed. And while they share a common plea for the stabilisation of aggregate demand, this shared stance towards reflationism is far from supported by the same type of policy devices. Solving this puzzle will require a thorough analysis of their respective understanding of the functioning of a monetary economy, with a particular attention given to their respective treatment of the expectations issue.

For the moment being, let us see a few avenues of reflection for a better understanding of the current crisis that can be identified through Keynes' and Friedman's own interpretation of the Great Depression.

The parallel with the 1929 crisis

In the middle of the 1930s, some of those economists who belonged to the London School of Economics felt rather embarrassed while Hayek and Robbins simply advocated for the liquidation to go on. One then saw people like Hicks joining the then-in-Cambridge (UK) interventionist camp. Much nearer to us, the former president of the US Federal Reserve Board Alan Greenspan (2008) acknowledges being in a "state of shocked disbelief". For him, the 2008 financial collapse represents the breaking down of what he founded until now at the same time sound monetary theory and wise political advice. In his words: "the whole intellectual edifice ... collapsed in the summer of last year" (Greenspan 2008). It is precisely because the 2008 watershed in financial places all over the world led in turn to such a severe real downturn that the comparison with the 1929 collapse appears as an obvious statement of facts. A contraction of GDP of such an importance has not been seen in developed countries since the early 1930s. Is the worst of the crisis behind us? Or are new shocks likely to arise due to uncorrected imbalances and because of a sovereign debt 'bubble'? It is hard to say, at least because the future is partly the result of our ability to act in a sound way. Now as before debates rage on the root causes of the crisis and, by the way, on the role public authorities played in creating the current recession (especially in the USA).

At the theoretical level, the recession that we currently experience raises first of all the issue of the root cause of what is happening. Second, it is also the occasion to re-evaluate the way as economists we conceive the world and to question the relevance of our standard toolkit: what is wrong with economic theory, and in particular with macroeconomics, to make the collapse so unexpected? Third, at the policy level too the current dramatic events reactivate debates on the duty of State authorities: how to stabilise a decentralised market economy?

The most critical issue at stake is the understanding of what is happening now, the very cause of the 2008 collapse. As during the Great Depression, the battlefield today is roughly divided into two camps. On the one hand, there is the explanation put forward by the non-interventionist wing of economists, i.e. those who oppose discretionary devices. For them, the very cause of the 2008 crisis is an unsound policy of monetary authorities, especially in the USA. The title of John Taylor's recent book is explicit: *Getting off Track: How Government Actions and Interventions Caused, Prolonged and Worsened the Financial Crisis* (2009). For him, "the Great Deviation killed the Great Moderation, gave birth to the Great Recession, and left a troublesome legacy for the future" (Taylor 2010, p. 1).[44] For Taylor, no doubt real disorders were purely and simply created by monetary disorders. It is striking that Taylor's book ends with an explicit reference to Friedman. His final chapter is devoted to "Frequently Asked Questions" and concludes as follows:

> Milton Friedman is often quoted as saying, "The Great Depression, like most other periods of severe unemployment, was produced by government mismanagement rather than by any inherent instability of the private economy." Does this statement apply to the current financial crisis and period of severe unemployment? Yes.
>
> (Taylor 2009, p. 76)

Actually, the parallel made (explicitly in the case of Taylor) between the 'Great Deviation' and Friedman's interpretation of the Great Depression does not withstand scrutiny. Indeed, Friedman is much more concerned with the dry-up of liquidity and the purchasing power shortage due to an unsound monetary *tightening* in early 1929 than with the bursting of an asset bubble due to excessive monetary *loosening* that might have occurred *before* 1929. To this extent, Taylor's interpretation rather echoes the Austrian view of what happened in the

1920s: central banks' mistakes leading to too low interest rates and along the way allowing a speculative boom.[45] So it can hardly be argued that the 2008 crisis developed in a Friedmanian fashion, quite the contrary.

What those who belong to the interventionist wing of economists, i.e. those who stand for discretion, have in common is the denial of this explanation in terms of mistakes in monetary policy put forward by Taylor. For example, Wade (2009) emphasises the role played by global imbalances: in short external deficits, globalised finance and floating exchange rates. Here is to be found the most prominent interpretation of the 2008 recession, namely a 'general saving glut'. As argued by Skidelsky (2011):

> A Keynesian analysis would put global imbalances at the heart of the current economic meltdown. Keynesian unemployment is triggered off by an imbalance between planned saving and investment that is liquidated off by a fall in output.... An increased desire to save (by the Chinese) subjected the US economy to deflationary pressure.
>
> (Skidelsky 2011, pp. 9–10)[46]

However, it must be recognised that "the current crisis developed in a manner quite contrary to that presupposed by Keynes in the *General Theory*" (Leijonhufvud 2009, p. 742) through the second-round effects of deleverage of banks and financial institutions instead of the sole effects of disturbing effects of speculation on real investment. It is the Keynes of the *Treatise on Money* (1930) more than the one of the *General Theory* (1936) that would help us to understand the financial side of a real collapse (Leijonhufvud 2009).[47] But once the real effects of a financial turnaround are acknowledged through the collapse of long-term expectations, a crisis of confidence as well as a liquidity crisis, the return to the theoretical construct framed in the *General Theory* appears essential to understand how the deflationary process easily becomes self-feeding in case of a large protracted external shock.

To sum up, what is certain is that the current crisis can hardly be seen as Friedmanian in the way it has developed. As for him, Keynes may be of help in grasping the original causes of the current turmoil, but in that case the analysis cannot be restricted to the theoretical framework of the *General Theory*.

The second feature of the analogy with the Great Depression refers to our ability as a discipline to provide useful tools to think about the world in which we live. Say's law found its place in history as the key hypothesis of the whole classical edifice to be removed in order to understand why a laissez-faire economy is not self-adjusting. It was hard to find an economist who would have explicitly relied on Say's law at that time. It was Keynes' flair (others would say Keynes' bad faith) to have flushed out such a tacit assumption. What about this issue now? Today, it is far from obvious to guess what will be the state of the macroeconomic art in the following ten years, especially concerning the potentiality of DSGE models. For some, "the recent crisis gives no reason to abandon the core empirical 'rational expectations/sticky price' model developed over the past 30 years" (Taylor 2009, p. 5). But one sees also pleas for the necessity to become better macroeconomists, such as Leijonhufvud's (2010) one. Involved in these debates one can find the way we conceive the economy as a linear and closed system, the underlying hypothesis of financial market efficiency, and the rational expectations approach launched with the New Classical Revolution. Beyond the idea of rational expectations itself, there is embedded a fundamental postulate, namely the assumption of continuously clearing markets. As stated by Laidler (2010a):

> It is not just that such macro-economic models cannot address the policy issues that the recent convulsions in financial markets have created, or that it is difficult for anyone brought up under their influence to conceive of such events occurring in the first place, but that also those who treat their market-clearing properties as defining the boundaries of scientific macro-economic place such questions outside of the sub-discipline's subject matter. That is why a crisis in macro-economics is an integral part of the current economic situation.
>
> (Laidler 2010a, p. 48)

As far as we see it, both Keynes and Friedman should be of some help if we are to review our way of conceiving the functioning of a monetary economy. Both of them are Marshallian in their approach to economics and built theoretical constructs that make ample room for market disequilibria and in which the rational expectations approach hardly fits. So both their respective ways of understanding how private expectations are formed and their respective approach of disequilibrium should be very helpful if one tries to grasp the functioning of a monetary economy.

Unsurprisingly, the third feature of the analogy between our contemporary period and the 1930s turns out to be the proper role that public authorities should play to restore a full employment equilibrium together with stable prices. In short: what should be done now? Regarding policy devices, 2008 seems to mark a clear turning point.

Before 2008, the 'New Consensus' that leading economists arrived at can be summarised as follows. First, monetary policy was considered much more agile than fiscal policy to counteract short-run fluctuations. Regarding fiscal policy, prior to the 2008 global economic downturn it was considered even by most New Keynesians "as playing a secondary cyclical role, with political constraints sharply limiting its de facto usefulness" (Blanchard *et al.* 2010, p. 200). In a word, Keynes' stance for discretionary fiscal policy seemed to have evaporated. This being said, this dismissal of fiscal policy should be moderated. If we consider policy advice and implementation, "in practice … the rhetoric was stronger than the reality" (Blanchard *et al.* 2010, p. 202). In particular, it did not exclude the fact that automatic stabilisers help: "fiscal policy is reduced to providing a prudent and sustainable regime of expenditure and taxation" (Dixon 2008, p. 43). Regarding monetary policy, it was considered as a much more powerful means to stabilise the economy.

Monetary loosening or tightening can be decided very quickly (no need of a Congress approval); central banks are almost everywhere 'independent' so that monetary policy is quite unlikely to be captured by certain pressure groups; and above all monetary counter-cyclical measures can be easily reversed.

The second thread of consensus ensued from the disqualification of short-term discretionary devices. State authorities were henceforth supposed to support stabilisation policies, the latter being conducted in terms of rules instead of discretion. Even for those who considered its potency, fiscal policy was considered much more efficient when thought of in terms of 'automatic stabilisers': "the advantage of automatic stabilisation lies precisely in that it is automatic; it does not get into difficulties that appear when a democratic government launches a recovery plan (or on the contrary a 'fiscal cooling')" (Solow 2002, p. 20).[48]

Because of their interventionist bias, those economists who are still confident in the State's ability to act efficiently are considered – and labelled – Keynesians. But because of both their disqualification of discretionary fiscal policy under normal circumstances and because of their confidence in monetary policy (to be conducted in terms of rules) the New Keynesians would also be considered as much more worthy of Friedman's name than of Keynes', as De Long (2000a) claims. In short, here are the terms of the fiscal and monetary consensus that prevailed until 2008.

Things became much more complicated *after* 2008. This consensus for monetary as well as for fiscal policy seems to have vanished. We have seen pleas for monetary loosening and even monetary 'unconventional' policies (Mishkin 2009). But with regard to the huge amount of liquidities accumulated by both private actors and the banking sector, the liquidity-trap scenario envisaged by Keynes appears to be in sight. We also have seen strong call for vigorous fiscal policy (Spilimbergo *et al.* (2008), to take but one example) and as a matter of fact counter-cyclical fiscal actions have been set in motion, such as the 2008 Economic Stimulus Act or the 2009 American Recovery and Reinvestment Act in the USA. Regarding fiscal devices, policy-makers seem to have obeyed 'old-Keynesian reflexes' rather than New Keynesian ones.

In a *New Palgrave* article presenting his "monetary and fiscal policy overview", one can find Kocherlakota (2008) arguing as a way to conclude his point:

> There is an old joke to the effect that if you ask 10 macroeconomists about a policy question, you'll get 11 different answers. This joke provided a disturbingly accurate picture of the state of the field in the 1970s and 1980s. To a remarkable extent, it was no longer applicable as of 2005. There is a profession-wide consensus on methods that did not exist in the early 1980s. *This consensus has led to a set of results about monetary and fiscal policy that are sharp, robust and surprising.*
>
> (Kocherlakota 2008, p. 713; emphasis added)

To be sure, such a contention could no more be used as a consensual conclusion for an entry in a dictionary of economics. The old jokesters are still among us. In line with the lack of consensus on what led to the 2008 crisis it can no more be argued that most of the economists would agree on what the policy mix should consist of. Those who call for large fiscal stimulus packages and ambitious loan-financed infrastructure projects still face what was called in Keynes' time the 'Treasury View'. By the same token, those who urge policy-makers to look beyond the here and now crisis still have to face the same type of objections Friedman had to when he tried to convince his contemporaries to avoid narrow and short-sighted devices. No doubt the current policy debates should gain a lot by returning to Keynes' and Friedman's respective policy advocacies.

3.5 Conclusion: Keynes' and Friedman's policy philosophy

One might be tempted to consider that an author's views would be shaped by dramatic historical events. As a matter of fact, this is not really the case for our two authors: "although both Keynes' and Friedman's analyses varied during their careers, their political philosophies and worldviews, their *Weltanschauung*, did not change in any important way" (Dostaler 1998, p. 319). In particular, whether they experience 1929 as a contemporary or rather as a historian both Keynes and Friedman hold an interpretation of the Great Depression that is rooted in their visions on the self-regulating properties of a laissez-faire system. That is, their respective appraisal of the Great Depression reinforces but does not really reshape their overall systems of thinking vis-à-vis capitalism.[49]

The economic policy advocated by Friedman is better understood with regard to his explanation of the Great Depression, even though his first advice largely predates his *Monetary History of United States*. Friedman never changed his mind concerning this dramatic historical episode. For him, the Great Depression is the example par excellence of how initiatives on behalf of public authorities (i.e. discretionary policies) prove inefficient and counterproductive. For him, the most severe depression ever known results purely and solely from mischiefs in the conduct of monetary policy. Not only did the financial collapse in 1929 directly result from the unfortunate tightening in monetary policy, but the Fed had also prevented the economy from benefiting from the rebalancing and equilibrating forces that it intrinsically possesses by *pursuing* this deflationary policy. So the policy guidelines Friedman designs for a market economy rule out from the outset any possibility for the authorities to take initiative: better 'rules' through biding law than 'discretionary' power. Yet, the economies we live in use money to facilitate exchange. Laissez-faire would not help regarding monetary affairs. Hence the design of a monetary authority in which private agents can have confidence in stabilising the system, and by the way which can help them to have confidence in the economic climate. Inevitably there would be economic fluctuations – they are not avoidable. The provision of a monetary stable background thus appears as a 'second-best' choice aiming to anchor short-term nominal expectations.

As for Keynes too, the employment policy he advocates is better understood with regard to the 1929 crisis even if his first call for public works largely predates the Great Depression. The substance of his explanation of this historical episode did not vary either: an unfettered market system does not inherently possess powerful re-equilibrating forces so that a laissez-faire economy might endure protracted slumps with no sign of recovery. On the policy side, the whole project is to ensure that the Great Depression will never happen again. On the theoretical side, there is the necessity to provide theoretical foundations for the policy project. It is true that an "inept" monetary policy, as Friedman and Schwartz call it, turned a standard recession into the great slump of 1930. But these monetary disorders gave rise to real disturbances through induced second-round deflationary effects. Because monetary expansion would not necessarily restore equilibrium by itself, especially in Great Britain where the recession lasted so long and where long-term real expectations were so depressed, Keynes calls for public works and for the socialisation of investment at a more general level. Ultimately, Keynes' overall policy guidelines can be viewed as a double-sided weapon with a common purpose: both fiscal and monetary policies aim at the management of the long-term state of real expectations.

What are the lessons to be learnt for the kind of liberalism Keynes and Fried-man respectively hold? On the one hand, Keynes considers that a free market economy is not able to stabilise by itself around full employment. As early as in 1919 in the *Economic Consequences of the Peace* he claims that the time of the old type of laissez-faire is over. Besides, he considers that the individualistic competitive system is increasingly replaced, for better or worse, by intermediate bodies. We should take advantage of this tendency to implement a 'new liberal-ism'. That is the reason why he claims: "For my own part I think that capitalism, wisely managed, can probably be made more efficient for attaining economic ends than any alternative system yet in sight, but that in itself it is in many ways extremely objectionable" (Keynes 1926, CW 9, p. 294). Yet, to properly under-stand this quotation it must be kept in mind that for Keynes "capitalism compris[ed] the entire set of institutions governing economic activity. Govern-ment was not separated from capitalism" (Backhouse and Bateman 2009, p. 653). This 'new liberalism' entails the set-up of new institutions to cope with the inability of a laissez-faire economy to absorb by itself large and protracted shocks.

As for him, Friedman utterly rejects such a diagnosis. His overall system of thought rests on the self-correcting properties that the system possesses by itself to absorb external shocks, provided that policy-makers let this temporary adjust-ment process develop (the cyclical process being supposed to converge). Viewed from the 1960s, Smith's 'invisible hand' principle is considered as relevant as ever. Incidentally, in their paper dedicated to Keynes' appraisal of capitalism Backhouse and Bateman argue about Friedman:

> In his classic *Capitalism and Freedom* (1962), Friedman provided a series of studies of different markets but, despite using the word capitalism in his title, he failed to offer any overarching analysis of the institutions that

underpin capitalism or of the social conditions that are necessary for its functioning. Friedman seems to imply that capitalism requires unfettered markets and nothing else.

(Backhouse and Bateman 2009, p. 651)

In our view, this assessment is not fair to Friedman's appraisal of capitalism. Just like Keynes, Friedman does not conflate unfettered markets with capitalism. He is well aware that a purely individualistic economy requires a particular institutional setting to function well. That is the reason why he advocates a system as competitive and as individualistic as possible, at both the political and the economic level. First, at the political level Friedman favours power as dispersed as possible, which means at the most local level. In his own words: "I am a liberal in the classical sense or, in the terminology that has become common in the United States, a libertarian in philosophy" (Friedman's interview in Snowdon and Vane, 1999, p. 132). Friedman is a true believer in free will. Yet, he is not an anarchist: he recognises the necessity of public authority for some tasks, the foremost of which is the need for a monetary authority. As his son David Friedman (2008) puts in his *New Palgrave* article dedicated to "Libertarianism", Milton Friedman is a good example of "someone who accepts both the utilitarian argument for redistribution from rich to poor and libertarian arguments against government intervention in the market" (D. Friedman 2008, p. 110). Second, at the economic level Friedman acknowledges that an unfettered market system is far from perfect and that temporary disequilibria are unavoidable. Yet, government initiatives to dampen these departures from the long growth trend are very likely to make matters worse. Hence Friedman's choice *not to* choose between market failures and government failures.

4 Keynes and Friedman on the employment policy
Structure and conduct

4.1 Introduction

Regarding the way we conceive the functioning of decentralised market economies, and especially the way we appraise their capacity to converge by themselves towards full employment at stable prices, regarding also the way we consider the role that should be respectively dedicated to fiscal and monetary policies, 2008 represents a clear turning point. Before the crisis, debates used to focus on how to soften the regular ups and downs of the business cycle. After 2008, the very question turns out to be the mere existence of self-correcting forces in the presence of a large and persistent external shock – as in the early 1930s. As stated by Laidler:

> A revival of the age-old debate about the inherent stability or otherwise of a decentralized economic system based on private property and voluntary exchange – a market economy as it is usually called – has been one of the very few positive consequences of the economic crisis that began in the summer of 2007.
>
> (Laidler 2010b, p. 2)

In short, the "modern theoretical consensus – known alternatively as the Neo-classical synthesis or the New Keynesian model of monetary policy" (Goodfriend 2007, p. 48)[1] – that prevailed until 2008 seems severely undermined by the latest financial collapse, and discretionary fiscal policy has returned to the centre of debates as was the case in the early 1930s.

Keynes and Friedman are at the origin of these contemporary debates regarding the role public authorities should play to sustain stability as well as the debates about the respective merits of fiscal and monetary policy. Although he was far from the first and even less the single economist to advocate public works at the time of the Great Depression, the name of Keynes is usually associated with discretionary fiscal policy and with the disuse of monetary policy because of liquidity traps. So when contemporary economists now refer to Keynes, it is because of his support for fiscal stimulus packages. As for him, Friedman is definitely associated with the dismissal of fiscal policy, the denial of discretionary devices and thus the plea for monetary policy conducted in terms of rules to sustain the self-equilibrating properties of a market economy.

The Keynes and Friedman we will portray in this chapter are far from the caricatured images one commonly gets from their advocacies. To show this, we will proceed as follows. First, if we are to investigate the employment policy advocated by our two authors, it is better to start with Keynes' and Friedman's respective understanding of the unemployment issue. In particular, how do Keynes and Friedman respectively define 'full employment'? And how do they explain unemployment during the Great Depression? This is the subject matter of the following section. The next two parts of the chapter are dedicated to Keynes' and Friedman's policy advocacies in terms of monetary policy and then fiscal policy. As we will see, whether one considers oneself today a proponent of 'discretion' or rather a proponent of 'rules' we should have great lessons to learn from our two authors. On the one hand, 'discretion' as this term is now understood is hardly advocated by Keynes as a *systematic* way of dealing with economic policy. In a way, Keynes too calls for economic policy guidelines, i.e. for rules. On the other, 'rules' as defined today hardly fit into Friedman's system of policy advices: contemporary rules are far too discretionary from Friedman's standpoint. We will close by showing how the return to both Keynes' and Friedman's original advocacies could help us to widen the debate from the single issue of rules versus discretion as understood nowadays.

4.2 Full employment and unemployment

Obviously, for both Keynes and Friedman the basic purpose of the economic policy is to ensure both and at the same time 'full employment' and price stability. For both Keynes and Friedman full employment does not mean a zero rate of unemployment. That is, both of them take well into account the market imperfections. As we will see below, their respective quantitative valuation of full employment is not so divergent. But it is on the duty for the State to know its target that they part company. Regarding 'abnormal' unemployment, and especially unemployment during the 1930s, neither of them would deny the possible existence of disequilibrium on the labour market. But the dynamic mechanisms behind this disequilibrium will appear in sharp contrast.

We will first examine Keynes' and Friedman's own definition of full employment. We will then turn to their respective analysis of the unemployment issue by looking at the way they respectively understand the origin of unemployment during the Great Depression. Concerning this second issue, sharp differences will be brought to light regarding the way they understand the dynamics at work between employment and wages in a monetary economy.

Keynes and Friedman on the definition of full employment

Let us start with a point that seems to have been almost completely forgotten. As a matter of fact, Keynes is highly concerned with imperfections in the labour market. His inquiry of "involuntary unemployment" relies on the critical distinction of this concept from what he calls "voluntary unemployment", that he defines as follows:

> In addition to 'frictional' unemployment, the [second classical] postulate is also compatible with 'voluntary' unemployment due to the refusal or inability of a unit of labour, as a result of legislation or social practices or of combination for collective bargaining or of slow response to change or of mere human obstinacy, to accept a reward corresponding to the value of the product attributable to its marginal productivity.
>
> (Keynes 1936, CW 7, p. 6)

During World War II Keynes deals explicitly with "structural unemployment" (Keynes 1943, CW 27, p. 354) that he clearly distinguishes from what he calls "special unemployment" (Keynes 1943, CW 27, p. 311).[2] Most noticeably, Keynes' concept of voluntary unemployment and the concept of full employment as its corollary (defined as the absence of involuntary unemployment) aim to disentangle unemployment due to effective demand failures from market imperfections (Leijonhufvud 1968a). Involuntary unemployment of course but also voluntary unemployment are supposed to be dealt with by the adequate policies.

As for Friedman, he is well known to consider that a market economy gravitates towards the 'natural rate of unemployment', that he defines as follows:

> The 'natural rate of unemployment' ... is the level that would be ground out by the Walrasian system of general equilibrium equations, provided there is embedded in them the actual structural characteristics of the labor and commodity markets, including market imperfections, stochastic variability in demands and supplies, the cost of gathering information about job vacancies and labor availabilities, the cost of mobility, and so on.
>
> (Friedman [1968a] 1969a, p. 102)[3]

As explicitly stated in Chapter 12 of his *Price Theory* (1962b), Friedman's concept of natural rate of unemployment aims to disentangle monetary causes from real causes of unemployment.

For our purpose here, two points of comparison are worth noticing. The first one applies to the rate of inflation consistent with full employment while the second one applies to State duties regarding the measurement of its full employment target.

First, is a zero rate of inflation compatible with full employment? Or is there necessarily an inflationary bias in a decentralised economy? Noticeably, Friedman's natural rate of unemployment does not correspond to any particular rate of inflation, since a vertical Phillips curve in the long run implies a natural rate of unemployment consistent with any given rate of price increase. In particular, full employment in Friedman's sense of the term is perfectly consistent with a zero rate of price increase. By contrast, Keynes' full employment target is not consistent with a zero rate of inflation. In Keynes' decentralised economy, prices rise before full employment is attained because of what he calls "bottle-necks" (Keynes 1936, CW 7, p. 300).[4] To put it the other way round: at Friedman's zero inflation rate there would still be involuntarily unemployed resources according to Keynes' full employment target. Besides, there is an overall effect of a rise in effective demand on both voluntary and involuntary unemployment regarding Keynes whereas monetary causes and real causes of unemployment are sealed-off concepts in Friedman's case. In Keynes' case, a general recovery that occurs through an increase in aggregate demand possesses second-round effects on structural unemployment insofar as it helps to deal with market imperfections such as misallocation of workers and firms – a point that is not emphasised in the *General Theory* but that is dealt with extensively in Keynes' political papers.

Their respective views on the full employment target in a decentralised economy no longer seem so divergent once the 'inflationary bias' in Keynes' economy is incorporated into the analysis. A much sharper contrast between our two authors lies in their opposing views on the need for authorities to gather information so that they might 'know' their full employment target. Keynes takes some trouble to measure his full employment target. For him, the need for the authorities to have "absolutely up-to-date information", the "best and latest information" (Keynes 1945, CW 27, pp. 409–10) is a crucial issue that largely predates the *General Theory*, actually. For Friedman, the reverse is the case. There are two distinct reasons for that. First, Friedman relies on what can be called a data-uncertainty argument. As we have seen in previous chapters, Friedman considers that in no way is the State more able to get information on time in comparison with private agents immersed in markets. A collective body is first and foremost constituted of individuals; there is no such thing as a 'collective rationality'. So there is no reason to suppose that a collective body would be able to get more relevant information than individualistic and competitive bodies. His second line of argument is a by-product of Friedman's confidence in the self-adjusting capacity of a market economy in the long run and corresponds to a model-uncertainty argument. If it is true that in the long run we know well the interactions between the monetary and the real sides of the economy (or rather precisely the lack of interactions between the two, the classical dichotomy being truly relevant in a long time horizon), in the short run it remains hardly conceivable to disentangle minor shocks from equilibrium dynamic adjustment processes. To the best of our knowledge Friedman did not explicitly support structural policies to deregulate the labour market, with the exception of Chapter 12 of *Price Theory* (1962b) where Friedman argues that the natural rate of unemployment "can be lowered by removing obstacles in the labor market, by reducing frictions" (Friedman [1962b] 2007, p. 228). As a matter of fact, there was no reason to deal at length with this sort of issue: from Friedman's standpoint, the reform of the dole, the abolition of a minimum wage level as well as the dissemination of trade unions' market power should be a matter of course. Obviously, a reform of the unemployment benefits would lower the natural rate of unemployment. Yet, the measurement of its numerical value should not be a matter of concern for policy-makers:

> As the coiner of the term, I am disturbed at its widespread misuse and mis-understanding. The natural-rate is not a fixed number. It is not 6% or 5%, or some other magic number ... The natural-rate is a concept that does have an empirical counterpart – but that counterpart is not easy to measure and will depend on particular circumstances of time and place.
>
> (Friedman 1996)

The natural rate of unemployment is the unemployment rate towards which the economy *naturally* gravitates provided policy-makers refrain from any action to boost aggregate demand. Trying to ascertain what it might be is therefore a pointless exercise.

All in all, if Keynes' and Friedman's respective valuation of full employment are quite similar (with the exception of an inflationary bias in Keynes' case), it is in the policy implications of their own definition that they definitely part company: while for Keynes it is an absolute necessity for State authorities to get knowledge on their full employment target, such an exercise might turn out to be quite dangerous in Friedman's eyes. Wouldn't it open the door for discretionary intervention once any departure from the natural rate is detected?

Keynes and Friedman on 'abnormal' unemployment during the Great Depression

With regard to their respective views on full employment, what are Keynes' and Friedman's respective analyses of unemployment during the Great Depression? What about 'abnormal' unemployment at that time? As we will see below, for both Keynes and Friedman the basic goal of the policy guidelines they call for is to ensure that the Great Depression would never happen again. We will have to wait for the next chapter dedicated to the study of the functioning of a monetary economy to get a thorough understanding of the theoretical underpinnings of their policy advice. For the moment, let us provide here an insight of Keynes' and Friedman's views on the ultimate causes of unemployment in the 1930s, with the view to better understand their policy advice analysed in the remainder of this chapter.

We have seen in the previous chapter that for both Keynes and Friedman the economy was in *disequilibrium* during the Great Depression – although they part company on the type of disequilibrium at stake: *monetary* disorders that prevented the self-correcting mechanisms to come into play in the real side of the economy for Friedman; a large-scale collapse in the *real* side of the economy –although the financial meltdown and the real collapse that ensued in this particular occasion was due to due mischiefs in the conduct of monetary policy – for Keynes (that is, a fall in the marginal efficiency of capital might have for Keynes other causes than the bursting of a speculative bubble and the latter might originate elsewhere than in an 'inept' monetary policy). Here below, we will sketch out Keynes' and Friedman's respective understanding of unemployment at that time.

First, what about Keynes' understanding of 'involuntary' or 'special' unemployment during the Great Depression? As we have seen, for him the severe 1929 financial collapse was due to an unduly restrictive monetary policy, which was precisely implemented to curb speculation on financial markets. This financial breakdown set into motion real mechanisms that led to an insufficient level in aggregate demand to ensure full employment. So the critical disorders to be cured lay in the real side of the economy, and critically on the investment market. In the language of the *General Theory*, the financial crash severely depressed the long-term state of expectations, which means too a low marginal efficiency of capital. In Great Britain, trying to lower the interest rate through monetary easing would have probably been in vain: it would not help to boost investment and thus to escape the depression. Yet, the case for monetary loosening was more arguable in the United States where the downturn was much more severe than in Great Britain but was preceded by a long period of expansion so that long-term expectations were probably less depressed. That is, in the United States an expansionary monetary policy through open-market operations would probably be sufficient to *indirectly* boost aggregate demand thanks to lower interest rates. In contrast, public works in Great Britain were absolutely needed to *directly* stimulate expected demand.

What about the labour market dysfunctioning? All the unemployment prevailing at that time was clearly not 'voluntary', understood as the result of market imperfections responsible for wage rigidity. If public works were launched the rise in aggregate demand expected by entrepreneurs would lead to a rise in prices *and* in output, even with the hypothesis of constant money wages which implies a fall in real wages.[5] For our purpose here, the point is that the workforce would not withdraw its supply of labour so that unemployment should be considered at that time to be to a very large extent 'involuntary'. And as is now well known, the fact that workers do not withdraw their labour supply when prices rise whereas they opposed money-wage cuts does not rely on money illusion. To put it in a nutshell, in a monetary economy, the labour force cannot bargain anything but the *money* wage. And in a decentralised market economy, adjustments are progressive so that cuts in money wages are progressive and exploratory. Actually, a cut in the money wage corresponds to a fall in the *relative* wage.[6]

We have seen in Chapter 2 that Keynes opposes inflationary remedies to unemployment. We can now focus in on our argument a little further. For Keynes, rising prices must be viewed as the *consequence* of the recovery: they are a "symptom of rising output and employment" (Keynes 1934, CW 21, p. 299), the signal of future profits. As such, this 'profit-inflation' renders the recovery easier. But "there is much less to be said in favour of rising prices if they are brought about at the expense of rising output" (Keynes 1933, CW 21, p. 292).[7] One cannot hope to increase output *through* inflationary remedies, i.e. try to barter inflation *for* unemployment. In brief, Keynes would not 'ride on' the steeper part of the Phillips curve to obtain an increase in the employment level.

Regarding Friedman, one faces two methodological problems. First, to the best of our knowledge Friedman never provided an explicit appraisal of unemployment during the Great Depression. To get a snapshot of his interpretation one has to combine, on the one hand, his analysis in terms of monetary disorders in his *Monetary History of the United States* (1963) co-written with Schwartz with, on the other, the dynamic explanation of the natural rate of unemployment. The analytical explanation of unemployment during the Great Depression can then be shaped in a symmetrical manner to the analysis of a monetary expansion: the starting point of the causal chain is a monetary contraction such as the one undertaken by the Fed in early 1929.

The second methodological difficulty is that the analytical argument of the monetary mechanism of transmission stated in Friedman's AER lecture in 1967 (published in 1968) appears quite confused once compared to the one put forward in his 1976 Nobel lecture (published in 1977). Laidler (2012) shows that in Friedman's (1968a) paper there are two intricate and hardly reconcilable arguments. There is first an analysis in terms of *disequilibrium*: monetary expansion leads to an increase in aggregate demand and thus in the output level. Wages and prices rise as a reaction to this increase in aggregate demand (consistently with Philips' analysis and in a highly Keynesian fashion). But this reasoning is inconsistent with Friedman's microeconomic theory of prices according to which individuals placed within a purely competitive setting react to price signals by modifying their quantity supply and demand in every market. The second line of argument is set in terms of individual *equilibrium*: individuals are viewed as misperceiving the price and wage dynamics. As for workers, they wrongly think that they are on their labour supply curve when they accept to offer more labour regarding the increased money wages offered by entrepreneurs to hire them. That is, workers perceive with delay the price rise of the goods they buy. Workers offer more labour at the initial prices but progressively react to price increases in demanding higher wages, which in turn reduces the labour demand on the part of entrepreneurs.[8] Friedman's (1977a) explanation dismisses the first line of argument and relies exclusively on the second one. The argument then runs as follows: monetary expansion leads to a rise of prices that employers wrongly consider as applying to their own activity (i.e. they confuse a rise of the general price level with a modification of relative prices) so that they want to produce more and thus to hire more labour. Firms do increase their supply price because of an increased marginal cost (including higher money wages necessary to cope with the hiring of additional labour). As for them, workers wrongly perceive the rise in money wages as a rise in real wages (which means that they perceive the increase of the general price level with delay), so that they offer more labour. There is a crucial hypothesis made here, that a perceived increased real wage is necessary for the labour force to work more. To put it plainly, this means that the labour force was initially on its labour supply curve – there was no unemployment in the strict sense of the word – when monetary expansion was launched. The – necessarily temporary – macroeconomic disequilibrium is rendered possible only by mischiefs in price perceptions. As soon as new prices (of goods, labour, and so on) are incorporated into individual expectations, we are back to the initial position, i.e. to the natural rate of unemployment – the general price level excepted. Here, macroeconomic disequilibrium is consistent with microeconomic equilibrium: people *think* they are on their curves.

Let us apply Friedman's definitive explanation of the dynamics around the natural rate of unemployment (i.e. the analytic argument of the 1977 Nobel lecture) to get a rationale of 'abnormal' unemployment during the Great Depression. Monetary tightening in 1929 lowered the nominal aggregate demand and thus the general price level. In Friedman's monetary framework, the aggregate supply curve is not vertical in the short run because of price misperceptions that allow for variations in the output level. This means that private actors reacted to the contraction in nominal aggregate demand in a twofold way. Employers wrongly perceived the fall in price as a decline in the relative price of the good they produced and decided accordingly to produce less. They dismissed workforce because of the increase in the perceived real wage they respectively faced (i.e. the real wage paid in terms of the product price they sold). A symmetric argument applies to the labour market: the fall in the general price level led to a fall in money wages but workers wrongly perceived the money-wage cut as a real wage cut (which means that they perceive the fall of the general price level with delay), so that they offered less labour. Were employers and workers in a capacity to correct their misperceptions and to adapt accordingly their inflationary expectations to the new level of money supply, the macroeconomic disequilibrium would have disappeared. In Modigliani's (1977) words: "output falls, not because of the decline in demand, but because of the entirely voluntary reduction in the supply of labor, in response of erroneous perceptions" (Modigliani 1977, p. 4).

How can we then explain the huge rates of unemployment attained during the Great Depression? In Friedman's own words in his Chapter 12 of *Price Theory* (1962b) dedicated to the labour market functioning, "the answer is not entirely clear" (Friedman 1962b, p. 236), a statement that echoes Lucas' acknowledgement that "the great Depression … remains a formidable barrier to a completely unbending application of the view that business cycles are all alike" (Lucas 1980, p. 697). Friedman acknowledges that "there was a series of sharp, unanticipated declines in aggregate demand, so that the recurrent and even bigger readjustments in anticipations were required" (Friedman 1962b, p. 236). The rationale behind Friedman's implicit analysis of the labour market is the following: the Fed did not give private actors a chance to correct their wage and price misperceptions since it pursued its monetary tightening from 1929 to 1933: the dramatic and prolonged fall in the monetary supply (M2) led to a fall in nominal aggregate demand, which meant a fall in prices and through this channel a fall in the output level. Ultimately, Friedman's rationale of unemployment "turns the standard explanation on its head: instead of (excess) employment causing inflation, it is the (unexpected component of) the rate of inflation that causes excess employment" (Modigliani

1977, p. 5). At the macroeconomic level no doubt the economy as a whole was in disequilibrium. At the microeconomic level equilibrium was at work, in the sense that the departure from the long-term vertical Phillips curve is explained by price misperceptions. Noticeably, while Friedman's main explanation of 'abnormal' unemployment relies on delays in perceptions of relative current prices (i.e. backward adaptive expectations), Lucas and Rapping (1969) extend Friedman's analytical approach by adopting a forward-looking framework (i.e. rational expectations) in the sense that for them individuals took time to adapt their expectations of prices and wages.[9] From 1933, the attention of policy-makers shifted towards fiscal stimulus. Paradoxically, from that time on the fact that the monetary policy potency was roughly ignored allowed monetary disorders to disappear. Price expectations adapted to the new level of money supply growth and the economy went at last back to the natural rate of unemployment as defined by the long-run vertical Phillips curve. Besides, the comparison with the 1873–79 sharp recession (prices and wages felt much more and output felt much less) leads Friedman to conclude that "clearly, in the intervening half-century, wages and prices had become much more rigid" (Friedman 1962b, p. 237). This line of argument in terms of nominal rigidities is noticeable to the extent that from Friedman's general standpoint market imperfections are usually viewed as nothing but a "catch-all excuse for all failures to provide a satisfactory explanation of observed phenomena" (Friedman 1962b, p. 213).

What are the lessons to be drawn from Keynes' and Friedman's assessment of unemployment during the Great Depression for the conduct of the economic policy? Despite their points of divergence, their explanations have in common that they stand in sharp contrast with Kydland and Prescott's (1982) purely real thesis that during the Great Depression optimising individuals were optimally responding to *real* shocks (such as technological shocks). Accordingly, both Keynes and Friedman would share the following advocacy in order to react to sharp contraction in aggregate demand:

> The only aggregative economic policy implications we see for events like the Great Depression are the standard ones: if possible, avoid the aggregate-demand shifts which cause them; failing this, pursue corrective demand policies to make them as brief as possible.
>
> (Lucas and Rapping 1972, p. 187)

In comparison with the proponents of real business cycle theory Keynes, Friedman (as well as Lucas) have in common that they consider the Great Depression as the result of a fall in aggregate nominal demand, the latter being interpreted as an aggregate disequilibrium that requires an unambiguous departure from equilibrium analysis as well as a careful understanding of the expectations issue. Even Lucas who adopts a forward-looking expectations procedure freely admits that one could hardly rely on purely technological shocks, changes in consumer tastes, and so on, not to talk of a too generous dole, to get a full explanation of the 1930s.[10]

Yet, on the precise causes of this contraction in aggregate demand and on the issue of the proper remedies to correct this macroeconomic disequilibrium, the positions held by our two authors are very different. As for Keynes, he insists on the second-round effects of monetary disorders on the real side of the economy: a too low long-term state of real expectations with regard to the prevailing interest rate requires direct State intervention to raise aggregate demand, and thus the level of output. When entrepreneurs are so pessimistic, there is no hope to be found in monetary policy to restore aggregate demand at its full employment level. Even if as a matter of principle monetary loosening can be considered efficient, this efficiency only applies to the USA (monetary policy would not be efficient in Great Britain). The remedy would in no way come from the *direct* rise in the general price level due to monetary loosening, but through the fall in interest rates. As for Friedman, his interpretation of the Great Depression in terms of purely monetary disorders together with his plea in terms of a constant nominal aggregate demand (i.e. monetary loosening to restore 'normal' prices) rely on his understanding of the effects of changes in the money supply on inflationary expectations. That is, private agents do take time to get information on the relevant prices and to adapt their nominal expectations accordingly. The best that economic policy can do to stabilise aggregate demand is to anchor nominal expectations so as to avoid misperceptions of relative prices.

Let us now see the economic guidelines advocated by Keynes and Friedman, which both aim precisely to stabilise aggregate demand. The following section is dedicated to monetary policy while the section after focuses on fiscal policy. We will close this chapter by drawing the avenues for reflection Keynes and Friedman offer us to reshape contemporary debates regarding the economic policy.

4.3 Monetary policy

Let us start our appraisal of Keynes' and Friedman's policy advocacies with the issue of monetary policy. There are two reasons for proceeding this way. First, Keynes' confidence in the potency of fiscal policy is a corollary of his distrust of monetary loosening to support the recovery in the short run. Second, most of Friedman's sharp critiques towards discretion apply to both monetary and fiscal policies although additional defects apply specifically to fiscal policy.

Regarding the way monetary policy can stabilise the economic system, regarding also the attention paid to the necessity to anchor private agents' expectations, the analysis carried out below will bring to light strong points of convergence between Keynes' and Friedman's advocacies. Precisely, for both of them monetary policy is concerned with the long-term prospects of a decentralised market economy. Yet, we will see that they have quite distinct manners of dealing with the practical issue (different target instruments) and that, most importantly, the kind of expectations to be managed in order to stabilise a monetary economy are not the same. Keynes is concerned with the long-term real expectations whereas Friedman aims to anchor short-term nominal expectations.

We will proceed as follows. We will start with the monetary policy advocated by Keynes, which is surprisingly defined in terms of rules, and we will then turn to Friedman's *k per cent* rule.

Keynes' discretionary rule

As a matter of fact, monetary policy is for Keynes a huge matter of concern. Yet, it is for him a long-term issue rather than a short-term weapon. See for example:

> I am far from fully convinced by the recent thesis that interest rates play a small part in determining the volume of investment. It may be that other influences, such as an increase in demand, often dominate in starting a movement. But I am quite unconvinced that low interest rates cannot play an enormous part in *sustaining* investment at a given figure, and when there is a movement from a higher rate to a lower rate in allowing a greater scale of investment to proceed over a very much longer period than would otherwise be possible.
>
> (Letter to M. Ezequiel, 7 June 1941; quoted in Moggridge and Howson 1974, p. 463)[11]

As the quotation above shows, two issues should be distinguished. First, there is the case of the initial recovery, when expectations are so pessimistic that monetary policy proves impotent by itself to boost investment. As we will see, the plea for public spending ensues from this finding. Second, there is the issue of the conditions under which the initial recovery can last. Here, low interest rates are critical. Hence, monetary policy according to Keynes does not aim at controlling the short-term dynamics of a monetary economy. As we will argue, monetary policy is for Keynes highly concerned with the issue of long-term uncertainty. That is, monetary policy aims to sustain the long-term growth tendency of a decentralised economy.

In our opinion the proper monetary policy Keynes calls for should be labelled a 'discretionary rule', in the sense of long-term guidelines that nonetheless leave room for short-term adaptations to circumstances. First, the 'rule' aspect of Keynes' advocacy comes from his basic opposition to the rise and fall of interest rates to control the boom, and in particular to dampen inflationary pressures. When inflation was feared at the end of the Great Depression, Keynes stated about dear money that "we must avoid it as we would hell-fire" (Keynes 1937, CW 22, p. 389). Keynes' rule corresponds to a slowly decreasing interest rate in order to follow the path of a necessarily decreasing marginal efficiency of capital: "the major purpose of the Treasury should be to establish stable conditions with a gradually declining rate over a long period of years ahead, a necessary condition of which is the creation of a reasonable expectation that this is, in fact, the probable course of events" (Keynes 1935, CW 22, p. 351). The necessity to encourage private actors to have confidence in this tendency, the need to wait for previous falls being well established before attempting a further decrease are constant matters of concern for Keynes. It might happen that "a consolidation of the existing position coupled with a greater degree of confidence in the maintaining of the existing rates of interest" (Keynes 1936, CW 22, p. 375) would be more needed than a further fall. For the implementation of this rule to be successful, it is critical that monetary authorities show confidence in this downward tendency of interest rates. To this end, they might come to accept to borrow on shorter durations than preferred to enforce private expectations: "the authorities are only fettered in their policy if they themselves have a counter-liquidity preference" (Keynes 1945, CW 27, p. 391), that is, if they prefer to borrow long term than borrow short term. It is their acceptance to borrow on short terms instead of raising long-term rates that contributes to fostering private actors' expectations. Thus, Keynes' monetary policy operates through two different channels: first by providing as much liquidity as necessary "to feed the market" (Keynes 1941, CW 22, p. 416); second by managing expectations, that is the liquidity-preference schedule of private actors. This twofold way monetary policy operates is critical to understand how it comes to be successful: "in practice, open-market purchases of securities may, almost at the same time, move market yields directly, thereby *cet. par.* enlarging the liquidity of the system correspondingly (liquidity channel), and successfully steer the convention itself downward too (expectational channel)" (Bibow 2000, p. 557). Basically, such a view of monetary policy is explained by the heterogeneity of agents and of their expectations, to be managed by public authorities.

During World War II, one can consider the implementation of Keynes' rule as successful. At that time the needs of the Treasury to borrow became huge. The target was a long-term rate of 3 per cent. In 1941 Keynes considered that "another revolution in our financial practice has followed from our great success in borrowing for the war at a low rate of interest" (Keynes 1941, CW 22, p. 303). As acknowledged by Moggridge, Keynes was for a large part responsible for the commitment of the authorities to a 3 per cent rate.[12] What was the right policy to reach and to maintain this 3 per cent target? The first step was to offer as much liquidity as required to the private sector: "the gilt-edged market can only be kept good by allowing holders to be just liquid as they feel to be" (Keynes 1941, CW 22, p. 414). Second, the Treasury had to be patient if they wanted to respect their commitment: "it is simply a question of waiting and of making it clear that loans will only be available at a modest rate of interest, becoming still more modest as time goes on" (Keynes 1939, CW 21, p. 540). The confidence of the Treasury themselves in their future policy was here considered as the key point. Now, during World War II the Treasury was in fact the principal borrower. Hence: "the ability to wait constitutes the signal advantage of the Treasury over private borrowers" (Keynes 1939, CW 21, p. 562). Centralised borrowing would first allow cheaper borrowing and second "facilitate ... the management of the market generally" (Keynes 1942, CW 27, p. 280). The Treasury had to be sufficiently patient to wait for the private sector to adapt to the present convention before trying to decrease the long rate to a lower level. If they had weak confidence in the downward tendency of the long rate of interest, private actors would start to keep liquid again, not the least through the rearrangement of their patrimonies in favour of shorter securities. As Moggridge and Howson (1974) argue, in a socialised economy in which public and semi-public bodies play an increasing role and in which centralised borrowing is by the way made possible, monetary controls are made easier than in a laissez-faire economy where the state plays a small part. Here at stake there is a critical mechanism that helps monetary authorities to achieve their target, namely the tap issue. Under this mechanism, "rates of interest and maturities were announced but no limits were set to the cash amount of any issue" (Tily 2006, p. 664). For Keynes, "it is the technique of the tap issue that has done the trick" (Keynes 1945, CW 27, p. 392).[13] This institutional mechanism appears as exactly symmetrical to Friedman's *k per cent* monetary aggregate rule: here monetary authorities target a rate of interest and provide the corresponding amount of bonds that individuals and institutions are willing to buy.

Now, Keynes' long-term interest rate rule has its discretionary side. As we see it, this discretionary aspect of Keynes' rule is to be found in the necessity to take account of circumstances in the implementation of the policy for the management of the market in general. Indeed, one can see for example Keynes arguing: "no dogmatic conclusions should be laid down for the future about the rates of interest appropriate to different maturities, which should be fixed from time to time in the light of experience" (Keynes 1945, CW 27 pp. 396–7). Contrary to Friedman, Keynes agrees to adapt his monetary rule to the particular circumstances of the time. In Keynes' views monetary authorities seem to be able to collect information on the current state of the economy: the Ministry of Trade and Production should be "charged with the duty of passing on absolutely up-to-date information to the Capital Budget division of the Treasury" (Keynes 1945, CW 27, p. 409). What is more, for Keynes and contrarily to Friedman (as well as Hayek), public authorities have the capability to behave wisely for collective efficiency.[14] This discretionary side of Keynes' rule involves the management of short rates much more than the management of long rates. In Keynes' view the rise of short-term interest rates is nothing but a *pis-aller* with regard to alternative means to break the boom such as rationing.[15] Quite surprisingly, monetary authorities might even decide to push up their long-term interest rate of borrowing in case of exceptional circumstances, if for example inflationary pressures appear after the transition stage of the recovery after World War II: "if the prevailing long-term tap rate becomes chronically too low, in the sense that it encourages new capital formation on a scale tending to inflation, the rate should, in general, be raised" (Keynes 1945, CW 27, p. 398).

What comes out of our analysis of Keynes' monetary policy? First, regarding the conditions to be fulfilled for monetary policy to be successful, monetary policy à la Keynes requires knowledge about the structure of the economy and information on its current state. Monetary authorities are considered sufficiently wise and competent to implement the rule advocated which means that Keynes' rule requires collective rationality on the part of the public body.

Second, regarding the framing of monetary policy, Keynes adopts a forward-looking approach. One can see him arguing:

> Perhaps the most important factor in the whole situation is the impression the Treasury itself creates concerning its objective and future policy.... At present the market does not know what to expect. ... The tendency is not for certain.
>
> (Keynes 1939, CW 21, pp. 563–4)

Taking this quotation seriously, it is hard to consider that Keynes advocates discretion, if by discretion one means monetary authority that "chooses the current rate of interest by reoptimizing every period" (Clarida *et al.* 1999, p. 1670). In Keynes' theoretical framework also, expectations can be considered as endogenous. In a way, for him also monetary policy turns out to be a strategic game between monetary authorities and economic agents.

Third, on the ultimate purpose of monetary policy, the issue is to sustain the long-term growth capacity of the economy. Accordingly, the relevant interest rate to be managed is thus the long-term one. Levels of short rates are relevant only to the extent that they give us information on private actors' expectations about long-term rates. Noticeably, monetary authorities should try to use their influence with the view to drive this long-term monetary rate of interest.

All in all, it is as if for Keynes monetary authorities were in a position to influence the long-term prospects of the economy – its growth path – which is an issue that largely encompasses the question of how to sustain the self-adjusting capacity of the economy (a short-run matter of concern once one considers the output level is ultimately determined by the natural real interest rate in the long run). Beyond that, Keynes in no way calls for ups and downs of interest rates to control inflation as the Moderns advocate.

For Keynes, it takes time to lower the long-term interest rate, because of its conventional nature. As a consequence, "the long-term rate of interest must be kept continuously as near as possible to what we believe to be the long-term optimum. It is not suitable to be used as a short-period weapon" (Keynes 1937, CW 21, p. 389). Monetary policy is definitely not, for Keynes, the proper instrument to fight inflationary pressures, even if he is a constant opponent of inflation.[16] Beyond the supply of monetary assets monetary policy should aim to manage private sector's real expectations. To this extent, the liquidity preference of private actors turns out to be a critical variable to be politically controlled by state intervention. That is the reason why monetary authorities are supposed to develop a long-term view.

Friedman's monetary rule in retrospect

Let us now turn to Friedman's *k per cent* monetary rule. Two issues should be disentangled. First, there is the issue of the policy *conduct*: what is the ultimate goal of monetary authorities? And what dose of leeway should be conferred to them in the practical implementation of policy? This first issue refers to "strategy" as Friedman (1982a, p. 100) calls it.[17] Second, there is the issue of the target of monetary policy: what is the relevant variable to manage? Is it a direct instrument, or are monetary authorities supposed to drive a proximate target? This second issue refers to the best "tactics" (Friedman 1982a, p. 100) to implement in order to achieve the strategy stated above.[18]

Conduct of monetary policy

Let us start with strategy. Friedman's starting point is twofold. In the long run we know quite well the "closeness, regularity, and predictability" (Friedman 1969b, p. 144) of the link between monetary aggregates, price level and output. This is an argument put forward by Friedman throughout his career. But in the short run the fact remains that

> we do not know enough to be able to recognize minor disturbances when they occur or to be able to predict either what their effects will be with any precision or what monetary policy is required to offset their effects.
>
> (Friedman [1968a] 1969a, p. 107)[19]

Monetary authorities should rely on these empirical regularities to provide an institutional framework invariant with respect to circumstances, whatever the ups and downs that might appear in the short run. So Friedman's purpose is definitely not to offer an optimal monetary policy, the best policy able to obtain the largest collective welfare at all times. On the conduct of economic policy in general, he explicitly acknowledges that "this is one of those cases in which the best can be the enemy of the good" (Friedman 1969b, p. 144). In his words: "the elimination of monetary uncertainty would promote healthy economic growth by providing a more stable environment for both individual planning and social action" (Friedman 1969b, p. 145). Such an assertion directly ensues from Friedman's assault against the Phillips curve: the lower the variations in the price level, the lesser important fluctuations around the natural rate of unemployment.

The ultimate goal of monetary policy is to promote economic stability through the stability in prices. The point is that a monetary policy rule properly defined would anchor private agents' expectations:

> Our economic system will work best when producers and consumers, employers and employees, can proceed with full confidence that the average level of prices will behave in a known way in the future – preferably that it will be highly stable.
>
> (Friedman [1968a] 1969a, p. 106)

*

Friedman's basic purpose is to provide a stable *monetary* framework. Indeed, inflation is always a monetary phenomenon. By contrast, "output is a real magnitude, not a monetary magnitude" (Friedman 2010, p. 116). Yet, erratic movements of money supply have dramatic consequences on fluctuations in the output level. As we have already seen and as Friedman (2005) again claims, the way the sharp contraction of money precipitated the Great Depression is evidence for that claim. Finally, there is Friedman's distrust towards collective bodies. See for example:

> Even granted the market failures that we and many other economists had attributed to a strictly laissez-faire policy in money and banking, the course of events encouraged the view that turning to government as an alternative was a cure that was worse than the disease, at least with existing government policies and institutions. Government failure might be worse than market failure.
>
> (Friedman and Schwartz 1986, p. 39)

Again, Friedman does not deny the existence of market failures, to the extent that the shocks involved are temporary and not large-scaled, probably uncorrelated and that they give rise only to a temporary departure from the natural rate of unemployment. What he points out is that government action is much likely to make matters worse. Hence his advocacy of a "government of law instead of men" (Friedman [1962c] 1968c, p. 190), that is strictly legislated rules instead of an independent central bank. Indeed, an independent monetary authority is contrary to the dispersion of political power dear to Friedman; it depends too much on personalities and, above all, it is highly likely to be captured by bankers.

What Friedman basically aimed at was to see central bankers' hands tied in advance. No special knowledge or wise advice should be necessary to apply a monetary rule.

Target of monetary policy

Let us now turn to tactics. What is the most relevant instrument consistent with the monetary rule argued above? And what is the best institutional setting mandatory for this rule to apply? Friedman does not deny that a day might come when monetary policy will be able to target explicitly the price level through the manipulation of the monetary base, i.e. that money would still be the instrument but price stability will become the explicit ultimate target. Yet, in the light of our present knowledge and institutional setting characterised by *fiat* money (i.e. money that the issuer does not promise to convert into anything) a rule formulated in terms of constant growth of money is the best achievable. There is one basic reason for that: "the most important magnitude that the monetary authorities can effectively control and for which they have primary responsibility is the stock of money" (Friedman 1960a, p. 88). That is, the instrument manipulated by authorities should conflate with the target formulated. This is not the case merely by chance: since its implementation in no way requires the slightest interpretation, such a rule completely avoids discretion. As we will see below, from his very initial pleas in the 1940s to the latest ones Friedman's positions regarding monetary tactics varied slightly. The amendments operated over time apply first to the monetary aggregate involved (is it the monetary base? Or M2? Even M3?), the precise rate of growth targeted (should we even consider a constant rate of fall of money supply?) and second to the institutional set-up mandatory for the monetary rule to fully operate. But these amendments should be viewed as practical qualifications needed to fix a monetary stable background rather than qualifications applying to the overall goal.

Let us first analyse the precise instrument involved in the implementation of a monetary rule à la Friedman. From 1948 to 1959 Friedman moved from a rule in terms of counter-cyclical fluctuations in the stock of money[20] to a rule in terms of a constant growth rate of money. The first rule would function quite well. Yet, such a scheme was later considered "more sophisticated and complex than is necessary" (Friedman 1960a, p. 90). That is the reason why Friedman turned to a "simpler rule" that consists in that "the stock of money be increased at a fixed rate year-in and year-out without any variation in the rate of increase to meet cyclical needs" (Friedman 1960a, p. 90). In contemporary wording, the later rule turns out to be a second-best option. This became the position he definitely stuck to.

A further point is which monetary aggregate should be controlled, as well as the path targeted for the aggregate chosen. When he introduces his *k per cent* rule Friedman specifies that "the precise rate of growth, like the precise monetary total, is less important than the adoption of some stated and known rate" (Friedman [1968a] 1969a, p. 109). Again, the point is to avoid discretionary intervention on the part of public authorities.

Without anticipating too much our study of the functioning of a monetary economy, which will be the subject matter of the next chapter, a particular point is worth noticing here with regard to Keynes' monetary guidelines investigated above. In his "Optimum Quantity of Money" (1969a) essay, Friedman considers three *scenarii*: a constant money supply, a constant rate of growth of money supply and a constant rate of fall. A positive rate of growth entails welfare loss since money enters both utility function and production function. When prices rise, cash balances yield a negative return. At the opposite, the effect of a continuous decrease in the quantity of money would be a welfare gain since a lower amount of cash balances would provide the same pecuniary and non-pecuniary services as before. As a matter of principle, Friedman claims that "our final rule for the optimum quantity of money is that it will be attained by a rate of price deflation that makes the nominal rate of inflation equal to zero" (Friedman 1969a, p. 34). With a rate of inflation solely determined by monetary factors, this overall goal means a rate of money supply growth equal to the opposite of the real interest rate as determined by real factors such as productivity of capital and thrift. This plea strikingly echoes the monetary guidelines advocated by Keynes, who also calls for a zero money rate of interest as a long-term target to be reached. This being said we hasten to precise that, as we will see in the next chapter, these similar pleas rely on highly distinct theoretical underpinnings.

Because of the practical difficulties encountered by the implementation of a monetary rule, Friedman ultimately favours a positive rate of growth in the quantity of money. What are these practical difficulties? According to Friedman: "Transition to a new policy would take time. Many prices are slow to adjust. Any decided change in the trend of prices would involve significant frictional distortion in employment and production" (Friedman 1969a, p. 45).

The fact is that "the major price rigidities are for factor services" (Friedman 1969a, p. 47), and particularly of course money wages. Hence a moderate and controlled rate of inflation would help to cope with rigidities in some relative prices (as for example in money wages). Here is to be found one of the few occasions on which Friedman acknowledges nominal rigidities (another exception is set as an aside to his monetary explanation of the Great Depression). In his AER Presidential Address Friedman (1968a) suggested a constant growth rate of 3–5 per cent for M2 or slightly less for M1 so as to ensure stability in the price of final goods. In 1969, he considered that a 2 per cent rate of growth in M2 might be achievable as a long-run policy goal. This is not surprising to the extent that, the longer the time period considered, the more frictions and rigidities can be considered as having been encompassed.

What about the particular institutional setting mandatory for the rule to apply? Friedman's point is that the complex and fractional reserve system might impede the central bank ability to control the total stock of money. In 1948 as well as in 1959, he called for a 100 per cent reserves requirement on demand deposits to avoid endogenous creation of money, a procedure whereby "the total of money and of high-powered money would then be the same" (Friedman 1960a, p. 69). The instability of the total stock of money due to changes in the forms in which the public holds money (i.e. currency or deposits) would be eliminated. Open-market operations would be the key instrument used to reach this target.[21] Lately Friedman (1984) abandoned the 100 per cent proposal and then advocated contemporary reserve accounting instead of lagged accounting, and this whatever the type of deposit. Friedman went back to this question in the early 1980s, at the time when a large instability of money demand was observed in the USA, at least with regard to the monetary base and M1. This occurred because of structural changes in the financial sector of the economy, especially the payment of interest on demand deposits. Friedman took note that "the Fed has been unable or unwilling to achieve such a target", i.e. M1, and henceforth acknowledged that "it is preferable to state the rule in terms of a magnitude but that unquestionably can be controlled with very narrow limits within very brief time periods, ... namely the monetary base" (Friedman [1984] 1987, p. 414). Viewed as something like "a Schelling point – a natural point at which people tend to agree" he then advocates "zero growth in high-powered money" (Friedman [1984] 1987, p. 422).

There is a counterpart to the freezing of the monetary base, which is to let the deregulation in the financial sector follow its natural course. The banking sector would then function as any other industry. Here is to be found a critical application of Friedman's overall claim that the economy system possesses endogenous correcting forces.[22] This is especially the case regarding the financial markets functioning, about which Friedman ([1960b] 1969a) denies the possibility of destabilising speculation: "the economic function of speculation is taken to be the reduction of inter-temporal differences in price" (Friedman [1960b] 1969a, p. 286). Indeed, financial markets are considered to work just like any others: "why should we not have variety and diversity in the market for borrowing and lending as in other markets?" (Friedman [1967] 1969a, p. 83). Clearly, the "loosening of the financial structure through continued deregulation" (Friedman [1984] 1987, p. 422) would increase the money multiplier (i.e. the ratio between monetary base and M2). At a hypothetical stationary state position (i.e. with real output constant), and with a zero growth rate for high-powered money, the other monetary aggregates would be kept constant, as well as the price level. But with a real output level growing at a stable rate, the behaviour of the nominal income and of the price level would depend on possible changes in the money multiplier: if financial innovations rise at the same pace as the real output (but without any necessary causality between the two), the money multiplier would rise too and prices would be kept stable; if not, prices will fall at the same rate that real output rises. As usual, what interests Friedman most of all is the dynamic adjustment process. For him, history teaches us that the "loosening of the financial structure through continued deregulation" (Friedman [1984] 1987, p. 422) is very likely to increase the money multiplier (i.e. the ratio between monetary base and M2) as well as the income velocity of M_1.[23] Within the institutional setting advocated, both the changes in the money multiplier and in the income velocity would change gradually, which amounts to the exact contrary of the so-called instability in financial markets that would prevent the implementation of his monetary rule. Friedman argues:

> In the system I have just described, the total quantity of any monetary aggregate would be determined by the market interactions of many institutional and millions of holders of monetary assets. It would be limited by the constant quantity of high-powered money available at ultimate reserves. The ratios of various aggregate to high-powered money would doubtless change from time to time, but in the absence of rigid government controls ... the ratios would change gradually and only as financial innovations or changes in business and industry altered the proportions in which the public chose to hold various monetary assets.
>
> (Friedman [1984] 1987, p. 423–4)

At the same time the capacity for any initiative on the part of monetary authorities would be negligible, and the long-run relationship between monetary income and M2 would be restored. Friedman freely admits that what he calls for, freezing "the quantity of high-powered money, and deregulat[ing] the financial system" (Friedman [1984] 1987, p. 425), is a far-reaching institutional change. Yet, he considers his dual programme worth discussing, especially insofar as "it construct[s] an ideal goal, so that incremental changes can be judged by whether they move the institutional structure towards or away from that ideal" (Friedman [1984] 1987, p. 424).

Such a manner of putting the issue and to frame his own position gives us a strong hint as to Friedman's stance in his policy advice. Friedman appears as not so much concerned with the practical issue. Rather, what he offers is an "ideal goal", an abstract idealised standpoint to which the actual regime can be compared. No doubt, from Friedman's standpoint, our modern economies are far from moving progressively towards his ideal type; policy-makers of the contemporary era do not advance along the right path. Traditionally, central bankers manipulate interest rates. They moved – temporarily – to monetary aggregates only from the mid-1970s to the early 1980s. Friedman (1982a) considers that even at that time central bankers were mainly paying lip service to his advocacy. What basically explains the return of central bankers to interest rate targeting is the instability in the velocity of money in the late 1970s: because of financial innovations, the relation between monetary base and other aggregates becomes much more difficult to predict.[24] This was considered as an insuperable argument against Friedman's monetary aggregate targeting.[25] So the move from one type of instrument to the other is seen as a change rendered necessary in modern times of financial markets development, a change respectful of the spirit of Friedman's rule if not literally. But this twist is merely heresy from Friedman's standpoint. For him "the talk about changes in the demand for money is simply a red herring introduced by the Federal Reserve. ... In each case it has turned out that there has been no change in the demand for money" (Friedman 1982b, pp. 73–4). So the instability in velocity of money is not for Friedman a direct matter of concern but rather an excuse used by interest rate rule proponents.[26]

Worse, the targeting of short-term interest rates can in no way be considered as a first rough estimate of monetary targeting. As Friedman (2010) claims, nothing can insure us that the interest rate targeted is the right one to achieve the desired inflation rate: the output or monetary growth might not be at their equilibrium levels. Again, Friedman leans against a model-uncertainty argument to claim that monetary authorities should refrain from discretionary interventions.

As we have done for Keynes, let us take stock of the main features of monetary policy à la Friedman. First, regarding the conditions to be fulfilled for monetary policy to be successful, monetary policy à la Friedman does not require the slightest information on the economic system to operate. For Friedman, "one problem is that [the monetary authority] cannot know what the 'natural' rate is. Unfortunately, we have as yet devised no method to estimate accurately and readily the natural rate of either interest or unemployment" (Friedman [1968a] 1969a, p. 104). Consistently with his overall policy advice, Friedman clearly leans on both an uncertainty-model argument and on a data-uncertainty argument: public authorities are ignorant of both the structure of the economy and of its current state. The economy might be on the upward tide of the business cycle while policy-makers take for granted the contrary. They might also be wrong about the process at work behind the current economic climate. The crucial point here is the difficulty to collect *on time* data on the precise situation faced by the economy, and by the way the difficulty to rightly grasp the mechanisms at work in the dynamics of a monetary economy. Because of delays, time lags, etc., deliberate action is likely to be pro-cyclical, with the risk of enhancing rather than reducing fluctuations. It is not merely by chance that the monetary authorities' target concurs with the direct instrument they control. Friedman's monetary rule requires no special knowledge or wise advice for the individuals in charge of their implementation: there is no leeway, no interpretation, and even less what is called today "constrained discretion" (Bernanke 2003).

Second, there is the complete absence of discretion left to monetary authorities in the implementation of a policy rule. For example, should monetary authorities intervene when the prices of primary goods rise? Regarding the inflation rate, how to 'choose' the right indicator: is it the GDP deflator? Or the consumer price index? For Friedman, this sort of questioning would give too much leeway to the authorities. That is precisely the reason why he opposes the price-level rule: "it is the wrong type of rule because the objectives it specifies are ones that the monetary authorities do not have the clear and direct power to achieve by their own actions" (Friedman [1962c] 1968c, p. 193). Basically, what Friedman aims at is to see monetary authorities tied hand and foot. He did not claim to have established an 'optimal' monetary rule that would cope with the regular and unpredictable ups and downs of the economy. Rather, what he elaborated was a second-best instrument that prevents public authorities from making matters worse. In this regard, policy rule according to Friedman belongs to 'autopilot' and mechanical prescriptions.

Third, in Friedman's theoretical framework the interest rate is basically a market phenomenon. For him monetary policy "cannot peg interest rates for more than very limited periods" (Friedman [1968a] 1969a, p. 99). Besides, interest rates are "a misleading indicator of whether monetary policy is 'tight' or 'easy'" (Friedman [1968a] 1969a, p. 101).[27] What matters is not merely the current interest rates but their trends. That is, the current interest rate incorporates expectations on future levels of inflation, and thus of the growth rate of the money supply. Viewed in this way,

> low interest rates are a sign that monetary policy has been tight – in the sense that the quantity of money has grown slowly; high interest rates are a sign that monetary policy has been easy – in the sense that the quantity of money has grown rapidly.
>
> (Friedman [1968a] 1969a, pp. 100–1)

His empirical investigations comfort Friedman in his view that monetary variability (say, of M2) is highly (and as a matter of fact positively) correlated with output variability. That is basically why he emphasised so much "the role of monetary variability – the one item that central banks can control" (Friedman 2010, p. 117).

Last, on the ultimate purpose of monetary policy Friedman considers that "the Fed exists to define a monetary system.... it has one and only one function: to keep the price level steady" (Friedman 2010, p. 116), which means that monetary authorities should in no way care about the real side of the economy. This comes as no surprise once one acknowledges that in Friedman's eyes the stability of the monetary side of the economy is a pre-condition for stability in its real side.

*

To conclude on this issue of monetary policy, it might be true that Keynes and Friedman possess a shared concern for the stability of a monetary economy and that they share the same consideration for potency of monetary policy in a long-term perspective to achieve this basic goal. Yet, beyond the surface points of agreement fall to pieces. Keynes is highly confident in the centralised authorities' capacity to act in a timely and wise manner on the grounds of good knowledge both of the structure of the economic system as well as of its current state while quite the contrary is true for Friedman. Besides, Keynes targets the long-term interest rate while Friedman focuses on the aggregate money supply. A hint for this sharply different approach to the conduct of monetary policy, which will be at the core of the remainder of our investigation in the following chapter, is that Keynes is concerned with the long-term expectations regarding the prospective returns on capital goods (i.e. long-term real expectations) whereas Friedman is concerned with the short-term expectations regarding the ongoing prices of the goods and factors of production each agent needs to buy and sell in a monetary economy (i.e. short-run nominal expectations).

For the moment, let us turn to the second weapon of the employment policy aiming to stabilise a monetary economy, namely fiscal policy.

4.4 Fiscal policy

As for Keynes, his pleas for State intervention are often viewed as an equivalent to Lerner's (1941) 'functional finance' principle. This means a very low concern regarding fiscal deficit, which is very likely to cause the sort of problem of sustainability in the public debt in the long run that we now experience. Besides, Keynes is also considered as the forerunner to fine-tuning as supported by Heller (1967). This implies a focus on the short-run issue at the expense of long-run concerns towards the growth trend of the economy. As for Friedman, he is usually considered as a long-standing and relentless critic of fiscal policy. Friedman is said to have constantly opposed counter-cyclical fiscal policy because of the specific defects from which it suffers beyond the common flaws of discretionary policies that it shares with monetary policy.

Let us review Keynes' and Friedman's original pleas to appreciate the scope of these assessments. On the one hand, we will see that Keynes' policy guidelines are a far cry from the insistence on short-term devices that is ascribed to him. To put it in a nutshell, the socialisation of investment advocated by Keynes corresponds to a long-term programme that focuses on the control of demand for capital schemes and does not entail budgetary deficit. On the other hand, we will show that Friedman has not always been the monetarist opposed to any type of fiscal device he claims to be.

Keynes on pump-priming and the socialisation of investment

As Keynes wrote to Robbins in 1943, "much less effort is required to prevent the ball rolling than would be required to stop it rolling once it has started…. After the slump has fully developed, the relevant figures get dreadfully large" (Keynes 1943,

CW 27, p. 316). To properly understand Keynes' views on fiscal policy, two issues must be disentangled. First, there is the case of the cure for unemployment as and when it arises as was the case during the Great Depression, but also during the whole 1920s in Great Britain: this is the reason why Keynes' plea for public works predated the 1929 collapse. Second, there is the basic purpose to maintaining the economy at its full employment level: what are the economic policy guidelines to be implemented so as to ensure that a dramatic episode such as the Great Depression would never happen again? The matter at hand is to secure a spendings flow consistent with full employment. Were these two basic issues carefully disentangled, a lot of misunderstandings would have been avoided.

We will proceed as follows. First, we will see what Keynes calls for to escape the slump once it has occurred. Second, we will see that, this first major hurdle being crossed, Keynes turns his attention to the crucial issue of crisis prevention: how to prevent the occurrence of slump? From this, we will be able to portray Keynes' overall programme for the 'socialisation of investment' that stands in sharp contrast with the commonly accepted idea one usually gets of fiscal policy à la Keynes.

Keynes on pump-priming

In the early 1930s, *before* the *General Theory*, there was an emergency, which was to *escape* the depression. As soon as he comprehended the seriousness of the situation, the situation appeared rather desperate in the eyes of Keynes: "we are violently out of equilibrium" (Keynes 1930, CW 13, p. 199). The first obvious remedy to discuss would be implementing wage cuts with the view to restoring the equilibrium on the labour market and letting the liquidation go on. As we have seen in the preceding chapter, Keynes strongly opposed this 'liquidationist' analysis. Keynes' first line of argument was that a deflationary wage policy could be hardly implemented because of the size of the adjustment needed: money-wages should be cut by about 40 per cent. Hence, money-wage cuts were simply "not worth discussing from the practical point of view" (Keynes 1930, CW 13, p. 198). The second line of argument, which takes place at the theoretical level, was much more ambitious: it consisted in denying the efficiency of wage cuts to cure unemployment. The point turned to demonstrate that money-wage cuts were a remedy of the kind that cured the patient by killing him. By the time of the *General Theory* Keynes' opposition to wage cuts relied upon their depressive influence on entrepreneurs' long-term expectations. That is the reason why money-wage cuts would not help. Here is the theoretical turning point in the genesis of the *General Theory*, a point "which has been too often forgotten over time by a number of (old and new) Keynesian economists" (Meccheri 2007, p. 716). Monetary loosening does not prove a convincing alternative to wage cuts, especially in the British case: when private initiative has almost collapsed and when confidence is very weak, "the response to what would have been in other circumstances a strong stimulus may be very reluctant" (Keynes 1930, CW 20, p. 346).

Hence, the benefit expected from a recovery programme by aim of fiscal stimulus is the restoration of business confidence through the "recovery of business profits" (Keynes 1930, CW 20, p. 444). Public works are not intended to substitute for private investment; they are rather supposed to "break the vicious circle" (Keynes 1933, CW 21, p. 158).

This objective set for the public works scheme raises some comments. First, in Keynes' eyes all private spendings are not the same: the point is to raise the autonomous demand for long-lived assets (i.e. investment) rather than the induced flow of spending of short-term goods (i.e. consumption). Second, Keynes' plea for public works in no way relies on static expectations on the part of private actors. It is true that Keynes distinguishes in the *General Theory* short-term and long-term expectations, perfect foresight being assumed for the former and the latter being considered as exogenously determined. But in no way are public works efficient to raise aggregate demand only so long as expectations are kept unchanged, quite the contrary. As argued below, fiscal policy aims to manage the long-term private state of expectations by encouraging entrepreneurs and investors to anticipate a high level of aggregate demand.

Keynes on capital budgeting

In the late 1930s, *after* the *General Theory*, Keynes' matter of concern was to *forestall* potential problems inherent in the broader tendencies of a market economy, in other words to implement economic guidelines to ensure that a market economy would be kept at its full employment level. This is precisely what Keynes means by the 'socialisation of investment'. We have dealt above with the monetary policy aspects of the socialisation of investment; let us focus on fiscal policy.[28]

In the various memoranda Keynes wrote during World War II with the view to shape an employment policy for a peacetime economy, one can always find a deep concern for the stabilisation of the long-term state of private expectations. Here is to be found the 'rule aspect' of Keynes' advocacies. After the Great Depression, Keynes' overall matter of concern is to develop long-term capital schemes that would stabilise spendings flows in a long-run perspective. Hence the plea for the setting of a Capital Budget,[29] with the aim to "balance and stabilise the Investment Budget for the national economy as a whole" (Keynes 1945, CW 27, p. 409). Capital budgeting entails recurrent programmes and long-lived capital schemes that are much more effective in fixing private expectations at the full employment target. The objective is to *prevent* large fluctuations in private investment through *long-term* public capital expenditure: "emphasis should be placed primarily on measures to maintain a steady level of employment and thus to prevent fluctuations" (Keynes 1943, CW 27, p. 323). For Keynes, about two-thirds of total investment would be involved (Keynes 1943, CW 27, p. 322), which seems quite comprehensive for a contemporary reader.

As is the case for monetary policy, Keynes' policy guidelines regarding fiscal policy have their 'discretionary' side, which is expanded in a twofold way. First, there is the issue of the discretion attributed to the Treasury in charge of the implementation of this long-term programme, which corresponds to, "the means of ensuring stability in the long-term investment programme coupled with proposals for adjusting its tempo to unforeseen changes" (Keynes 1943, CW 27, p. 357).[30] It might not be excluded that the economic climate changes, so that postponing or on the contrary quicker setting of capital schemes would be needed. This is consistent with Keynes' confidence in public bodies to take the right decision at the right time.

Consistently with this discretionary leeway attributed to policy-makers in the implementation of a general 'rule', Keynes advocates the creation of an institution designed to deal with short-term adjustments, namely Keynes' 'buffer stock' schemes. Remember that "Keynes's scheme from the outset focused on stabilizing commodity prices in order to reduce producer risk and to smooth the trade cycle" (Dimand and Dimand 1990, p. 121). Indeed, Keynes is well aware that huge fluctuations in prices of commodity goods discourage their holding, with dramatic effects in terms of large-scale business fluctuations. On the one hand, low levels of commodity holdings on behalf of entrepreneurs entail shortages and thus 'semi-inflation' much more rapidly. This precipitates the downturn of the cycle because of the sudden collapse of inflationary expectations when it happens. On the other hand, low stocks of commodities retard the recovery because of the shortenings and bottlenecks they entail. Keynes considers buffer stock schemes as an efficient way to dampen the trade cycle, to vanquish "the fundamental malady of the trade cycle" (Keynes 1942, CW 27, p. 121) with the savings of financial means. Thanks to these buffer stock schemes, a short-term weapon against output and employment fluctuations is available, a weapon that is subordinate to the long-term fiscal policy. It should not be too difficult to get information on time on the amounts of commodity stocks stockpiled by private actors; information on price fluctuations is available without any delay. Accordingly, the trade cycle would be dampened through the fight against speculation on commodity markets.

The socialisation of investment

With regard to the fiscal policies undertaken after World War II, which were labelled Keynesian, it is worth emphasising the following points. First, during the Great Depression or after, Keynes' matter of concern was directed to controlling the flows of capital goods needed to ensure full employment. As shown in Chapter 2, Keynes was highly dubious about the efficiency of short-term devices that aim to raise consumption spending. On this issue, Keynes' stance is quite ironic. He answered for example to Meade:

> I should much deprecate trying to ... reduce taxation on drink and smoke with a view to making people drink and smoke more when they were tending to be out of work, or to dealing with income-tax, where there is a huge time lag and short-run changes [are] most inconvenient.
>
> (Keynes 1943, CW 27, p. 319)

Friedman would probably not argue otherwise while relying on his permanent income explanation of the consumption function.

Second, while Keynes' buffer stock scheme combines a short-run perspective – aiming to lower commodity price fluctuations – with a much longer one which consists in decreasing uncertainty on future commodity prices – the fact remains that Keynes' fiscal guidelines entail a long-run perspective hardly reconcilable with the fine-tuning of the economy advocated by Heller. In other words, fiscal policy according to Keynes does not aim at 'gap closing'. It does not aim to *counteract* output and employment actual deviations from some target path. Fiscal policy does not aim to smooth out the trade cycle; this is a task much more easily – and indirectly – performed through the control of commodity prices. Next, Keynes is highly dubious regarding 'automatic stabilisers' when he comes to comment on Meade's social security proposal for counter-cyclical variations of both employers' and employees' social security contributions. This rejection of Meade's proposal is to be explained by Keynes' strong reservations regarding devices aiming at consumption-boosting programmes and his strong concern for the control of investment. The only advantage in Meade's proposal noticed by Keynes is that fluctuations of contributions would contribute to balance the Social Security Budget. Indeed, Keynes strongly opposes what he calls "deficit budgeting" for being a "particular, rather desperate expedient" (Keynes 1943, CW 27, p. 354). For him, "the capital budgeting is a method of maintaining equilibrium; the deficit budgeting is a means of attempting to cure disequilibrium if and when it arises" (Keynes 1943, CW 27, pp. 352–3).

The third point to be emphasised applies to the modalities of State intervention regarding the ownership of the capital schemes developed. As noticed above, Keynes considers that about two-thirds or three-quarters of the total amount of national investment would be concerned with his 'socialisation of investment' plans, which seems to be at first sight a huge amount. Yet, one can find here a peculiar field of application of Keynes' conceptions regarding the 'State', that is consistent with his 'Middle Way doctrine' we investigated in Chapter 2. As Skidelsky (2011) notices, "by 'socialisation of investment' Keynes did not mean nationalisation" (Skidelsky 2011, p. 11). As a matter of principle, Keynes confidently relies on the ability of private bodies to cooperate with public authorities, especially regarding major infrastructures. His general policy advice for capital schemes development can be considered as pre-dating what we now call 'public-private partnerships': the ownerships of the means of production as well as the initiative might be kept private. Yet, in terms of State responsibilities towards the control over national investment, from the late 1920s to his last pleas, Keynes' policy advice moved from a 'semi-autonomous' body to organise the cooperation between private, semi-private and public initiatives towards a strictly public body under the responsibility of the State. This is unsurprising if one keeps in mind that the powers coming within the scope of this National Capital Budget became larger and larger as time elapsed.

Another characteristic of Keynes' fiscal guidelines rarely brought to light shows how large is the gap between his initial pleas and later 'Keynesian' advocacies to 'fine-tune' a market economy. By focusing on long-term capital schemes that are supposed to be profit-earning (even if indirect benefits must be taken into account to balance the Capital Budget), the schemes advocated by Keynes improve the competitiveness of the economy. That is, a capital-scheme programme would have an aggregate-demand effect when launched but it would later have also a feedback effect on the supply side of the economy. Arestis and Sawyer (2004) do not argue otherwise when they state:

> The supply-side equilibrium can itself be influenced by the path of aggregate demand. The size and distribution of the capital stock is a determinant of the productive capacity of the economy, and a larger capital stock is a determinant of the productive capacity of the economy, and a larger capital stock would be associated with the supply-side equilibrium involving a higher level of output and employment. The level of aggregate demand (including the change in economic activity and profitability) has an impact on investment expenditure, and thereby on the size of the capital stock.
>
> (Arestis and Sawyer 2004, p. 458)

Last, by distinguishing between the Ordinary Budget and the Capital Budget, and by calling for a balanced Ordinary Budget Keynes' fiscal policy budgetary secured ample room for manoeuvre when needed, what we now call 'fiscal space'.

All in all, Keynes' main concern with fiscal policy is to forestall the occurrence of slumps through the design and the implementation of long-term capital schemes that aim to stabilise the private sector's long-term real expectations around full employment. This implies an ever-growing role played by the State in the economy, at the demand side both of the market for newly produced capital goods and of the loan market. Fiscal policy is thus closely intertwined with monetary policy.

The 'socialisation of investment' means a large amount of public debt with major infrastructures projects, which are profit-earning and have a supply-side effect in the long run: this is definitely not to be confused with deficit in the Ordinary Budget. Even when the matter at hand is to escape a recession (as was the case in the early 1930s) Keynes would not rely on consumption devices. Obviously, the stimulus of the demand for non-durable goods is really unlikely to possess a strong and long-lasting effect on the long-term state of expectations.

Keeping in mind these main features of Keynes' plea for a long-term capital budgeting, which is Friedman's position vis-à-vis fiscal policy?

Friedman against fine-tuning and State invasiveness

As a matter of fact, Friedman had not always been the radical opponent to fiscal policy he became in the 1960s. As shown below, the early Friedman was quite wary of the tide for fine-tuning at stake in the post-World War II optimism but he was not distrustful of stabilisation fiscal devices. From the 1940s to the 1960s, Friedman moved from an opposition to fiscal discretionary policy towards a wholesale rejection of fiscal policy per se. In this sense, Friedman's opposition to Keynesian advocacies strengthened as the standard Keynesians departed from Keynes' original programme.

Let us start with the early Friedman. As we have seen in Chapter 2, Friedman reviewed and sharply criticised Lerner's (1944) *Economics of Control* in 1947. He offered his own alternative to Lerner's 'steering wheel' principles in 1948. At that time, he blamed the Keynesians for focusing on short-term considerations, leaving aside long-term concerns such as long-term efficiency and growth potential of the economy. Friedman took the completely opposite view and offered a long-term programme to stabilise the business cycle while avoiding discretionary manipulations on the part of government.

Friedman's long-term stabilising programme runs as follows. First, and consistently with his general concern for political freedom according to which State intervention should be value-free, government expenditures should be defined independently of the economic climate. From the start, this "policy of determining the volume of government expenditures ... entirely on the basis of the community's desire, need, and willingness to pay for public services" (Friedman [1948] 1953, p. 136) constitutes a diametrically opposed way of defining the extent of State intervention with regard to 'functional finance'.[31] The same would apply for the transfer programme and for the (progressive and mainly personal) tax system.

Second, the budget principle would rely on a hypothetical level of income, not necessarily confounded with the full-employment level of output:

> The budget principle might be either that the hypothetical yield should balance government expenditure, including transfer payments (at the same hypothetical level of income), or that it should lead to a deficit sufficient to provide some specified secular increase in the quantity of money.
>
> (Friedman [1948] 1953a, p. 137)

The scope of discretion would be limited to the definition of the targeted income level, on the basis of a time horizon of about five to ten years. Were this hypothetical income level targeted at a higher level than the full employment level, a secular inflationary bias would be entailed. Again, implicit in Friedman's plea there is the view that a small dose of inflation, so to say, would overcome the inefficiencies due to rigidities in both the price of goods and in the price of factors of production. According to this budget principle, State taxes and spendings would vary counter-cyclically and would automatically contribute to dampening the business cycle through the offsetting of aggregate demand fluctuations. Stabilisation would also rise from the monetisation of deficits and demonetisation of surpluses. A last critical point to emphasise is the indirect effect of such a scheme on private state of expectations in "stimulating a psychological climate favorable to stability" (Friedman 1948 [1953a], p. 148).

Friedman's early plea appears as an updating of sound finance principles: "the principle of balancing outlays and receipts at a hypothetical income level would be substituted for the principle of balancing actual outlays and receipts" (Friedman 1948 [1953a], p. 138). At that time, he did not claim for full employment and he considered that prices and wages flexibility was the right policy to ensure full employment. By the same token, Friedman did not claim that cyclical fluctuations would be fully eliminated by his long-term stabilising scheme. Instead, what he claimed was that his automatic adjustment plan would avoid most of the defects involved in the functional finance principles, especially delays: first delays between a fall in aggregate demand and its recognition; and second delays between the decision to counteract shifts in demand and its effect in terms of aggregate demand stabilisation programmes. Thus the early Friedman was at the same time worried about delays involved with discretion but highly concerned about stabilisation. While he opposed short-run devices in terms of the 'steering wheel' that would counteract aggregate demand fluctuations, Friedman's programme is quite similar to the 'automatic stabilisers' advocated by Meade: thanks to the programme he advocated, large wheel-running deviations would be automatically prevented.

In the 1960s, the Keynesians' stance about the welfare state was well established; discretionary fiscal policies were undertaken in most developed countries to smooth out the business cycle. At that time, Friedman's opposition to fiscal policy was much strengthened regarding his initial positions, despite his own claim to the contrary.[32] Far from sticking to his 1948 stabilising budget programme, he argued in his popular book *Capitalism and Freedom* (1962) that "unfortunately, the balance wheel is unbalanced" (Friedman 1962a, p. 76). Friedman again referred to lags in the implementation of fiscal policy to argue that fiscal schemes are very likely to be pro-cyclical; but the distinction he made previously between 'automatic stabilisers' (such as unemployment benefits) and variations in tax receipts simply disappeared.

Next, in opposition to his initial tolerance towards a slight dose of inflation displayed in his 1948 policy advice, the Friedman of the 1960s opposed fiscal stimulus because of the inflationary bias it introduces in government spendings. Indeed, a lesson to be learnt from the 'new public economics' is that fiscal stimulus is hardly reversed in periods of expansion. The difficulty of implementing government spending cuts during the boom clearly represents another weakness of fiscal policy with regard to monetary policy, which is definitively more easily reversed. Noticeably, this argument anticipates our modern relative preference for monetary policy to dampen the business cycle.

Third, it was only in 1962 that Friedman relied for the first time on what would become his famous model-uncertainty argument, which easily applies to both fiscal and monetary policies: "We simply do not know enough to be able to use deliberate changes in taxation or expenditures as a sensitive stabilizing mechanism. In the process of trying to do so, we almost surely make matters worse" (Friedman 1962a, p. 78).

Lastly, the definitive argument put forward by Friedman against fiscal policy is the 'crowding-out' effect due to the rise of government borrowing on the credit market. In order to isolate the dynamics entailed by fiscal measures as distinguished from variations in monetary aggregate (a distinction seldom made by the Keynesians in Friedman's eyes), Friedman considered a loan-expenditure programme, which would involve in the general case a rise in interest rates. As a matter of fact, in 1962 Friedman took pains to avoid the two extreme views: on the one hand, the extreme Keynesian case for a liquidity trap and/or for an interest-inelastic private investment is not very credible; on the other, he did not consider that a pure crowding-out effect would render fiscal policy entirely inoperative.

Seven years later, when he came to debate with Heller, who was famous for his advocacy for 'fine-tuning' in his *New Dimensions of Political Economy* (1967), Friedman's denial of fiscal policy became as sharp as ever. Because of its crowding-out effect "fiscal policy has, in [his] view, been oversold in a very different and more basic sense than monetary policy" (Friedman and Heller, 1969, p. 50). Indeed: "the state of the government budget determines what fraction of the nation's income is spent by individuals privately" (Friedman, in Friedman and Heller 1969, p. 50). Besides, it "has a considerable effect on interest rates" (Friedman, in Friedman and Heller 1969, p. 50). All in all, Friedman's definitive position turns out to deny any ability of fiscal policy to counteract deficiency in aggregate demand. Ultimately, fiscal policy is simply neutral, without any effect on real output or even inflation.

Let us briefly take stock of our results regarding Friedman. At the very beginning of his carrier, Friedman considered that government expenditures were able to stabilise aggregate demand. What he insisted on were delays and lack of information for fiscal stimulus to properly operate. After having considered a partial crowding-out effect on the credit market (through the rise in interest rates due to State borrowing), so that public expenditures are less efficient than thought by the Keynesians but still non-neutral, the crowding-out effect became a complete one, which operates only through the credit market. While monetary policy influences interest rates *and* prices, fiscal policy has a full influence only on the former and no effect at all on the latter. Friedman's initial concern for stability instead of year-to-year devices would have probably been shared by Keynes. In a sense, the same applies to Friedman's strong concern for the need to collect on time information about the economic climate. Remember that from the 1920s to his latest pleas, Keynes tirelessly called for the collection of information and statistics on the state of the economy. But between Keynes' overall fiscal guidelines and Friedman's late appraisal of fiscal policy the gap ultimately appears insuperable.

What ultimately comes out in Friedman's papers is the 'Treasury View' in its crudest form that Keynes faced in the 1930s.

4.5 Conclusion: Keynes' and Friedman's policy guidelines – convergences and divergences

Regarding the fundamental issue of whether we may need to stabilise a decentralised market economy, Lucas (2004) rightly points out that Keynes and Friedman share the "agreed-upon view" that: "We should stabilize spending flows, and the question is really one of the details about how best to do it. Friedman's approach involved slightly less government involvement than a Keynesian approach, but I say slightly" (Lucas 2004, p. 24).

It is true that Keynes' and Friedman's respective approaches to economic policy have several layers in common. First and foremost, the commonalities between them are easily brought to light when one acknowledges that both their policy advice aims at stabilising aggregate demand. In contrast to the contemporary analyses in terms of permanent market clearing offered by the proponents of the real business cycles such as Kydland and Prescott (1982) who follow the path initiated by the Austrians during the 1930s, neither obviously Keynes but also nor Friedman would consider that at the time of the Great Depression, with unemployment rates above 20 per cent, individuals were optimally reacting to technological shocks by lowering their labour supply so that equilibrium was at stake at both the aggregate and the individual levels. Second, Keynes and Friedman share the willingness to implement long-term policy guidelines. This is a particularly strong result regarding Keynes: as a matter of fact, Keynes is not concerned with fine-tuning as well as he does not call for *counter*-cyclical policy. In a way, Keynes and Friedman share a strong concern for *anti*-cyclical policy guidelines. And crucially, for both of them the impact of State intervention on private expectations is a crucial issue to be carefully addressed by policy-makers.

Yet, in many respects there are also critical points of divergence in their respective policy guidelines. Keynes' concern for the management of the long-term state of expectations, which directly ensues from his overall distrust towards the self-adjusting capacity of a decentralised market economy, would hardly cover Friedman's worry that State intervention might disrupt the self-correcting forces that spontaneously come from unfettered competition. To put it differently, the basic goal of Keynes' employment policy is the management of the long-term state of expectations with the view to sustain the demand for newly produced capital goods whereas Friedman worries about the fact that erratic policy would destabilise private expectations of future prices (and of course wages). That is, Keynes is concerned with long-term real expectations while Friedman is concerned with short-term nominal expectations. Another line of explanation of their respective standpoints refers to their own confidence in the ability of centralised authorities to behave efficiently. This reflects contrasted relationships towards conceptual issues such as the knowledge possessed by private actors about the future 'states of the world', and by the way their treatment of uncertainty. Last, there remains the issue of the way an expansionary policy alters output and prices in the short run as well as in the long run. This point refers to the issue of the dynamics between, on the one hand, the employment level and, on the other, price and wage levels.

What constitutes the 'monetary' character of the economy, the dynamics between employment and output as well as the treatment of uncertainty and the ensuing modelling of expectations will be the base material of the next chapter.

What can be learnt for today from Keynes' and Friedman's pleas? The very first lesson offered by both our authors is that stabilisation is really a serious issue for policy-makers in the decentralised market economies we really live in. Even a strong advocate of laissez-faire like Friedman would not let monetary affairs fall into private hands. A monetary economy does need policy guidelines to stabilise itself around full employment at stable prices.

Second, for both authors nominal rigidities are *not* at the heart of their pre-occupations, far from it. Neither of them considers nominal rigidities as the ulti-mate causes of departure from a position of equilibrium. For Keynes, in the absence of nominal rigidities the system would certainly endure much less stability so that they hopefully prevent too wide fluctuations. For Friedman, nominal rigidities are nothing but a "catch-all excuse for all failures to provide a satisfactory explanation of observed phenomena" (Friedman 1962b, p. 213).

Most critically, what is at the heart of their preoccupations for the stabilisa-tion of a monetary economy is for both of them the control of private agents' expectations. Depending on the way one formulates the issue of the guidance of these expectations, Keynes and Friedman offer us different avenues for reflec-tion. Keynes compels us to consider how long-term real expectations are formed in a world in which uncertainty prevails and how accordingly these expectations can be guided by the aim of public intervention. As for Friedman, he reminds us that private agents do not instantaneously adapt their inflationary expectations to a new policy regime and that the anchorage of short-run nominal expectations too should be an issue for policy-makers. Regarding the sudden twist in policy-makers' matters of concern in the last few years (from the fight against inflation-ary pressures in 2007 towards the current fears of deflationary spirals) that echoes Friedman's point, as well as the current difficulties for both private agents and governments to guess what the future *might* potentially bring forth in the coming years that echoes Keynes' case, it clearly appears that the preoccupa-tions developed by our two authors should be seriously taken into account today.

To conclude, those who claim to follow in the footsteps of the Friedmanian tradition when they call for 'strict' policy rules seem to have almost completely forgotten Friedman's distrust towards State authorities' ability to act wisely and timely and above all his model-uncertainty argument. As for those who claim to follow in the footsteps of Keynes' tradition, they may want to reconsider Keynes' strong concern for long-term issues (a slowly falling long-term interest rate and the necessity to control the demand price of long-lived capital schemes, to cite but a few examples) as well as his aversion to devices aiming at boosting consumption and deficit spending when they call for counter-cyclical policies.

5   The functioning of a monetary economy

5.1 Introduction

The previous chapter brought to light significant points of agreement between our two authors, especially regarding their common grasp of a decentralised market economy as a macroeconomic system, their shared concern towards long-term issues and their shared purpose for obtaining full employment together with price stability. Yet, this is not to deny the great divide that remains between some of their basic claims. Regarding their respective positions about the efficiency of fiscal policy, regarding also the way they conceive how monetary policy should be conducted and above all regarding their respective confidence in the ability of centralised authorities to impede market failures, the gap might appear insuperable. Hence, we come finally to the last step of our inquiry, which is that of the theoretical underpinnings of Keynes' and Friedman's pleas regarding economic policy.

As we will argue below, money as well as the 'monetary' character of a decentralised market economy, the treatment of uncertainty as well as the modelling of expectations and finally the dynamics underlying the interactions between the real and the monetary spheres of the economy are at the heart of the analytical problems to be considered here.

Strikingly, neither Keynes nor Friedman formulates the terms of the debate between their own positions and the ones of their opponents in terms of value judgements or moral principles. They develop the same attitude in that for both of them the issue to be settled is about *theory*. Keynes formulates very well the debate at stake in his 1934 paper entitled "Poverty in Plenty: Is the Economic System Self-Adjusting?" (CW 13, pp. 485–92). When he targets his opponents, Keynes claims:

> [They] do not, of course, believe that the system is automatically or immediately self-adjusting. But they do believe that it has an inherent tendency towards self-adjustment, if it is not interfered with and if the action of change and chance is not too rapid.
>
> (Keynes 1934, CW 13, p. 487)

In Keynes' views, the rationale behind this 'belief' is the classical theory of the interest rate, which considers the interest rate as the key variable able to freely adjust itself so as to bring the inter-temporal price system to its full employment level. As for Friedman, he takes the same step as Keynes in his introduction to *Dollars and Deficits* (1968c), which is entitled "Why Economists Disagree". Friedman would not deny that differences in value judgements might play a role, especially when for example the distribution of income arises in the debates. But as a matter of principle, "the major reasons for differences of opinion among economists … are not differences in values but differences in scientific judgements about both economic and non-economic effects" (Friedman 1968c, p. 10).

Following Keynes' and Friedman's own suggestions to focus on theory, in what follows we will analyse the similarities as well as the differences in the theoretical background underlying the economic guidelines respectively advocated by our two authors. Our idea is the following: if one attempts to provide a better understanding of Keynes' and Friedman's views on the self-adjusting capacity of the economic system, and by the way if one seeks to rationalise their 'policy philosophy', it is imperative to examine carefully the way they understand the *monetary* character of a decentralised market economy.

We will divide this issue into two parts. We will first analyse Keynes' and Friedman's positions regarding money and uncertainty through in particular their understanding of the demand function for money. In a second step, we will provide rationales, from both Keynes and Friedman, of the role the State is supposed to play in a monetary economy. Our results can be summed up as follows. The essential point that explains the great divide between Keynes' and Friedman's pleas to stabilise the economic system refers to their respective way of grasping the monetary character of the economy. For Keynes, the essential feature of a monetary economy is that private agents might want to stockpile liquid assets, that is assets the value of which is unlikely to be revised in case of a sudden revision (but yet not foreseeable from today's perspective) in our long-term state of expectations. For Friedman, there is no basic difference with a real economy in the sense that monetary assets are substitutes for a large spectrum of real assets; the demand for a "temporary abode of purchasing power" is highly stable and expectable, and does not fundamentally impede the functioning of the real side of the economy. This means a sharp contrast in their respective understanding of the type of uncertainty faced by private agents: Keynes relies on 'uncertainty' whereas Friedman deals only with 'risk'. In the final analysis, the treatment of this issue of uncertainty made by Keynes and Friedman determines their respective positions towards State duties in a monetary economy. In Keynes' eyes the State is precisely the very agent able to cope with our lack of knowledge about the future 'states of the world'. State authorities are supposed to convince private agents that the future is not so unknown, and that full employment is highly probable. By contrast, the ignorance about the true structure of the economic system faced by civil servants together with their inability to disentangle an initial external shock caused to the system from the necessarily convergent adjustment process implied by this shock (which will restore an equilibrium position along the long-term growth path but which is not necessarily monotonic), are both arguments that definitely disqualify

State authorities' temptation to enhance the stability of a decentralised market economy.

5.2 Keynes and Friedman on money and the interest rate

First of all, what are the key features of an economy that uses 'money' to facilitate exchanges? That is, what is money according to our two authors and why hold an asset that pays nothing? Second, can we safely rely on the classical theory of the interest rate to understand how a monetary economy achieves the inter-temporal coordination of savers' and investors' plans? This will provide us with the required material to analyse the issue of the 'transmission mechanism' of State impulse to both the monetary and the real sides of the economy, which is the main subject matter of the next section of this chapter.

Not surprisingly, contrasted theoretical underpinnings of demand for money despite *similar* functional expressions will provide a highly contrasted theory of the interest rate. Let us make that more precise – by the 'real' interest rate we simply mean the nominal rate charged on bonds minus a price deflator. As simple as this may seem, defining the 'real' interest rate this way raises from the outset a basic problem: which is the proper price deflator to be taken into account? Since Keynes distinguishes capital goods from consumption goods, the former being long-lived in comparison to the latter, the relevant rate is for him the long rate. And the relevant price deflator should be the price index of capital goods. In Friedman's case, there is no disentanglement between the two rates. Because he considers implicitly a single aggregated good, there is no basic reason to consider the long rate instead of the short one. And Friedman is easily allowed to use a 'price level index' deflator in his measurement of the 'real' interest rate – a radical simplification that, as the author of a whole chapter in the *General Theory* dedicated to the "Choice of Units" issue, Keynes would hardly take at face value. Beyond that technical issue, as we will see below it is the causality between the real and the monetary sphere that is at stake here.

Keynes' monetary theory of the 'real' interest rate

Keynes' overall policy guidelines rely on a theory of the interest rate that contrasts with the classical interest rate of course, but also with what is commonly considered today as a 'Keynesian' theory of the interest rate. The stance taken by Keynes for long-term programmes, his deep concern for the management of the long-term state of expectations and his insistence on the necessity to foster a climate of confidence cannot be understood but with regard to his understanding of the factors that determine the long-term interest rate.

To see this, we will proceed as follows. First, we will outline the main features of a monetary economy in Keynes' meaning of the word. Second, Keynes' peculiar concept of liquidity, which again stands in sharp contrast with its commonly accepted meaning, ensues from this. We will then provide an assessment of Keynes' theory of the interest rate as a monetary theory of the 'real' interest rate.

What is a monetary economy à la Keynes?

It has been rightly argued that Keynes is more interested in the elaboration of a *monetary economy* than in the elaboration of a theory of *money* as such (Dos Santos Ferreira 2000). Indeed, in the preparatory works to the *General Theory* Keynes distinguishes three types of economy: a *cooperative* or *real-wage* economy, a *neutral* economy and an *entrepreneur* or *money-wage* economy. In the first "the factors of production are rewarded by dividing up in agreed proportions the actual output of their cooperative efforts" (Keynes 1933, CW 29, p. 77). In a neutral economy factors of production are rewarded in money. However "there is a mechanism *of some kind* to ensure that the exchange value of the money incomes of the factors is always equal in the aggregate to the proportion of current output which would have been the factor's share in a co-operative economy" (Keynes 1933, CW 29, p. 78). Clearly, this mechanism 'of some kind' actually corresponds to the classical theory of the interest rate. According to the latter, there exists a unique interest rate determined by non-monetary factors such as productivity and thrift, to which the long-term money interest automatically adjusts. A neutral economy functions *as if* factors of production were remunerated in kind.

By opposition to a real economy or to a neutral economy, Keynes' definition of a monetary economy, also called a money-wage economy or an entrepreneur economy, runs as follows:

> Money is par excellence the means of remuneration in an entrepreneur economy which lends itself to fluctuations in effective demand. But if employers were to remunerate their workers in terms of plots of land or obsolete postage stamps, the same difficulties could arise. *Perhaps anything in terms of which the factors of production contract to be remunerated, which is not and cannot be a part of current output and is capable of being used otherwise than to purchase current output, is, in a sense, money.* If so, but not otherwise, the use of money is a necessary condition for fluctuations in effective demand.
>
> (Keynes 1933, CW 29, p. 86; emphasis added)

Hence, in a money-wage economy factors of production are rewarded in terms of money but the 'mechanism of some kind' ensuring that the actual product will in turn be bought is absent. It will be only by mere chance that effective demand will coincide with full employment. This means that the exchange value of the remuneration to factors of production is independent of the scale of aggregate output. In other words, factors of production are now capable of *hoarding* the asset in which they are paid.

As the quotation above shows, the same problem would arise if factors of production were paid in 'something else' than money. If they were to be paid with obsolete stamps, they would be able to stockpile and thus defer purchasing power for an indefinite time in terms of obsolete stamps. In such an economy obsolete stamps would be held as a reserve of wealth precisely because they are the means of exchange. Indeed, since contracts are formulated in terms of obsolete stamps individuals seek to defer purchasing power in the same standard. This statement will be made again in the *General Theory*: "so long as there exists any durable asset, it is capable of possessing monetary attributes and, therefore, of giving rise to the characteristic problems of a monetary economy" (Keynes 1936, CW 7, p. 294).

What are these monetary attributes? First, the monetary asset is supposed to have a zero elasticity of production, in the sense that no more labour would be employed if its demand-price rises. This is clearly the case for 'money' – its supply depending on the behaviour of the central bank – but also for plots of land or obsolete stamps. The stock of these monetary assets is thus given during the current period and their future supply is easily predictable. Second, the monetary asset is characterised by a zero elasticity of substitution. The monetary asset is demanded 'for itself' so that demand would not fall when its price rises. Why then would individuals prefer to keep purchasing power in terms of the monetary asset (which provides no yield) rather than to purchase consumption or capital goods? What is the price of this monetary asset and why does its demand price not necessarily decrease when the quantity supplied rises? Precisely because of its liquidity, which we discuss briefly below.

To properly understand Keynes' point about liquidity one must rely on his peculiar treatment of 'uncertainty' – as distinct from 'risk' to use modern terminology. When one does not fully know the entire set of the 'states of the world' and, worse, when one does not even know to which extent our knowledge is lacking, the problem that immediately arises is not only to make forecasts, but also to attribute weight, to be more or less confident, in these forecasts. Hence the "two-tier theory of belief" (Runde 1994, p. 133) held by Keynes.[1] The more complete the information becomes, the more relevant evidence we can acquire, the higher will be the weight of the argument under consideration.[2] Since the knowledge and evidence available to each of us is not the same, it should be noted that both the propositions examined and the degree of rational belief in them (namely its probability) will differ from person to person.

By no way does liquidity according to Keynes' meaning of the term correspond to what we consider today as 'marketability' or 'easy convertibility' in money.[3] That is, "an asset with low convertibility may have high liquidity, and *vice versa*, however counter-intuitive this may now seem" (Hayes 2012, p. 46). Keynes himself provides us with a hint for such a claim when he states: "it may be that in certain historic environments the possession of land has been characterised by a high liquidity premium in the minds of the owners of wealth" (Keynes 1936, CW 7, p. 241). As far as we see it, Hayes is right in arguing that:

> Keynes's implicit definition of liquidity is the degree to which the value of an asset, measured in any given standard, is independent of changes in the state of expectations. Liquidity risk is therefore the possible ... loss of value

as a result of a change in the state of expectation, which includes the state of confidence.

(Hayes 2012, p. 47)[4]

In addition, liquidity applies to all assets: "there is, clearly, no absolute standard of 'liquidity' but merely a scale of liquidity" (Keynes 1936, CW 7, p. 240). Strikingly, it cannot be excluded that "money itself loses rapidly the attribute of 'liquidity' if its future supply is expected to undergo sharp changes" (Keynes 1936, CW 7, p. 241).

Keynes' demand for money function

Let us draw the lessons of the analysis above for understanding Keynes' conception of the demand for money. Keynes' demand function for money as formulated in the *General Theory* is stated as follows:

$$M_1 + M_2 = L_1(Y) + L_2(r) \tag{1}$$

In its simplest form, the first component of this money-demand function M_1 is roughly assimilated to the quantitative theory of money in its Cambridge cash-balances version. In the rough interpretation presented in textbooks, the second component M_2 corresponds to the speculative demand for money understood as follows: the interest rate is the borrowing cost of a new investment project and wealth owners prefer to hold cash rather than bonds (i.e. they prefer to stay 'liquid') if they expect the interest rate to fall (they thus stand as 'bears' on the bond market). But things are more complicated in Keynes' original writings.

Two points are worth noticing to properly understand Keynes' conception of the demand for money: the first applies to the aggregation procedure chosen by Keynes; the second refers to the meaning he attributes to the liquidity-preference schedule.

The first critical point to be emphasised is that in a monetary economy à la Keynes wealth owners do not only arbitrate between the holding of money and the holding of bonds, but between the holding of 'money' (i.e. monetary assets that yield nothing) and the holding of non-monetary assets (including bonds but also equities and physical capital schemes) all of them being supposed to offer the same yield at the equilibrium. This reasoning requires a clear distinction between consumption and capital goods. Leijonhufvud (1968a) shows that, capital goods being by definition long-lived, they are much more sensitive to long-term rates than to short-term ones. For wealth owners newly produced capital goods are supposed to compete with the existing stock of capital goods, but also with other existing wealth assets such as equities, bonds, and so on. Aggregation over assets requires that they have the same prospective returns.[5] As for wealth owners, bond streams and equity streams are roughly perfect substitutes at equilibrium; capital goods and debts can be lumped together in the 'non-monetary asset' aggregate. This non-monetary asset can be viewed, in the simplest case, as a title which pays a stream of *a* dollar per year during T years. The price of this asset then depends on 1) the discounting rate of these streams (in short the interest rate) and 2) the prospective value of *a*. The current value of these prospective streams roughly corresponds to what Keynes calls the marginal efficiency of capital. Hence, Keynes' representative non-monetary asset should be considered as a long-lived one. In other words, capital goods are clearly imperfect substitutes for short-term financial assets.[6] With the marginal efficiency of capital being considered as given, the interest rate then plays the role of an (inverse) index of the non-monetary aggregate price. Capital schemes being long-lived, the relevant interest rate to be considered here is the long rate rather than the short one. By the way, the investment level is elastic to the interest rate. Indeed:

> In Keynes' language, 'a decline in the interest rate' *means* 'a rise in the market prices of capital goods, equities, and bonds'. Since the representative non-money asset is very long-lived, its interest-elasticity of present value is quite high. The price-elasticity of the output of augmentable income sources is very high.
>
> (Leijonhufvud 1968a, p. 42)

Keynes' analysis does not make room for a homogeneous output, the "shmoo" as Leijonhufvud (1968a, p. 132) calls it. So the aggregative structure to be found in the *General Theory* is quite different from the 'old' Keynesian one (say, IS-LM) but also from the one of the New Keynesian models.[7] Hence, in the equation of the demand function for money stated above, the interest rate must be seen as an (inverse) index of the non-monetary asset price. A too high interest rate means a too low valuation of the stock of non-monetary assets.

The second point worthwhile emphasising regarding Keynes' demand function for money refers to his original treatment of the liquidity-preference schedule. Too often the precautionary motive is conflated with 'risk' whereas the speculative motive is conflated with 'uncertainty'. What are actually at stake here are two complementary motives of the liquidity preference involved with 'uncertainty'. It is seldom noticed, as for example Runde (1994) does, that after the *General Theory* the speculative and the precautionary demand for money are lumped together as the demand for inactive balances. In Keynes' words:

> The demand for liquidity can be divided between what we may call the active demand which depends on the actual and planned scales of activity, and the inactive demand which depends on the state of confidence of the inactive holder of claims and assets.
>
> (Keynes 1937, CW14, p. 221)

This addendum should have proven crucial for later debates. Keynes' precautionary motive for liquidity preference means "to provide for contingencies requiring *sudden* expenditure and for *unforeseen* opportunities of advantageous purchases" (Keynes 1936, CW 7, p. 196; emphasis added); this actually depends on the existence of 'true uncertainty' as opposed to 'risk'. The point is to avoid capital loss because of a sudden revision of long-term expectations (that is, of our expectations of future non-monetary asset prices), the magnitude of this revision being yet unforeseen from today's perspective. A similar demonstration applies to the speculative motive for liquidity preference. In case of the existence of organised markets for non-monetary assets, such as the bond market, an individual wealth owner can be distrustful towards the long-term state of expectations as expressed by the market: he becomes a 'bear' when he considers a future rise of interest rates (i.e. future fall in prices of non-monetary assets, as Leijonhufvud (1968a) puts it) more probable than a future rise (i.e. a rise in prices of non-monetary assets); otherwise he becomes a 'bull'. In Keynes' words, this means "knowing better than the market what the future will bring forth" (Keynes 1936, CW 7, p. 170).[8] Here is to be found the explanation of Keynes' change of terminology when, after the *General Theory*, the precautionary and the speculative motive of demand for money were lumped together in the 'inactive' balances: if we are distrustful towards our own long-term expectations (which corresponds to the precautionary motive) or towards these expectations as expressed through the market price of non-monetary assets (which corresponds to the speculative motive), the result will be the same, that is, the holding of monetary assets.

Let us take stock. When he does attribute very low weight to his expectations of future value of assets or to the market valuation of these assets as provided by their market price, the wealth owner might decide to hold assets with shorter maturity, i.e. he might decide to stay 'short' rather than 'long': the longer the time to maturity, the most likely is a – *yet unexpected* – change in the long-term state of expectation to occur.[9] Second, this wealth owner might decide to hold bonds instead of equities or physical assets, since the former carries fixed income streams whereas the yields provided by the latter have to be expected. Hence the illusion of 'liquidity' that prevails on the organised market for debts, epitomised by the famous parable of the beauty contest. Hayes (2006) would ask the reader to notice the inverted commas, so as to distinguish the *illusion* of liquidity provided by marketability from *true* liquidity provided (as a matter of convention, however) by an asset the value of which *in any given standard* is unlikely to be subject to unforeseen re-evaluation. Last, this wealth owner might precisely decide to hold an asset that does not provide any yield by itself, but the value of which is weakly dependent on an unforeseen change in the long-term state of expectation; that is, he might decide to stay liquid in holding monetary assets.

Keynes' monetary conception of the 'real' interest rate

Let us conclude this appraisal of Keynes' monetary theory by making explicit his understanding of the determination of the interest rate. As rightly pointed out by Smithin, "Keynes's notion of liquidity preference … should properly be regarded precisely as an alternative theory rate determination, rather than simply as a theory of money demand, as in the textbooks" (Smithin 2003, p. 9).

Within an economy à la Keynes, wealth owners do not look for a particular amount of money – or even a particular amount of liquidity – to be held. That is, there is no specific amount of 'buffer stocks' that individuals seek to accumulate, any additional liquidity being henceforth used to demand financial or real physical assets, or even durable consumption goods. Rather, to retrace the line of reasoning taken by these wealth owners, it might be convenient to consider the composition of their balance sheets as passively reacting to their expectations of non-monetary asset prices. They are individuals who make the best forecasts they can in relation to the knowledge they possess about the future valuation of the assets they hold; as seen above they also have to place some confidence in their own forecasts. Accordingly, they will hold assets of a longer or shorter maturity, assets more or less easily convertible in money (physical or financial assets), assets that pay flexible or fixed income streams (equity or bond). Again, all these non-monetary assets must be considered as roughly perfect substitutes at equilibrium and can be lumped together in the 'non-monetary asset' aggregate. The equilibrium achieved at the market level is a stock equilibrium and not a flow equilibrium of newly issued assets. To say it differently, newly produced capital schemes have to compete with the existing stock. As shown by Leijonhufvud (1968a), once the prospective income streams of this composite aggregate are considered as given in the short run (let say a given marginal efficiency of capital, as supposed in all the first 18 chapters of the *General Theory* except precisely in Chapter 12) 'the' interest rate plays the role of an inverse index of the price of this non-monetary assets aggregate.

The wealth owners who populate an economy à la Keynes take time to revise their judgement about future prices of non-monetary assets. This echoes the general inclination of entrepreneurs and of investors to interpret the current economic climate as part of a general tendency. That is, individuals take time to get more reliable knowledge and to form accordingly firmer judgement. As a result, it can be considered that expectations tend to be extrapolative. As for wealth owners, the relative rigidity of their expectations regarding asset price levels leads them to take time to accept parting with liquidity, that is to accept to undergo capital losses that are unforeseen from today's perspective. More precisely, they need time to revise their judgement in favour of an upward movement of asset prices that could be more likely than the reverse. The downward rigidity of the interest rate follows from its conventional character: "*any* level of interest which is accepted with sufficient conviction as *likely* to be durable *will* be durable" (Keynes 1936, CW 7, p. 203). That is precisely the reason why the money interest rate (i.e. the rate charged on money loans) "rules the roost" (Keynes 1936, CW 7, p. 223) in a monetary economy. Other assets (and critically newly produced capital goods) have to compete with the return offered by money loans. That is precisely also the reason why "it is conceivable that there have been occasions in history in which the desire to hold land has played the same rôle in keeping up the rate of interest at too high a level which money has played in recent times" (Keynes 1936, CW 7, p. 241). A very low elasticity of substitution and a quite nil elasticity of production, here are to be found the two critical characteristics of a monetary asset.

All in all, the interest rate is not determined by a confrontation between the true motives of lenders and borrowers on a supposed 'real' credit market. The whole structure of interest rates is the result of the financial markets functioning together with the provisioning of liquidity by the central bank, the "green cheese factory" (Keynes 1936, CW 7, p. 235) of the *General Theory*. As put by Smithin:

> In that case, the implied argument is that rate of interest is first determined in the financial system (hence a monetary theory of interest) and that both the marginal physical product of capital and the rate of time preference must adjust to the money rate of interest, rather than the other way around.
>
> (Smithin 2003, p. 118)

That is the reason why regarding Keynes one can rightly speak of "a monetary theory of the *real* rate of interest" (Burstein 1995; emphasis added). The consequence of this monetary determination of the interest rate is the complete reversal of causality between the monetary and the real sphere of the economy: "the real economy must adjust to interest rates rather than vice versa" (Smithin 2003, p. 119).

Friedman's 'neutral' monetary economy

At first sight, the theory of money demand held by Friedman appears as more 'complete', or more sophisticated with regard to the simplest one held by Keynes, especially if one considers that it is too often believed that for Keynes the demand for money would 'only' depend on two variables, that is money income and the 'interest rate'. That is, as he himself claims Friedman would have 'generalised' Keynes' initial theory of money demand by incorporating more arguments in the M_2 component, i.e. more substitutes to money, so that the demand for money would be rendered elastic to the interest rate. Actually, we have seen above that Keynes' theory of the demand for money function is more sophisticated than it appears at first glance. And what Friedman actually does is much more subtle. At the same time that he considers many more substitutes for money than only bonds, he makes significant modifications to the analytical framework in which he comes to study the motives for money demand. As we will see below, "Friedman treated money ... 'as if' it was a service-yielding consumer durable to which the permanent income hypothesis of consumption could be applied" (Laidler 1982, p. 6).

Friedman's demand for money function

While defending the thesis that "the function of money [is] a temporary abode of purchasing power" (Friedman and Schwartz 1982, p. 25), Friedman himself claims to have extended Keynes' theory of liquidity preference to a larger set of assets than only the bonds taken into account by the 'Keynesians'. Along the lines of the Quantity Theory of Money, a Friedmanian demand function for money for an individual wealth owner, which can be found in Friedman and Schwartz (1982, p. 39) but also in Friedman (1970c, p. 13), is written as follows:

$$\frac{M}{P} f(y, w, R_m^*, R_B^*, R_E, g_p^*; u) ,$$ (2)

where M is the stock of money, P an index of price level as commonly used to estimate current income, y the income level of the individual, w his wealth, R_m^* the expected return on money (probably zero), R_B^* the "expected nominal rate of return on fixed value securities, including expected change in their prices" (i.e. bonds), R_E^* the "expected nominal rate of return on equities, including expected change in their prices" (Friedman and Schwartz 1982, p. 39) and g_p^* the expected rate of inflation. Strikingly, the last term u refers to a "portmanteau symbol standing for whatever variables other than income may affect the utility attached to the services of money" (Friedman and Schwartz 1982, pp. 39–40). Neglecting in particular distribution effects, this demand function for money is easily aggregated for the economy as a whole.

According to this Friedmanian version of the Quantity Theory of Money in its cash-balances version, why does one want to hold money? From the outset, the point to be emphasised is that the demand for money is measured in 'real' terms through the use of a price index deflator. As is well known, holding a certain proportion of our income in the form of money helps us to encompass the problem of the double coincidence in exchange. On the one hand, dedicating resources to the holding money instead of 'real' assets lowers collective welfare (hence the plea for a slowly decreasing supply of money that we have seen in the previous chapter). But on the other hand, it can be easily argued that an economy that allows for monetary exchanges is more efficient than a barter-based system, so that the argument for considering a monetary economy as less efficient than a real one turns to be strongly qualified. As the second argument (the non-human wealth w) makes clear, a demand function that depends on the total wealth and not only on current income is much more stable than a 'Keynesian' one. Regarding the expected rate of return on the various assets taken into account, money is considered by Friedman as a substitute to a wider spectrum of assets than merely bonds. This is precisely the way Friedman claims to have enlarged the analysis carried out by the Keynesians (a claim that is not relevant regarding Keynes, as we have seen above). But Friedman himself is well aware that these rates of return are not independent, that is, that they should be equal at both the individual and the market equilibria.

As a matter of comparison with our analysis of Keynes' appraisal of money carried out above, the crucial parameter to be discussed is the last one, the portmanteau variable u. By the latter, Friedman claims to take account of the "other variables determining the utility attached to the services rendered by money relative to those rendered by other assets – in Keynesian terminology, determining the value attached to liquidity proper" (Friedman and Schwartz 1982, p. 38). Included in these variables is "the degree of economic stability expected to prevail in the future" (Friedman and Schwartz 1982, p. 38). Both the expected returns on various assets and the *u* 'portmanteau' parameter provide the second basic reason to hold money, i.e. the fact that money is "a reserve for future emergencies" (Friedman 1969a, p. 3). But Friedman hastens to add: "In the actual world, money is but one of many assets that can serve this function … This reason corresponds to the 'asset' motive stressed in the literature" (Friedman 1969a, p. 3).

Friedman on uncertainty

At this stage, it could be easily considered that Friedman's demand function for money is a generalised version of the liquidity-preference function of the 'Keynesians' – but yet not so dissimilar to the 'original' one framed by Keynes – with two main exceptions regarding Keynes: first, the demand for money is expressed in real terms; second, wealth is an explicit argument of the demand function. Yet, by making reference to some of Friedman's other writings one can show how dissimilar the theoretical underpinnings of Friedman's account of liquidity actually are regarding Keynes'. To make this point, let us refer to Friedman's essay "The Optimum Quantity of Money" (1969a). The fifth characteristic of Friedman's "hypothetical simple society" (Friedman 1969a, p. 2) runs as follows: "The society, though stationary, is not static. Aggregates are constant but individuals are subjects to uncertainty and change. Even the aggregates may change in a stochastic way, provided the mean values do not" (Friedman 1969a, p. 2).

This is precisely what Friedman calls "individual uncertainty" (Friedman 1969a, p. 3), and which corresponds to 'risk' in Knight's (1921) terminology. A similar hint can be found in his "Theoretical Framework for Monetary Analysis" (1970c). Dealing with the 'adjustment process' (to which we will return later), Friedman states that "at a long run equilibrium position, all anticipations are realized, so that actual and anticipated, or measured and permanent magnitudes, are equal" (Friedman 1970c, p. 48; Friedman and Schwartz 1982, pp. 59–60). Again, it is 'risk' that is actually at stake here.

In our view, this second basic reason to hold money, i.e. the fact that money is "a reserve for future emergencies" (Friedman 1969a, p. 3) corresponds neither to the precautionary motive nor to the speculative motive for liquidity preference according to Keynes' meaning of the term. In Keynes' theoretical framework, 'liquidity risk' is the "possible … loss of value as a result of a change in the state of expectations, which includes the state of confidence" (Hayes 2006, p. 21). In contrast, 'actuarial risk' corresponds to variance, which requires that the entire set of the 'states of the world' are fully known. While at first sight Friedman's *u* portmanteau variable seems to take account of uncertainty in Keynes' meaning of the term, this claim does not withstand scrutiny and close examination. That is, Friedman's 'uncertainty' is nothing but 'actuarial risk'. As Davidson (1972) notices in his appraisal of Friedman's "Theoretical Framework for Monetary Analysis" (1970c), "the essence of uncertainty" is clearly one of Keynes' basic factors omitted by Friedman. By ignoring the true signification of 'liquidity risk' as opposed to 'actuarial risk' and by the way the true motive of liquidity preference, Friedman passes over the specificity of Keynes' theory of demand function for money.

Friedman's 'real' determination of the interest rate

In sharp contrast to Keynes' conception, Friedman undoubtedly considers the interest rate as determined on the real side of the economy. For him monetary policy "cannot peg interest rates for more than very limited periods" (Friedman [1968a] 1969a, p. 99). Friedman sticks to a Wicksellian distinction between the 'natural' and the 'market' interest rates when he states that "the monetary authority can make the market rate less than the natural rate only by inflation" (Friedman [1968a] 1969a, p. 101). The natural rate as defined by Wicksell (1998) corresponds to the 'real' return of new capital, the rate that we would obtain in a barter economy without any banking system. As it is analysed by Friedman, the real interest rate corresponds to a modified version of Robertson's loanable funds principle.

As elaborated by Friedman in his *Price Theory* (1962b), the 'real' interest rate is determined through the confrontation between a demand for funds emanating from firms and a supply of funds emanating from owners of resources in a barter economy. As for firms, their demand for funds is written as: $r = f(W, I)$ as a downward-sloping curve in the W-r axes, where r stands for the interest rate, W for total wealth and I for investment. As for wealth owners, the supply of funds is written as: $r = g(W, S)$, where S stands for saving. The account of wealth in the demand for and the supply of funds is set to escape the stock-flow flaws of the initial 'loanable funds' principle. But, as seen below (Figure 5.1), the curves are drawn for $S = 0$ and $I = 0$ so that, at the long-run stationary equilibrium, the basic problem of capital accumulation has been evacuated. Besides, in a monetary economy, we simply have an S' curve, where any gap between S and S' corresponds to the demand for money.

In a real exchange economy, wealth owners might want to accumulate a certain amount of real assets as a buffer stock against life's little surprises even in the case of a negative return on their loans. Hence, a negative real interest rate is possible to ensure full employment (the case represented above where S and I intersect for a negative real interest rate). But in a monetary economy, the same would not apply: the minimum feasible rate of return on money is zero, which may set a floor to the equilibrating market mechanisms. Yet, as the Pigou effect shows, there always exists a price level such that the stock of wealth desired by wealth owners in real terms can be attained, however high this amount might be. So the existence of monetary arrangements and financial intermediation does not modify in substance the argument set in real terms: in the long run there exists a real interest rate that ensures full employment through the inter-temporal

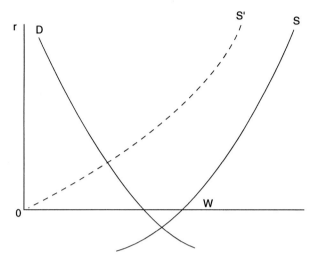

Figure 5.1 Friedman on the determination of the interest rate in a monetary economy (source: Friedman [1962b] 2007).

coordination of savers' and investors' plans and the corresponding market monetary rate is necessarily a positive one. In his "Theoretical Framework for Monetary Analysis" (1970c) as well as in his *Monetary Trends* (1982) written with Schwartz, Friedman roughly considers a constant long-term real rate assimilated to the marginal productivity of capital, which implies that there is no fixed factor of production (Smithin 2003, p. 115).

As a result, in Friedman's theoretical framework there cannot be any basic flaw in the inter-temporal price system: whatever the paucity of investment opportunities in a monetary economy subject to 'individual uncertainty', expectations are always fulfilled in the long run. As a consequence, there is always a real interest rate able to match thrift with productivity, i.e. to coordinate the 'true' motive of lenders and borrowers. There is also no reason to hoard buffer stocks of money beyond a certain amount, which is both and at the same time easily predictable in terms of few variables and highly stable in the long run (i.e. a stable demand function for money) since "at a long run equilibrium position, all anticipations are realized, so that actual and anticipated, or measured and permanent magnitudes, are equal" (Friedman 1970c, p. 48; Friedman and Schwartz 1982, pp. 59–60). That is the reason why money is nothing but a *temporary* abode of purchasing power. Friedman applies the standard principle of the decreasing marginal utility attributed to consumer goods. Contrary to Keynes' point that money is demanded 'for itself', so that its demand price does not fall with the stock of money in circulation, Friedman considers that the amount of cash balances private agents wish to hold is necessarily finite. Crucially, this also explains why "the price of money ... is the inverse of the price-level – not the interest rate. The interest rate is the price of credit" (Friedman, in Friedman and Heller 1969, p. 75). Ultimately, we are back to the loanable funds principle: although he does not explicitly accept the terminology, there is no doubt that for Friedman the interest rate equilibrates the demand for funds to finance newly produced capital schemes with the supply of funds. In short, there is from the outset no room for coordination failures in a decentralised market economy, despite its monetary character.

What about the interactions between the real and the monetary sides of the economy? In sharp contrast with Keynes' theoretical construct, the causality goes for Friedman from the real sphere to the monetary side of the economy: the whole structure of interest rates adapts to the time preference as displayed by lenders and productivity as estimated by borrowers. In his theoretical essays (Friedman 1970c, Friedman and Schwartz 1982), Friedman considers a *fixed* real interest rate, roughly identified with a *constant* marginal productivity of capital.[10] This idea of a constant real of interest determined by a constant marginal productivity of capital is "based on the 'Chicago modification' of traditional neoclassical capital theory, which eschews the usual diminishing marginal productivity arguments to generate an effectively constant marginal product of capital" (Smithin 2003, p. 115). From Keynes' perspective, such a simplification is nothing but a *petition principii* that evades the issue: for Keynes there is no such thing in a monetary economy as a *unique* real interest rate, let alone a interest rate determined by external factors.

Noticeably, from an Austrian perspective too such a shortcut evacuates the critical issue of the inter-temporal preferences of households as well as the inter-temporal character of the structure of production, which both might change over time and thus require adjustment in the monetary sphere of the economy. As stated by Garrison:

> The monetarist counterrevolution strongly downplayed the psychological factors that might color investment decisions and, in effect, turned a blind eye to the consumption-investment itself. These two magnitudes were combined into an all-inclusive magnitude summarily called output and symbolized by Q in the equation of exchange. ...
>
> The focus on real output puts into eclipse the division of that output between consumption goods and investment goods. Even more deeply into eclipse is the Austrian construction of a temporally defined structure of production. The very basis on which the natural rate is conceived is simply absent in modern, highly aggregated macroeconomic theorizing.
>
> (Garrison 2006, pp. 62–3)

What comes out of our analysis of Keynes' and Friedman's respective understanding of the interest rate determination? On the one hand, Keynes holds a monetary theory of the 'real' interest rate that relies on his conception of uncertainty and on the corollary concept of liquidity. What Keynes aims to construct is a theory of the functioning of an *entrepreneur* (also called a *money-wage*) *economy* that makes room for coordination failures between the inter-temporal plans of savers and investors. In a monetary economy left to its own functioning, the real side of the economy (and crucially the employment level) will have to adapt to its monetary side. On the other hand, Friedman holds a real theory of the interest rate that is based on the premise that the economic system stabilises by itself around a full employment equilibrium, at least if a long-term perspective that allows for all the necessary adjustments is adopted. What Friedman actually constructs is a theory of the functioning of a *neutral economy* according to Keynes' meaning of the word that evades from the outset coordination failures. In the long run, the classical dichotomy holds well for Friedman.

5.3 Coordination and stabilisation: the role of the State in a monetary economy

We are now in possession of almost all the elements needed to provide the requested rationales to the economic guidelines Keynes and Friedman advocate respectively. With no surprise, the way one regards the monetary character of the economy, the nature of the knowledge one considers that private actors possess regarding the structure of the economy, its 'states of the world', all these lines of comparison prove critical to identifying true points of agreements, outward similarities and irreconcilable positions in the policy pleas of our two authors. Indeed, what renders a public works programme or monetary loosening able to have a long-lasting effect on unemployment or on the contrary only a short-lived one, if not their effects on the expectations held by private actors?

For the last part of our inquiry, we will proceed as follows. In the first step, we will briefly outline Keynes' and Friedman's respective understanding of the dynamics at work in a monetary economy, with the view to better grasp the precise mechanisms through which State intervention is supposed to operate. We will see that they hold highly different views on the dynamics between prices and quantities, that is highly different explanations of the upward slope of the aggregate supply curve. We will then frame the rationales behind their advocacies regarding economic policy: on the one hand, Keynes' plea for a long-term stabilisation programme is to be explained by his strong concern towards inter-temporal coordination failures; on the other, Friedman's plea for the stabilisation of short-run nominal expectations by aim of a monetary rule fixed once-for-all is to be explained by his unconcern towards inter-temporal coordination that leads him to postulate the stability of the system. Finally, we will close this chapter by applying these results to Keynes' and Friedman's understanding of the financial markets functioning: what turns out to be a crucial cause for concern for Keynes is simply set aside in Friedman's case.

Dynamics and stability: first elements towards an understanding of State impulse in a monetary economy

We have seen that Keynes' and Friedman's respective thought about economic policy takes place in varying theoretical frameworks, especially regarding their understanding of the monetary character of a decentralised economy as well as the type of uncertainty faced by private agents. In our view, it should be possible to go even beyond these features that characterise the theoretical models built by our two authors. Our hypothesis is that behind an economic policy, there is an analysis of the dynamics at work in a market economy.

Take for example, the Great Depression. For Friedman, 'abnormal unemployment' at that time came from the fall in money supply that cuts the general level of prices and thus aggregate demand; private actors confused a general price level fall with a modification in relative prices and reduced their offer of goods and labour. The growth rate of money supply does not affect the real side of the economy but variations in the rate of growth of money supply greatly matter for the stability of the system: money is neutral but not 'super neutral'. By contrast, for Keynes monetary disorders were not at the core of the trouble, although bank failures and freezing of money markets undermined business confidence and thus sharply raised the liquidity-preference schedule of both banks and private actors. In Keynes' eyes the seeds of the recession lay in the dramatic fall in the financial assets price, which represented a large real shock on the long-term state of expectations. In other words, monetary disorders had a real effect through the collapse in the relative price level of capital goods measured in terms of money wages.

In order to facilitate understanding and interpretation of our findings below regarding economic policy, let us briefly outline Keynes' and Friedman's views on the aggregate supply curve. This should help us to grasp the interactions between employment and prices, and thus the ultimate rationales behind their policy guidelines.

In Keynes' theoretical framework, the aggregate supply curve is non-vertical, but neither non-horizontal. That is, there is no room for an inverse L-shaped aggregate supply curve. Besides, in the original case made in the *General Theory*, the upward slope of the supply function is not explained by price sluggishness, rigid wages, and so on.[11] Here, there is a departure from perfect competition in the sense that it is not supposed that at the current level of prices the individual firm would sell whatever quantity it wants to. Instead, it faces a downward-sloping demand curve. Imperfect competition and constrained demand means that firms are making expectations regarding the goods they will be able to sell. Depending on these sales expectations, the question they face is to decide their supply price. This is a well-known argument for a Marshallian scholar. For our purpose here, three points are worth noticing.

First, Keynes distinguishes the short-term from the long-term expectations: while he assumes perfect foresight for the short-run expectations (i.e. expected sales equal to actual sales), the long-term state of expectations about future levels of effective demand (let us say the marginal efficiency of capital) is made exogenous – which means a highly different thing than given.

Second, the equality between the real wage and the marginal productivity of labour is supposed to be interpreted as a 'wage curve', which should not be interpreted as a demand curve for labour but which is valid only at the market equilibrium. That is, the employment level is not *predetermined* by the labour market functioning.

Third and consequently, fluctuations in the price level should be viewed as an aside of fluctuations in real magnitudes. To put it quite plainly, it does not make sense in Keynes' perspective to try to raise output (and thus employment) by aim of a rise in prices, what is called an inflationary policy.

So the dynamics at work between prices and real magnitudes in a monetary economy à la Keynes is at variance with the one we are accustomed to, especially in contemporary New Keynesian models. Undoubtedly, this will entail varying policy guidelines.[12]

What about Friedman? His aggregate supply curve actually corresponds to the equilibrium version of the old expectations-augmented Phillips curve, which can be written as follows:

$$\pi_t = E_{t-1}\pi_t + \alpha(y_t - y^*) \tag{3}$$

where π_t is the inflation rate, $E_{t-1}\pi_t$ stands for the expected current inflation rate, y_t the actual level and output and y^* the target level of output – let say the natural level of output. In the case of adaptive expectations in its simplest form, $E_{t-1}\pi_t = \pi_{t-1}$.

Along Friedman's line of analysis, equation (3) is an aggregate supply function. There is perfect competition but imperfect information about the true relative prices. There are thus lags in the adjustment process that allow the output level to deviate *temporarily* from its natural level. If relative price movements were disentangled from variations in the general price level (i.e. in the case of scalar effects), the Phillips curve would be vertical in the short run. So there might a short-run trade-off but it disappears as soon as expectations adapt to the new monetary regime. It is precisely this type of rationale in terms of *equilibrium* within imperfect information that lies behind Friedman's 1977a paper. In our view, Laidler (1982) is right in arguing that:

> To say that the Phillips curve is an aggregate supply curve is to say that fluctuations in output and unemployment represent the voluntary choices of individuals operating in markets which are continually clearing but in which agents make expectional errors about prices.
>
> (Laidler 1982, p. 16)

Because deviations from the natural rate of unemployment are costly in terms of collective welfare the plea that naturally ensues from such an interpretation of the 'old' Phillips curve is, to put it in a nutshell: keep the price-level rise under control to anchor the private actors' inflationary expectations. So Friedman's plea goes further than the one behind the neo-classical expectations-augmented Phillips curve, which relies on forward-looking expectations: it requires not only to avoid 'policy surprises' as Lucas (1972) calls them (by carefully announcing credible changes in monetary regimes, changes which might be large-scaled) but also and most importantly to keep the inflation level under control through pro-gressive and gradual changes in this monetary regime – insofar as such changes came to be needed. A Friedmanite plea regarding economic policy necessarily incorporates from the outset gradualism as a general principle of intervention.

What appears from our discussion carried out above? According to Keynes' Marshallian dynamics, a non-vertical supply curve falls within a *disequilibrium* framework. At the market level, prices variations are the result of quantity dise-quilibria. And firms react to quantity signals by adjusting their price supply. By contrast, Friedman's dynamics looks highly Walrasian: firms react to price signals by adjusting their quantity supply. Friedman's non-vertical supply curve falls within an *equilibrium* framework that incorporates at the same time slow adjust-ments in inflationary expectations, i.e. imperfect information on relative prices.

Let us now bring together all the threads of analysis we have got so far to ultimately provide the rationales behind Keynes' and Friedman's policy guide-lines. As we will see below, coordination failures are the very rationales behind Keynes' overall advocacies whereas Friedman's economic guidelines are better understood with regard to his analysis of the 'adjustment process', which leads to a cyclical but yet converging pattern.

Coordination failures as the rationale behind Keynes' economic guidelines

Keynes' policy guidelines are better rationalised if one keeps in mind the strong concern he has towards long-term expectations and the stress he leads on the issue of investment expenditure and capital accumulation. Keynes' *General Theory* offers two parables to highlight the coordination failures problem that comes up in a monetary economy: the first one is concerned with the marginal efficiency of capital while the second applies to the liquidity preference. First, the parable of the deferred diner to be found in Chapter 16 runs as follows:

> An act of individual saving means – so to speak – a decision not to have dinner to-day. But it does *not* necessitate a decision to have dinner or to buy a pair of boots a week hence or a year hence or to consume any specified thing at any specified date. Thus it depresses the business of preparing to-day's dinner without stimulating the business of making ready for some future act of consumption. It is not a substitution of future consumption-demand for present consumption-demand, – it is a net diminution of such demand.
>
> (Keynes 1936, CW 7, p. 210)

This parable of the deferred diner illustrates well the market incompleteness for commodities (i.e. the absence of forward markets for a wide range of goods), hence the coordination failures between long-term production and consumption plans. That is, an act of saving does not automatically create the corresponding investment. Roughly stated, entrepreneurs have to expect the state of effective demand in the long run, i.e. the marginal efficiency of capital. Worse, an increase in the propensity to save is likely to induce a fall in the marginal efficiency of capital since one is very likely to extrapolate the current tendency due to the inertia in expectations. As Leijonhufvud (1968a) or Dos Santos Ferreira (2000) show, the market system is not able to reconcile the inter-temporal choices on the respective part of savers and investors: "the actual information mechanism composed of existing markets lacks certain 'circuits' (Leijonhufvud 1968a, p. 280). Thus, marginal efficiency of capital might be too low regarding the current propensity to save.

Second, as the parable of the beauty contest illustrates, financial markets as they really function do not provide the proper interest rate able to coordinate saving and investment. Let us remind ourselves of this famous parable to be found in Chapter 12 of the *General Theory*:

> ... professional investment may be likened to those newspaper competitions in which the competitors have to pick out the six prettiest faces from a hundred photographs, the prize being awarded to the competitor whose choice most nearly corresponds to the average preferences of the competitors as a whole; so that each competitor has to pick, not those faces which he himself finds prettiest, but those which he thinks likeliest to catch the fancy of the other competitors, all of whom are looking at the problem from the same point of view. It is not a case of choosing those which, to the best of one's judgement, are really the prettiest, nor even those which average opinion expects genuinely thinks the prettiest. We have reached the third degree where we devote our intelligences to anticipating what average opinion expects the average opinion to be. And there are some, I believe, who practice the fourth, fifth and higher degrees.
>
> (Keynes 1936, CW 7, p. 156)

As this metaphor shows, the second information problem that might arise in a monetary economy is whether "the existing 'circuits' will in any case transmit information that will induce producers to undertake the appropriate volume of investment" (Leijonhufvud 1968a, p. 280). That is, the interest rate is not able to coordinate the inter-temporal plans of savers and investors. In other words, when the marginal efficiency falls, the interest rate does not necessarily fall as well to restore the inter-temporal price system corresponding to full employment.

What do these two parables teach us regarding the rationales behind Keynes' policy guidelines? In Keynes' political view, both fiscal and monetary policies are supposed to deal with long-term expectations. They must be seen as highly complementary. For example, monetary loosening would hardly succeed in case of a restrictive fiscal programme. By the same token, a large capital-schemes package is very likely to be thwarted by an erratic monetary policy. This being said, fiscal policy can be considered as meeting primarily the first information problem (i.e. the heading of the marginal efficiency of capital) that gives rise to coordination failures whereas monetary policy meets more easily the second information problem (i.e. the heading of the liquidity preference). When the States launches an investment programme, it increases directly the demand price for newly produced capital goods, and through this way encourages private actors to revise their long-term state of expectations, i.e. to raise the marginal efficiency of capital. As for monetary policy, the provision of monetary assets through an open-market programme is directed towards convincing private investors to revise their judgements on the future interest rates (i.e. to revise their judgements on the future price level of non-monetary assets once the marginal efficiency of capital is considered as given) and, by the way, convincing them to part with liquidity at lower rates, that is to ask for a lower liquidity premium.

The rationale behind Keynes' fiscal policy

Let us first focus on fiscal policy. The stress Keynes puts on investment projects and the strong doubts he expresses about the relevance of consumption-boosting devices have to be explained by the distinction he makes between consumption goods and capital goods: the former are short-lived and their demand price is thus less sensible to the long-term state of expectations. That is, State impulse aiming to raise consumption would not have in Keynes' eyes the same lasting effect on aggregate demand as investment stimulus. At the core of this analysis one finds the autonomous demand for long-lived real assets in a monetary economy. It is not because the long-term state of expectation is considered as given as a short-run simplification that it cannot be endogenously influenced by State intervention. The point at stake is to increase the demand price of newly produced capital schemes by seeking to increase the schedule of the marginal efficiency of capital – increased consumption will follow suit. More precisely, this means raising the market valuation of the marginal efficiency of capital. The State therefore plays a central role in encouraging the market, i.e. entrepreneurs and investors, to re-evaluate the prospective streams of long-term capital assets. The fact that the key issue is for Keynes to reverse pessimistic expectations clearly appears in the following quotation:

> Unfortunately the more pessimistic the Chancellor's policy, the more likely it is that pessimistic anticipations will be realised and *vice versa*. Whatever the Chancellor dreams, will come true! We must begin by resuscitating the national income and the national output.
> (Keynes 1933, CW 21, p. 184)

Thanks to public works, long-term expectations are revised, effective demand rises and via this way the employment as well as the price level does so. Remember that 'uncertainty' here means that private actors do not know the entire set of the 'states of the world', that they do not have perfect knowledge of the structure of the economy. Thus, the very purpose of public works is to encourage private actors to modify their long-term expectations. To put it the other way round, in an economy à la Keynes the effect of a public works scheme on aggregate demand is weaker when it is less anticipated and less advertised. The least impact is to be expected in case private actors are taken by surprise (which is simply the opposite of the case made by the proponents of the rational expectations approach like Lucas).

What about the 'crowding-out' effect, the fact that government spending would squeeze aggregate demand on the part of private actors? The way public spending might crowd private spendings out operates through the rise of interest rate on credit market. As Dimand (1988) shows, the answer to the 'Treasury View' is one of the crucial clues that pave the way from the *Treatise on Money* to the *General Theory*. As stated above, the answer consists in the finding of an alternative to the loanable funds theory of the interest rate. Once savings depends on income and aggregate income becomes the equilibrating variable between savings and investment, fiscal policy is able to provide the purchasing power needed to finance the investment projects. Besides, monetary policy can now become 'accommodating' by providing to private actors the surplus of liquidities needed by this increase in the income level: the size of the crowding-out effect also depends on the monetary authorities' behaviour.

The rationale behind Keynes' monetary policy

Let us now turn to the precise issue of monetary policy. Regarding Keynes' economic system, the point is that:

> The most basic conclusion ... would be that in the credit economy there is no natural rate of interest. Interest rates are determined in the financial sector proximately by the decision of the ultimate provider of credit, in other words the central bank.
>
> (Smithin 2003, p. 126)

The restatement of the meaning of liquidity we suggested above entails far-reaching implications for our restatement of the rationales behind monetary policy. With a long-term interest rate determined on the monetary side of the economy through the confrontation of the liquidity-preference scheme on the part of private actors (both private individuals and banks) with the provision of liquidity on the part of the central bank, there is no *unique* real interest rate towards which the economy would converge in the long run. When he retrospectively looks at his *Treatise in Money* in which he accepted the existence of a natural rate of interest that equilibrates savings with investment, Keynes acknowledges in the *General Theory* that:

> I had overlooked the fact that in any given society there is, on this definition, a different natural rate of interest for each hypothetical level of employment. And, similarly, for every rate of interest there is a level of employment for

which the rate is the 'natural' rate, in the sense that the system will be in equilibrium with that rate of interest and that level of employment.

(Keynes 1936, CW 7, p. 242)

If there is no unique natural rate of interest in a monetary economy, what is the basic purpose of monetary policy? Remember that the previous chapter has shown that a 'monetary rule' according to Keynes' meaning of the term means a slowly decreasing long-term interest rate, each fall being secured and thus considered as 'definitive' by private actors. In line with our reassessment of liquidity stated above, the very purpose of monetary policy according to Keynes can be understood as follows: to part with liquidity at lower and lower long-term interest rates, that is to ask for a lower and lower liquidity premium, implies that individuals attribute higher and higher weight to their expectations of future prices of non-monetary assets. In short, monetary policy aims to convince private actors that the future is less unknown than they could have feared and that undertaking new capital schemes is henceforth worthwhile. In a world of uncertainty, monetary policy is thus able to manage the 'real' interest rate through the management of long-term expectations as well as through the provision of liquidity. The corollary of monetary policy understood this way is to tackle the problem of speculation on financial markets and to deal with it. This means "to eliminate the baneful influence of private speculators and the volatility of expectations, thereby reducing risk premiums and increasing the capital stock" (Meltzer [1981] 1983, p. 449).

No doubt this dampening of speculation should not be too difficult if Keynes' 'Middle Way' doctrine were applied: the State would be directly or indirectly in charge of a large bulk of total investment in the economy (not necessarily through State ownership) and would by the same token become the main borrower. Viewed as an "agent of social responsibility" (O'Donnell 1989, p. 301), the State is precisely the very entity in the economy able to take long-term views, and by the way long-term commitments. As Carabelli (2003) argues, this means to not follow the rules dictated by habits and conventions but instead to rely on autonomous judgement, to form "genuine and reasonable judgement concerning the future" (Carabelli 2003, p. 224).[13]

Friedman on the 'adjustment process', or why State impulse is necessarily destabilising

Regarding Friedman, we thought it easier to divide this issue of the rationales behind the policy guidelines he advocates into two main headings that do not cover the conventional distinction between fiscal and monetary policy we used about Keynes.

There is first the study of the mechanisms at work in case of a discretionary device, either a fiscal policy or a monetary policy. As we will see below, there is not really a persuasive argument to be found here in order to substantiate

Friedman's general distrust of optimal control devices, especially regarding the transmission mechanism of monetary policy. That is the reason why we will focus in a second step on Friedman's understanding of a possibly cyclical adjustment process, i.e. a non-linear convergence path towards the long-term trend. In our view, here is to be found the ultimate rationale behind Friedman's overall advocacy for stable State devices, together with his plea for gradualism in the corrections applied to these devices.

Friedman on the transmission mechanism of discretionary policies

How does a monetary economy really function in Friedman's eyes so that discretionary devices do not stabilise the economy around full employment but merely muddy the waters? And through which precise channels do fiscal or monetary stimuli operate if they only give rise to an increase in the general price level or in the nominal interest rates, the real side of the economy remaining unchanged?

We will analyse below the three types of discretionary demand-boosting programmes considered by Friedman. There is first the issue of a loan-financed fiscal expansion, which corresponds to a standard fiscal policy. Second, there is the issue of open-market programmes, which correspond to a standard monetary policy. Third, there is also the case of a 'helicopter drop' of money (either launched once for all or continuously), which is usually viewed as an unconventional monetary policy, but which actually corresponds to an unconventional *fiscal* programme. We will bring to light the analytical inefficiencies of Friedman's line of reasoning, which makes it necessary to find the ultimate rationales behind Friedman's plea elsewhere.

Regarding the first issue, namely a fiscal programme financed by State borrowing, we have seen in the previous chapter how Friedman's position towards fiscal policy strengthened as time elapsed. The early Friedman in the 1940s and 1950s was not so opposed to loan expenditures as part of a general scheme for automatic stabilisation. Rather, what he pointed out were the mere practical difficulties encountered by public authorities in the implementation of a stabilisation programme (lack of information, delays, and so on). The Friedman of *Capitalism and Freedom* (1962a) highlighted the very special hypotheses upon which fiscal policy would be perfectly efficient (i.e. a nil crowding-out effect) through the highly unlikely hypothesis of the liquidity trap as well as the hypothesis of a perfectly inelastic private investment demand with respect to the interest rate (i.e. a vertical IS curve).

But Friedman went even further. In his debate with Heller published as *Monetary versus Fiscal Policy* (1969), what Friedman held corresponds to a pure crowding-out effect in its extreme version:

> ... fiscal policy has, in my view, been oversold in a very different and more basic sense than monetary policy.
>
> I believe that the state of the government budget matters: matters a great deal – for some things. The state of the government budget determines what

fraction of the nation's income is spent through the government and what fraction is spent by individuals privately.... *The state of the government budget has a considerable effect on interest rates.* If the federal government runs a large deficit, that means that the government has to borrow in the market, which raises the demand for loanable funds and so tends to raise interest rates.

If the government budget shifts to a surplus, that adds to the supply of loanable funds, which tends to lower interest rates.... I come to my main point – in my opinion, *the state of the budget by itself has no significant effect on the course of nominal income, or inflation, or deflation, or on cyclical fluctuations.*

(Friedman, in Friedman and Heller 1969, p. 50; emphasis added)

In Friedman's eyes, fiscal policy does not raise, even temporarily, aggregate demand. Strikingly, its impotency does not rely on a crowding-out effect of the type of the real balance effect: in case of fiscal impulse the general price level does not rise. At worst, what we could observe is a change in the relative price level for the goods the demand of which has increased because of government spending to the disadvantage of the goods foreclosed because of the increased cost of credit. Here, crowding-out appears instantaneously due to the squeezing of private demands for funds when State demand for funds is superimposed on the private flow. Except for a rise in the market interest rate, both the monetary and the real sides of the economy remain unchanged. The loanable funds principle is doing well.

Yet, if Friedman's contribution to debates surrounding the issue of economic policy had resulted in the identification of a pure crowding-out effect attributable to fiscal policy, no doubt the originality of his contribution would be considered quite limited.

There is a rather distinct rationale behind Friedman's advocacies regarding conventional monetary policy.[14] In "The Role of Monetary Policy", (Friedman 1968a) Friedman considers a very standard monetary policy through the buying of securities on the open market. The very first question Friedman asks is: "how can people be induced to hold a larger quantity of money? Only by bidding down interest rates" (Friedman [1968a] 1969a, p. 100). Yet, from Keynes' perspective this is puzzling: the individuals who populate an economy à la Keynes do not seek for a peculiar amount of money, either in real or nominal terms. For Keynes, the issue would be just the reverse: how to bid down interest rates? Only in making people hold more money. Be that as it may, Friedman acknowledges that open-market operations prove successful, so long as individuals do not revise their inflationary expectations. At first, interest rates decline and investment rises, just like in the Keynesian case. But a second transmission channel is added. Since "the function of money [is] a temporary abode of purchasing power" (Friedman and Schwartz 1982, p. 25), at the current inflationary expectations individuals hold more money than they wish to. To see what is happening, one can refer to the simple formulation suggested by Smithin (2003). The Keynesians would write the demand function for money as:

$$\frac{M}{P} = L(i,Y), L_i < 0, L_Y > 0 \tag{4}$$

where i stands for the nominal interest rate and Y the real income. Friedman would remind us that the proper interest rate to be considered is the real one:

$$r = i - \pi^e \tag{5}$$

where π^e stands for the expected rate of inflation (the relevant rate of inflation at the maturity date of the loans). From Friedman's perspective, the relevant demand function for money is thus stated as:

$$\frac{M}{P} = L(r + \pi^e, Y) \tag{6}$$

At their current inflationary expectations, individuals hold a too large amount of money. The real balance effect operates due to the increased opportunity cost of holding money and people ask for more goods and services. Aggregate demand increases, aggregate income too, unemployment falls, and so forth. Unfortunately, the story continues:

> But one man's spending is another man's income. Rising income will raise the liquidity preference schedule and the demand for loans; it may also raise prices, which would reduce the real quantity of money. These three effects will reverse the initial downward pressure on interest rates fairly promptly, say, a year or two, to return interest rates to the level they would otherwise have had.
>
> (Friedman [1968a] 1969a, p. 100)

Once the rise in the general price level is acknowledged and incorporated in expectations, individuals rearrange their portfolio and restore their initial real balances of money. Again, it is not the current level of prices that matters but the expected one.

By the same token, the expansionary open-market policy might produce higher market interest rates: if the actors on financial markets expect the rise in prices to be pursued, lenders will ask higher rates of return that borrowers will agree to offer. Noticeably, Friedman's reasoning makes it possible to offer a good rationale to the pro-cyclical movements of both real and nominal interest rates that he observed in his empirical work.

But at the same time, his analysis of the 'transmission mechanism' allows for changes in the rates of interests, which opens the door for an indirect channel of transmission of monetary policy through its effects on financial markets. That is, Friedman has opened the door for an interaction between the monetary and the financial sides of the economy that might ultimately render discretionary monetary policy operative. This is precisely the approach to the problem of the transmission mechanism investigated by Tobin (Bainar and Tobin 1968; Tobin 1969) by aim of the q concept. Remember that q corresponds to the market valuations of capital assets to their replacement costs for an individual firm. The higher q, the higher the market value of capital assets relative to their financial costs, the higher the inducement to invest. Open-market policies then appear as *financial* policies that can boost the demand for newly produced capital schemes thanks to the boosting of the existing stock market valuation of capital assets.[15] Tobin's line of argument by aim of his q effect severely undermines the case made by Friedman for a purely monetary transmission mechanism.

At the analytical ground, the very problem for Friedman is that his overall concern aims to prove that monetary loosening can do nothing in the long run but only cause a higher rate of inflation. As the 1977 Nobel lecture will later show, the short-run non-neutrality of money must come from private actors' misperceptions of relative prices due to the unexpected changes in money supply. In this regard, Friedman's appraisal of conventional monetary policy (i.e. open-market devices) in 1968 is at an impasse. Hence the necessity to isolate the effects of a monetary expansion on the goods market from its indirect effects on financial markets. That is how the 'helicopter drop of money' metaphor comes into action.

Accordingly, let us analyse the third heading concerned with discretionary policies, which is elaborated precisely by Friedman to disentangle the *direct* effects of monetary loosening on the general price level, which he aims to isolate from the *indirect* effects of monetary loosening through the changes in interest rates we discussed above.

The parable of the helicopter drop of currency corresponds to the issuance of base money; it is used by Friedman for the first time in his "Optimal Quantity of Money" (1969). In the "hypothetical simple society" considered, there is no lending nor borrowing; the credit market issue is clearly set aside. The initial position is an equilibrium one, where expectations are fulfilled. Then, "one day a helicopter flies over the community and drops an additional $1,000 in bills for the sky, which is, of course, hastily collected by members of the community" (Friedman 1969a, p. 4). Let us first suppose that this drop occurs just once. Everyone being taken by surprise, the real balance effect is quickly put into operation: since there is no credit market, one can be sure that individuals will get rid of the whole of their surplus cash balances in spending more goods. Unsurprisingly, the real long-term position of this economy is unchanged. In the case of a single drop, the inflation rate will come back to zero after the initial jump in the general price level. Yet, Friedman acknowledges that "it is much harder to say anything about the transition" (Friedman 1969a, p. 6), namely to disentangle in the transmission mechanism the real effects from the monetary ones. Noticeably, the case is even more complicated when the rise in the money supply is continuous (i.e. the dropping of money persists). In that case, the inflation rate will rise at the same pace as the money supply as soon as individuals adjust their inflationary expectations but not necessarily at the very beginning of the process, opening the door for a cyclical adjustment process, the 'overshooting' proposition that we will analyse extensively below.

With the parable of the helicopter drop, Friedman shows that a monetary economy is able to escape so severe a slump as the Great Depression: suffice it to provide private actors with base money to restore nominal aggregate demand. There is no 'liquidity trap', as the Keynesians argue. But there is a basic defect in Friedman's reasoning. While any indirect effect of monetary loosening through changes in interest rates on the credit market has been carefully set aside thanks to this helicopter drop metaphor, the counterpart of this issuance of base money through currency is actually the purchase of *goods* and not the purchase of *bonds*. That is a perfect equivalent of a tax relief financed by money issuance. Ironically, this unconventional monetary policy turns out to be a quite unconventional fiscal stimulus package, i.e. a money-financed fiscal policy. As the author of the parable of the buried bottles with banknotes,[16] Keynes would not disagree: while the economy has reached full employment, the aggregate supply curve being then vertical, any rise in effective demand has no real impact whatsoever but only raises prices. Such a scenario is all the more probable in an economy in which there are no financial markets. Clearly, the helicopter drop parable was not the proper way to settle the issue.

Friedman already demonstrated that a loan-financed fiscal policy would only raise the market interest rates. What he obtains with the helicopter drop parable is the denying of the efficiency of a money-financed fiscal policy. So the transmission mechanism of a conventional monetary policy is still an open issue to be answered.

Overshooting and cyclical pattern as the ultimate rationale of Friedman's overall guidelines

In our view, the ultimate rationale behind Friedman's plea for stabilisation policy through stable money supply growth is to be found in the study of two pieces of work that are explicitly dedicated to the issue of the transmission mechanism of monetary policy, his "Theoretical Framework for Monetary Analysis" (1970c) and its revised version included in his *Monetary Trends* (1982) co-written with Schwartz. These theoretical pieces aim to answer the objections raised by the 1967 AER lecture (Friedman 1968a) as well as by the 1969a essay including the helicopter drop metaphor. Friedman takes up there the issues previously identified: how does monetary policy operate in the short run? How does the economy move from its initial position just after the monetary shock to its long-run equilibrium? And how to disentangle the effects of this shock on output from its effects on prices?

In his 1970c essay one can rightfully consider that the monetary policy under consideration is a standard one, through the purchase of bonds on the open market. Friedman provides a general model in between the extreme 'Keynesian' case of an absolute liquidity trap (with its corollary, a highly unstable demand function for money) and the extreme 'classical' case of a fixed velocity of money and pure neutrality of money in the short run. As we have seen, in Friedman's model money is a close substitute to a large spectrum of assets. The specifications of the demand function for money entails both and at the same time a highly predictable but not necessarily a constant velocity of money, which allows for short-run non-neutralities. But the crucial problem of this 1970c essay (as well as of the 1982 one) is that both the real and the nominal interest rates are considered as given in both the short run as well as in the long run. The real interest rate is predetermined by the secular growth tendency. And the nominal rate is the predetermined real rate plus the anticipated inflation rate, based on past experience or outside the model, which means that market rates are supposed to incorporate very quickly new inflationary expectations. Both saving and investment which depend on the real interest rate turn out to be fixed. By the aim of this very strong hypothesis, the transmission mechanism fully operates through the general price level with no indirect influence on the credit market. Again, the critical issue of the indirect effect of monetary policy through financial markets, and the way it operates through its influence on private actors' expectations, is fully set aside.

The first type of critique that Friedman's 'in-between model' raises applies to the time span of Friedman's dynamic analysis, since "he tells us very little about timing and speed of adjustment or the length of run to which his models apply" (Brunner and Meltzer 1972, p. 64). The second line of critique, which appears much more harmful for Friedman's theoretical construct, is the ignorance of the fiscal policy issue, a point raised by Brunner and Meltzer but also by Tobin: "changes in government expenditures and taxes, apparently, have so little effect that they can be ignored entirely" (Brunner and Meltzer 1972, p. 64). Questioning the efficiency of a fiscal programme within Friedman's framework leads to surprising results, which are closely connected to the hypothesis of predetermined real and nominal interest rates. This point is at the core of Tobin's critique, which emphasises how loan-financed fiscal policy proves efficient to raise real output in Friedman's theoretical framework:

> ... the model is bizarre. So here is a model that acknowledges the interest sensitivity of the demand for money but preserves the quantity theory by the simple expedient of fixing interest rates. But the cost of this expedient is to concede fiscal policy more control over output and employment than virtually any Keynesian would claim.
>
> (Tobin 1972a, p. 89)[17]

All these critiques being well founded, there is a crucial proposition in the theoretical framework built by Friedman that provides in our view a crucial rationale for his overall economic guidelines principles. Tobin (1981) summarises well these policy principles to which we have to provide rationales:

With stable policies, ... the economy itself will be stable. Exogenous non-policy shocks, including entrepreneurial expectations and spirits, are assigned comparatively little empirical importance. To those shocks that do occur market adjustments are swift and convergent. Policy variations are more likely to amplify than to dampen natural fluctuations, misallocating resources in the process.

(Tobin 1981, p. 34)

Friedman's three purely theoretical essays, namely the 1969a essay dedicated to the "Optimum Quantity of Money", the 1970c "Theoretical Framework for Monetary Analysis" as well as the 1982 *Monetary Trends*, conclude with the idea of an 'overshooting' during the adjustment process. This idea of a cyclical reaction pattern applies to the changes in the rate of inflation in the 1969a piece of work whereas it later applies to the rate of change in nominal income when Friedman renounces disentangling changes in real income from changes in the price level. Crucially, this idea of overshooting and cyclical patterns is in the eyes of Friedman the "key element in monetary theories of cyclical fluctuations" (Friedman 1969a, p. 13).

The idea is quite simple. When the rate of growth of money increases, the rate of inflation will increase at the same pace in the long run (Figure 5.2). But in the short run things are more complicated. Let us first suppose that the rise in the money growth rate is not anticipated, but that people instantaneously adapt their inflationary expectations once the change is perceived. The higher rate of inflation raises the market interest rate. The opportunity cost of holding money becomes higher (the desired velocity increases) so that the real balances desired fall, which adds an additional pressure to the price level.

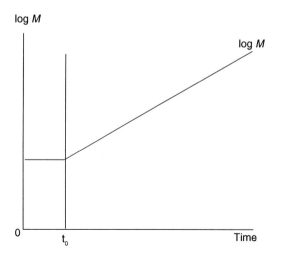

Figure 5.2 Time path of money stock before and after t_0 (source: Friedman and Schwartz 1982).

The equilibrium path of nominal income is thus given by the solid line rather than the dashed line (Figure 5.3).

What happens if people take time to understand what is happening and do not revise their inflationary expectations immediately? In the case of adaptive expectations, there must be an overreaction during the adjustment process, an overshooting, in the rate of change in nominal income. Indeed, at the very beginning of the process individuals are not necessarily able to disentangle a transitory rise in the money growth rate from a permanent one. The real interest being constant, the perceived cost of holding money is not fully adjusted and the current balances exceed their long-term desired level. That is, the nominal interest rate does not rise as much as in the case where inflationary expectations are revised without delay. Once the rise in the money supply is perceived as permanent, expectations are revised, which leads to a higher nominal interest rate. The desired cash balances fall through the increased demand for goods. Hence the overshooting phenomenon. There is no reason for the process to be smooth, so that cyclical patterns are possible (Figure 5.4).

This explanation of 'cyclical' fluctuations has to be compared with Friedman's contention in his 1999 interview with Snowdon and Vane. He there argues:

> I really don't believe that there is a business cycle, it is a misleading concept. The notion of a business cycle is something of a regularly recurring phenomenon that is internally driven by the mechanics of the system. I believe that there is a system that has certain response mechanisms and that system is subject over time to external random forces (some large, some small) that play on it and it adapts to those forces.
>
> (Friedman's interview in Snowdon and Vane 1999, p. 134)

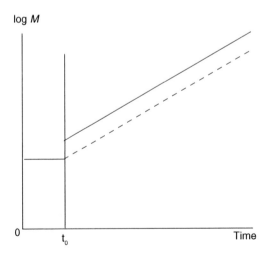

Figure 5.3 Equilibrium path of nominal income before and after t_0 (source: Friedman and Schwartz 1982).

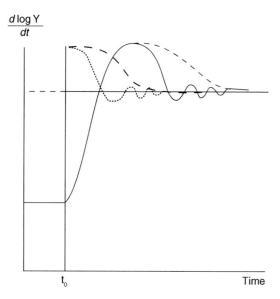

Figure 5.4 Possible adjustment paths of rate of change of nominal income (source: Friedman and Schwartz 1982).

In Friedman's eyes, both the real and the monetary sides are very likely to respond to external shocks in a cyclical fashion, of course because of some nominal rigidities and delays (which are nothing but a Keynesian 'excuse' for interventionism) but much more crucially because of lags in inflationary expectations. Regarding monetary policy, the best that monetary authorities can do is to avoid sharp swings in the money supply growth. In the long run there are no basic defects in the inter-temporal price system to be relied on to justify discretionary policy; there is no liquidity trap. Besides, in the short run public authorities 'do not know' the basic structure of the economy. Accordingly, they are very likely to confuse the 'cyclical' pattern of the adjustment process that ensues from a small real shock (as it is the most probable) with the external shock itself. This sort of ill-timed measure on the part of ignorant policy-making cannot but be disastrous.

It thus comes as no surprise that the best State authorities can do in a monetary economy is to prevent themselves from disturbing the stabilisation process brought into force in an economic system that intrinsically possesses the required self-correcting forces. The commitment of the State not to intervene by optimal control devices in case of a (necessarily temporary) departure from the dynamic equilibrium growth path can only reinforce the confidence that private agents can place in the economic climate. This commitment towards anti-cyclical policies provides a feedback effect that, in turn, underpins the system stabilising properties.

*

Such is probably the ultimate rationale behind Friedman's overall stabilisation plea. The very issue regarding Friedman is whether he succeeds in accounting for the transition from short-run impact to long-run effects of a monetary shock, whether also he succeeds in accounting for non-neutralities which are valid only in the short run, and most importantly whether he finally achieves his attempt in disentangling the adjustment path in output from the adjustment path in prices. Regarding the critiques his contribution raised and regarding also Friedman's success in his attempts to answer them, the last word can be given to Friedman himself who acknowledges:

> A major unsettled issue is the short-run division of a change in nominal income between output and price. The division has varied widely over space and time, and there exists no satisfactory theory that isolates the factors responsible for the variability.
>
> (Friedman 1992, p. 49)

Our quest for market foundations to the adjustment process has highlighted the precarious basis of Friedman's policy advocacies: his reasoning rests on too strong hypotheses (such as fixed interest rates in the short run as well as in the long run); and the argument of a cyclical but yet necessarily converging adjustment process that follows an external shock (i.e. the idea of a general equilibrium necessarily stable) turns out to be a *petition principii*. Unfortunately, in the final analysis Friedman's ultimate recommendations in terms of stabilisation devices are divorced from the results obtained through his theoretical investigations.

5.4 Conclusion: financial markets in a monetary economy

In Keynes' explanation of under-employment the functioning of financial markets plays a critical role. In a world in which the entire set of the future 'states of the world' is not fully known, individuals have to make expectations, but they also have to attribute a certain weight, a certain degree of confidence in these expectations. An open-market operation will not succeed if investors are not convinced by the downward tendency of the long-term interest rate. That is, an injection of liquidity would be ineffective if at the same time the liquidity-preference schedule shifts upward. Worse, the 'beauty contest' parable tells us about the specular dimension of financial markets that monetary policy will not succeed if investors are not convinced that the 'market' will remain unconvinced by this downward tendency: "the rational attitude cannot then be distinguished from the conventional attitude. Indeed, expectations are rational – and will prove correct – in that they coincide with the majority expectations" (Dos Santos Ferreira 2000, p. 276). It is not only the private expectations on future rates (i.e. on the future demand price of capital assets) that must be revised but rather, and much more critically, the individual expectations on the future conventional market valuation of these asset prices. In a world of uncertainty, financial markets as they really work do not coordinate the inter-temporal plans of savers with the ones of investors. There is no 'natural' rate, which would be fully determined by the 'real' values of productivity and thrift. The interest rate appears as the result of a conventional attitude regarding what the future will bring forth:

> It might be more accurate, perhaps, to say that the rate of interest is a highly conventional rather than a highly psychological phenomenon. For its actual value is largely governed by the prevailing view as to what its value is expected to be. *Any* level of interest which is accepted with sufficient conviction as *likely* to be durable *will* be durable; subject, of course, in a changing society to fluctuations for all kinds of reasons round the expected normal.
>
> (Keynes 1936, CW 7, p. 203)

Keynes' plea for the socialisation of investment ensues from this identification of the dysfunction of financial markets. Indeed, if investments were rendered as fixed and indissoluble as marriage this would impede the marketability of capital assets, and would thus depress their liquidity premium. The set of new institutions Keynes designs aim at the dampening of *speculation*, i.e. "the activity of forecasting the psychology of the market" (Keynes 1936, CW 7, p. 158) with the related aim of the encouragement of *enterprise*, i.e. "the activity of forecasting the prospective yield of assets over their whole life" (Keynes 1936, CW 7, p. 158). Ultimately, this means encouraging individuals to revise their judgement on the long-term state of the economy, that is contriving them to expect with strong confidence a future state of full employment. The long-term state of expectations will thus be quite high and the liquidity premium attached to money will be strongly abated.

Within an inherently unstable economy which lacks self-adjusting mechanisms in case of large and prolonged external shocks, when the State becomes a major player in the management of capital schemes (remember that for Keynes the 'State' in the widest sense might be concerned with two-thirds or three-quarters of the newly produced capital schemes) private actors can safely hold firmer judgements since the ultimate goal of State authorities is to "increase the partial knowledge available to individuals and the whole society" (Carabelli and Cedrini 2012, p. 28).

Regarding the efficiency of financial markets for providing the 'right' signals to individuals, which means their ability to coordinate savers' and investors' plans, no doubt Friedman takes a stance opposite to Keynes'. Isn't Friedman the author of an article called "In Defense of Destabilizing Speculation" (1960b)? Apart from the 'other' participants in a market, Friedman considers in this paper an additional *group* of individuals that he calls 'speculators' while Keynes distinguishes the *activity* of speculation from the one of the enterprise. This makes a great deal of difference. Indeed, Friedman considers that a 'fundamental' price can be identified:

the activities of speculators do not affect the quantities demanded and supplied by other participants in the market at current price. This implies that
there is a well-defined price that will clear the market at each point in the
absence of speculation and that this price is not affected by speculation.

(Friedman [1960b] 1969a, pp. 286–7)

Friedman's speculators exist *in addition to* the usual actors on markets. It is 'as
if' speculators were making bets in "gambling houses" entirely disconnected
from both the spot and the forward markets. Strikingly, the speculators Friedman
considers resemble the gamblers Keynes dealt with in his 1910 lectures dedicated to speculation, those who do not possess superior knowledge in comparison
to the other players (Carabelli and Cedrini 2012). Besides, from Keynes' perspective there is no such thing as an external "well-defined price". Such a short
cut is not defensible from Keynes' standpoint: what the 'beauty contest' parable
shows precisely is that wondering about the *true* prettiest faces is a pointless
exercise. 'Fundamental' values provided by the 'real' characteristics of the
system as distinguished from their 'conventional' valuations simply do not exist.
Again, the rational attitude cannot be disentangled from the conventional one.

In this paper dedicated to speculation, the gap between the two authors
widens even more when Friedman considers the case where speculation is not
stabilising, i.e. when it happens that the group of speculators take their decisions
in such a way that they do not reduce the inter-temporal differences in price, so
that they incur *systematic* losses. Apart from the existence of gambling houses
that exist to satisfy the risk-loving instinct of some of us who are willing to pay
to take risk,[18] the only example given by Friedman corresponds to the case of
"avoidable ignorance" (Friedman [1960b] 1969a, p. 287): before making my bet
I might ignore that the coin possesses two heads or that the coin is not fair. This
is a lack of knowledge that can be easily and readily cared about. Avoidable
ignorance opens the door for State intervention, but only to the extent that government officials possess better knowledge regarding the rules of the games. In
that case, "the appropriate solution is then for the government officials to make
their knowledge available either by providing the information on which their
price forecasts rest or by making and publishing the price forecasts themselves
(Friedman [1960b] 1969a, p. 288). Strikingly, all the metaphors given in this
paper dedicated to speculation come under the heading of risk instead of Keynes'
heading of uncertainty: heads or tails, the roulette wheel like in Monte Carlo or
lottery tickets. In all the cases mentioned by Friedman, the full distribution as
well as the likelihood of occurrence is fully known. It is not possible for the
markets under consideration *not to* provide the right signals to private actors.

Friedman's paper dedicated to speculation explicitly applies to the commodity markets and to the exchange rates as related to the balance of payments issue;
buffer stocks of commodities or fixed exchange rates are dismissed as mere Keynesian excuses for justifying State intervention. Friedman's dismissal of coordination failures between individual plans in these examples is easily extended to
financial markets as a whole. On the premise that financial markets function in

such a way to coordinate well the inter-temporal plans of savers and investors, Friedman considers that there is a natural interest rate as given by the true motives of borrowers (i.e. productivity) and of lenders (i.e. thrift) towards which a monetary economy gravitates. He also considers that there can be deviations in the short-term nominal rate but only so long as individuals take time to revise their inflationary expectations. And when he makes the hypothesis of both a constant real and a constant nominal rate of interest, as is the case in the two theoretical pieces of work we studied in this chapter (Friedman 1970c; Friedman and Schwartz 1982), he simply considers that the precise way how these inter-temporal plans are coordinated through the equilibrium of stock asset markets can be set aside with no loss of generality. As we have seen, the real interest rate is there considered as a constant determined by a fixed marginal productivity of capital. Here, "the vision is one in which there are ultimately no fixed factors, or in which technological advance may be presumed to offset whatever physical limits" (Smithin 2003, p. 115).[19]

The irreconcilable gulf between on the one hand Keynes' political plea for the socialisation of investment and on the other Friedman's stabilisation guidelines limited to a constant growth rate in the money supply ultimately comes through their respective concern for the inter-temporal price system.

For Keynes, the interest rate "may fluctuate for decades about a level which is chronically too high for full employment" (Keynes 1936, CW 7, p. 204). It turns out to be the 'villain of the piece' – to borrow Leijonhufvud's (1981) words – which ultimately bears responsibility for protracted unemployment. Hence the necessity to design institutional devices to restore when needed and most essentially to keep equilibrium in a monetary economy.

As for Friedman, the failure of the inter-temporal price system to provide the right signal is far from an issue. In this respect, the most extreme hypothesis made by Friedman to evade this issue is to be found in his "Optimum Quantity of Money" (1969a), which comprises the parable of helicopters dropping money over an economy in which possibilities for borrowing and lending have been abolished by decree. This hypothesis of the non-existence of an inter-temporal price system is later relaxed in Friedman's analyses. But in his "Theoretical Framework for Monetary Analysis" (1970c) as well as in the *Monetary Trends* (1982), real interest rates are considered as fixed, given by a constant marginal productivity of capital. Again, the possibility for inter-temporal market failures are there evaded from the outset. With no surprise, "the case for monetary growth rate rules, as initially stated by Friedman ..., was put in terms of the capacity of such a policy to *maintain* stability in an already stable economy – it was a policy prescription for *staying out* of trouble" (Laidler 1982, p. 30). The case for *restoring* equilibrium in a monetary economy in case of a large external and prolonged shock remains unsettled in his case.

6 Conclusion
Where to draw the line between laissez-faire and planning?

Historians of economic analysis frequently like to remind that "continued relevance is a fundamental rationale for history of economic thought" (Hoover 1995, p. 677). We hasten to add that this does not mean ventriloquism. In the present case, our purpose is not to wonder what Keynes and Friedman would have diagnosed as the root causes of the current recession or what they would have called for today. Rather, it seems to us that a return to their texts should help us to pursue avenues of reflection at both the theoretical and the policy level, and in particular to better frame the issues of the debate currently at stake. Both Keynes and Friedman should help us to reshape our questionings regarding the relationships between public institutions and private agents; they should also help us to rethink the policy alternatives at our disposal.

Here below, we provide our results under three main headings. Under the first heading there is Keynes' and Friedman's invitation to reflect upon the critical link between expectations and policy guidelines. Our two authors have complementary lessons to teach us with regard to our contemporary treatment of expectations as rationally formed. On the one hand, Keynes is highly concerned with the way State authorities could be in capacity to guide long-term real expectations in a world of uncertainty. On the other, Friedman asks us to remember that private agents do really take time to adjust even their short-term nominal expectations (which are better seen as adaptive) so that the anchoring of inflationary expectations should be an imperative matter of concern for policymakers.

Second, it seems to us that Keynes and Friedman could help us to reframe the terms of the debates surrounding the right economic policy for a decentralised market economy. Both of them invite us to go beyond the 'rules versus discretion' alternative as it is set today and to go even beyond the 'fine-tuning versus anti-cyclical devices' we used to refer to until the 1970s. In our view, a highly relevant way of putting the issue is the alternative set by Simons in the 1930s between 'authorities' and 'rules'. Stated this way, Keynes and Friedman offer us great lessons. On the one hand, Keynes' stance for 'authorities' means that the State is the very agent able to cope with uncertainty in a monetary economy and to help us to escape harmful conventional judgement, which is at the opposite end of what is nowadays called 'discretion'. On the other hand, Friedman's stance for 'rules' means that the provision of strict and highly rigid guidelines enforced by law with the view to anchor nominal expectations is the best that centralised authorities can do to stabilise a monetary economy. From this perspective, both Keynes and Friedman have great lessons to offer for the economic policy in times of crisis: a call for the design and the implementation of a renewed institutional setting to cope with large-scale external shocks regarding Keynes; a plea *against* short-term devices that are likely to prevent the activation of self-adjusting mechanisms as well as a plea *against* reversals of priorities within a short interval of time, which means a plea for lowliness, regarding Friedman.

Under the third heading, the question Hayek would ask to our two authors is: ultimately, where to draw the line between laissez-faire and planning? Putting the issue in this way brings to light the varying concerns underlying Keynes' and Friedman's overall policy guidelines. On the one hand, Keynes is highly concerned with the practical issue: we ought to take advantage of the current turmoil to reform here and now the monetary economies we live in. On the other, Friedman's standpoint is not so pragmatic: at a quite abstract level, what he offers us is an idealistic objective and what he gauges in the final analysis is our capacity to follow the right track.

Let us present the avenues of reflection Keynes and Friedman offer us along the lines of these three main headings.

6.1 Expectations and economic policy

At the theoretical level, it comes as no surprise that the very lesson we might learn for today from Keynes and Friedman is related to the issue of the interaction between the economic policy designed and the behaviour of private agents' expectations.

The contemporary rational expectations approach relies preliminarily on the idea of 'rational' behaviour on behalf of agents seeking to maximise their own objective function subject to constraints while being fully aware of all the alternatives they face. Beyond, a general characterisation of the concept of rational expectations approach is summed well in the following quotation:

> The rational expectations idea had it that agents' expectations about the future should be treated 'as if' based on as much knowledge of the structure of the economy and the time series properties of the shocks impinging upon it as was available to the economist building the model used to analyze their behaviour.
>
> (Laidler 2006, p. 56)

What can be said of this contemporary treatment of expectations from the perspective of the theoretical frameworks developed by our two authors? Regarding Keynes, from the outset the crucial issue of continuous market clearing, which underlies the principle of exhausted possibilities of mutual beneficial exchanges, is hardly reconcilable with his analysis in terms of aggregate disequilibrium. As regards expectations, Keynes clearly disentangles short-term from long-term expectations, a Marshallian distinction that has been precisely erased by the New Classical use of rational expectations (Hoover 1984). Keynes has so little interest in short-term expectations that he assumes what one would call today 'perfect foresight', i.e. that expectations are always fulfilled within the short period. By contrast, the long-term *real* expectations as incorporated into the marginal efficiency of capital are a key issue for Keynes (despite the fact they are generally considered as exogenous in the analysis carried out in the *General Theory*). That is, Keynes does not assume that private agents are likely to make systematic errors of foresight. Besides, they are not irrational in the sense that they do try to pursue their self-interest. Truly, Keynes seldom refers to the 'waves' of optimism and pessimism on financial markets as well as to 'animal spirits' and the like. But in our opinion, this point should not be carried out too far.[1]

With regard to rational expectations, there are two slightly different ways to locate Keynes' distanced position. First, it can be considered, as Meltzer (1996) does, that in Keynes' theoretical framework information is costly, which results in delays in adjustment, the speed of individuals' reactions depending partially on the dissemination of the information. This is a way to rationalise why "Keynes was concerned with the design of institutions that reduce risk or uncertainty to the minimum required by nature and market processes" (Meltzer 1996, p. 42). Another way to state the issue is to insist on the lack of knowledge faced by individuals regarding the future 'states of the world', which is an intrinsic principle in any monetary economy. Individuals hold their expectations with a certain weight, depending on the evidence they can get and their degree of confidence. That is precisely the reason why individuals take time to revise their judgements (which leads commentators to commonly interpret these long-term expectations as 'backward-looking' and anchored in historical judgements instead of being 'forward-looking') and why expectations tend to be extrapolative, which adds to a deflationary process. This is also why the concept of rational expectations does not make room for Keynes' 'degree of belief', the idea that each individual might form his own judgement, which is at the basis of the diversity in expectations among individuals.[2] Private agents do not know the structure of the economy and, to a certain extent, what will be possible or probable in the future is the product of our current decisions.

At their level, individuals might be trapped in conventional valuations, which are very likely to be harmful at the collective level. What the beauty contest parable reminds us is that conventional behaviour easily conflates with the 'rational' one, especially on financial markets. But for collective agents the matter at hand should be entirely different. If one disentangles reasonable expectations from conventional expectations, the former being "not grounded on rules, but on logical probabilities, i.e. 'real', limited knowledge or upon reasons in which we really believe" whereas the latter are "practical answers to the existence of total ignorance and uncertainty" (Carabelli and De Vecchi 2001, p. 280), it immediately follows that the duty for collective agents is to escape harmful conventions at the social level: "long-term professional investors could – and public institutions should – form reasonable expectations, grounded upon 'real' and 'genuine' partial knowledge" (Carabelli and De Vecchi 2001, p. 282).

As a Marshallian, Friedman too sharply disentangles the short-run from the long-run issue. In a way, Friedman takes exactly the opposite view to that developed by Keynes. He assumes adaptive *nominal* expectations in the short-term analysis, so that as a matter of fact foresights are seldom fulfilled. Private agents take time to revise their short-run nominal expectations, which is precisely the way money becomes non-neutral. But in the long run, Friedman assumes that expectations are always fulfilled, so inter-temporal coordination troubles à la Keynes simply vanish. Rational expectations are commonly seen as a refinement of Friedman's idea of adaptive expectations: when changes in policy regimes are announced and credible, i.e. when individuals are not taken by surprise, inflationary expectations adapt instantaneously and monetary policy is neutral even in the short run.

What about the relevance of the rational expectations approach from a Friedmanian perspective? It has been noticed that the underlying idea of continuous market clearing behind the concept of rational expectations hardly fits into Friedman's monetary explanation of business cycles too (Leijonhufvud 2000). Likewise, Friedman's overall policy guidelines hardly fit into this new paradigm that treats money as even 'super non-neutral'.[3]

Regarding the unknown faced by private agents and the formation of expectations, it is interesting to note that Friedman himself expresses on some occasions strong reservations concerning the concept of rational expectations. In the last chapter of *Monetary Trends* (1982), he takes the example of the free silver movement in the late nineteenth century. At that time, the point at stake was whether the United States would go off the gold standard, with the concomitant rise in inflation to be expected. Before 1896, the anticipation was inflation (as expressed in the higher interest rates in the USA than in Great Britain) while the reality was deflation. After 1896, just the reverse occurred: the anticipation was stability or deflation while the reality was inflation. It took about 20 years to see the end of this persistency in expectations errors. For Friedman, this example raises a threefold question. First, as economists we face historical time, which means that the 'free silver movement' episode is an experiment that cannot be repeated. It can be hardly stated that investors were wrong in their forecasts: "in a way the probability of anything happening ex post is always one" (Friedman's interview in Snowdon and Vane 1999, p. 132). Second, and correlatively, rational expectations conflate an assumed objective probability distribution of outcomes with the subjective probability held by individuals. Hoover (1984) clearly shows that the matter at hand here refers to the crucial distinction between 'risk', in which case the probability distribution is perfectly known so that there are no systematic and correlated errors, and 'uncertainty', which means in Knight's terminology unmeasurable uncertainty. On this issue of uncertainty and expectations, Friedman argues:

The only probability notion I can make sense of is personal probability in the spirit of Savage and others. Keynes's degree of belief is in the same family. In fact I believe that Keynes's contribution in his *Probability* book has been underrated and overlooked.

(Friedman's interview in Snowdon and Vane 1999, p. 132)[4]

Investors who experienced the 'free silver movement' faced uncertainty in the short-period perspective and the relevant time period considered to be allowed to properly rely on risk was about 20 years. Again, relying on rational expectations amounts to conflate the short run with the long run. As Hoover (1984) argues about this example, "Friedman *implicitly* defends the importance of uncertainty" (Hoover 1984, p. 71; emphasis added). As a result of the two previous points, the third and major defect of the rational expectations approach from Friedman's standpoint is that it downplays the role played by the monetary side of the economy in the transmission of shocks. What a long-run empirical perspective shows us is that, as a matter of fact, individuals do really take time to revise their inflationary expectations. In this regard, the rational expectations approach does not prove really helpful in understanding the disequilibrium dynamics of a monetary economy, concerned as it is with equilibrium: "it is not the open sesame to unraveling the riddle of dynamic change that some of its more enthusiastic proponents make it to be" (Friedman and Schwartz 1982, p. 630).

To put it somewhat as a paradox: in Friedman's eyes it is precisely because we know well that in the long run expectations are always fulfilled and that the economic system is ultimately self-adjusting that we should have our attention focused on the short-run disturbances. State duties can be summed up as follows: to forestall temporary departures from the dynamic growth path of the economy, the best that policy-makers can do is to prevent themselves from interfering within the free-play of the self-correcting forces that Friedman assumes the economic system to possess. The anchoring of nominal expectations, which is obtained by enhancing the stability of the policy regime, is the best achievable policy goal for those policy-makers most concerned with the building of confidence in the economic climate.

6.2 How to frame the debate about economic policy?

At the policy level too, Keynes and Friedman have great lessons for us today. To show this, we can first try to locate Keynes' and Friedman's respective overall advocacies with regard to the contemporary alternative of 'rules versus discretion'. If we do so, it immediately appears that both authors invite us to enlarge the terms of the debate as they are formulated today. We can also try to locate their positions within the 'fine-tuning versus anti-cyclical policies' alternative that prevailed until the 1970s. If so, both appear as true opponents to optimal control devices while they are at variance regarding the precise meaning they respectively confer on stabilisation. Third, we can refer to the 'rules versus authorities' way of putting the issue that was ongoing during the 1930s. In our view, this last way of framing the debate regarding State duties is highly fruitful in locating Keynes' and Friedman's own essential message. Ultimately, this 'rules versus authorities' way of framing our questioning provides us with renewed perspectives of reflection regarding the economic policy in times of crisis.

Rules versus discretion

Regarding the issue of how to stabilise a decentralised market economy, the terms of the debate have been thoroughly revised after the 'rational expectations' revolution launched by the New Classical economists. As it is framed today, the debate is set in terms of 'rules versus discretion'. Within this particular context discretion refers to day-to-day operations on the part of State authorities without any commitment towards private actors. There is no care for expectations or, to put it more precisely, private agents are considered as myopic, so that policy-makers can roughly ignore the precise way private agents form their expectations at the time the discretionary stabilisation policy is designed. Private agents' expectations are backward looking, i.e. anchored on history, or based on recent and past events. This means that public bodies can easily reoptimise every period and that "any promise made in the past does not constrain current policy" (Clarida *et al.* 1999, p. 1670).

By contrast, policy-makers who design rules-based policies explicitly integrate the interaction between the strategy they formulate and the behaviour of the rational agent: "policy making within a rational expectations framework becomes a strategic game between the policy maker and economic agents" (Snowdon and Vane 2002, p. 638). Today, what is meant by policy rule is "a systematic policy reaction function" (Laidler 2010c, p. 124). This means that today's rules-based policies are not mechanical schemes disconnected from the current economic climate. To take but one example, whether in its backward-looking form or in its generalised and forward-looking form, the baseline Taylor rule is definitely not a fixed once-for-all prescription. Rather, a generic Taylor rule must be regarded as a feedback rule, a policy reaction function that smoothes the business cycle while fully integrating the private actors' reaction to the policy regime designed.[5]

The very problem of this approach to stabilisation policy is that "the 'rules versus discretion' debate has taken a peculiar twist that presents discretion as the realm of lunatics" (Bibow 2009, p. 9). Indeed, 'discretion' does not appear as a convincing policy to pursue, in the light of the non-rational behaviour that such an approach assumes: how can private agents accept to endure systematic foresight errors? That is the main reason why today the debate concerns by and large the proper dose of leeway that is reasonable to impart to public authorities: a low one in the case of the classic Taylor rule and a larger one for the generalised or forward-looking rules.

Neither Keynes nor even less Friedman would have accepted to frame the debate how it is set today. Both the terms of the contemporary 'rules versus discretion' alternative are merely alien to the policy frameworks shaped by our two authors.

First, regarding Keynes there is no doubt that discretion as it is understood today hardly fits into his policy framework. It is a profound irony to associate the name of Keynes with devices that roughly dismiss such a crucial issue as expectations, that take private actors 'by surprise', and the effects of which persist only as long as individuals do not revise their expectations. Keynes' overall policy guidelines precisely aim to "defeat the dark forces of time and ignorance which envelop our future" (Keynes 1936, CW 7, p. 155), which means the guidance of private actors' real expectations regarding the long run. From this perspective, the more erratic and the less able a discretionary policy is to convince private agents to revise their judgement regarding the remote future, the more short-lasting it will be, with very small benefits for both output and unemployment. Discretion according to Keynes means neither short-term impulse nor the cheating of – temporary – myopic agents.

Next, what is now called a 'rule' is far too discretionary from Friedman's standpoint. Regarding the knowledge possessed by public bodies and the collective rationality that these institutions might benefit from, Friedman's position strongly echoes Hayek's. As is the case for Hayek, Friedman denies that institutions know more than individuals. The statement made by Carabelli and De Vecchi (2000) regarding Hayek, that public institutions "share with individuals a condition of ignorance, which impedes autonomous judgement" (Carabelli and De Vecchi 2000, p. 237), easily applies to Friedman. The implementation of a rule such as a baseline Taylor rule requires knowledge on the structure of the economy and information on its 'true' current state, the economic climate of the day, which public institutions are far from possessing. Besides, there is the issue of the willingness of the people who belong to public authority to act wisely and towards collective welfare. Friedman is deeply influenced by the 'new public school' economics. Everywhere and at every time, we are always and first and foremost individuals who look out for our own interest, how benevolent we might be otherwise. Hence, in Friedman's eyes the implementation of what one calls today a rule leaves much too leeway to policy-makers.

Both Keynes and Friedman would invite us to reframe the terms of the contemporary debates surrounding the issue of stabilisation in a monetary economy. They would also invite us to reconsider the theoretical underpinnings of these debates.

Regarding Keynes, even if discretion as understood nowadays hardly fits into his overall policy guidelines, this is not to say that he would take sides for rules as defined today. From his standpoint, in an economy that does not possess the required self-stabilising mechanisms for absorbing large and long-lasting external shocks the very problem faced by policy-makers is away from a short-run concern for stabilisation around the long-term equilibrium position (a concern for intervention that is viewed today as ensuing from nominal rigidities in general and staggered prices in particular).

Regarding Friedman, it is not only that he would reject the terms of the debate as stated today; he would also reject the theoretical underpinnings of this debate.

Friedman (1977a) already denied the existence of an inflation unemployment trade-off in the long run.[6] Lately, Friedman (2010)[7] also denies explicitly the existence of an empirical trade-off between variability of real income and variability of inflation. There are two basic reasons for that. First, the dynamics of the New Keynesian model of the Phillips curve (especially monopolistic competition and staggered prices) is alien to his theoretical background that only makes room for perfect competition. Second, the simple idea of a trade-off (even if between variability in output and variability in inflation) opens the door for fine-tuning. Friedman's statement that "treating the Fed as having two separate objectives is an open invitation to engage in fine-tuning, something that has almost always proved a mistaken practice" (Friedman 2010, p. 116) echoes his point made in 1977 about the existence of a medium-term positive relation between inflation and unemployment.

Optimal control versus anti-cyclical devices

If we go back to the 1960s or the 1970s, the debate was framed at that time in terms of 'optimal control versus anti-cyclical devices' or in terms of 'fine-tuning versus stabilisation'. It is noticeable that almost anyone today would call for 'fine-tuning'; only 'stabilisation' is still considered relevant as a policy issue. As is well known, Lerner (1941, 1944) used the metaphor of the 'steering wheel' to express this idea of 'fine-tuning': the State is able to 'drive' the economy through fiscal and monetary *counter-cyclical* policies. In Lerner's views, instead of conforming to the liberal principles of sound finance, the State should apply this new 'functional finance' principle to obtain full employment together with stable prices: monetary loosening and fiscal stimulus if there was unemployment, and the opposite if there was inflation. As for the first term of the alternative, the type of discretionary policies was considered appropriate to dampen the trade cycle until the 1960s but fine-tuning became wholly disqualified when developed economies became much more unstable.

The principle of 'stop-and-go' policies that was associated with the idea of fine-tuning as well as the idea that a lower rate of unemployment can be bargained in exchange for a higher inflation rate, has been definitely abandoned. Yet, it seems to us that the implicit confidence in our ability to design and to implement short-term devices to smooth out the business cycle and to implement counter-cyclical policies, which lies behind Lerner's idea of fine-tuning, is still present in the contemporary concern for stabilisation policy rules, although attention has shifted from fiscal policy to monetary policy. It is considered today that a central bank board is able to collect on time data on the current state of the economic system and on its future trend, and that the board possesses the required knowledge on the structure of the economy as well as on the delays encountered by the effect of a rise or fall in the very short interest rates on the monetary and the real sides of the economy. This allows in particular the board to disentangle an external shock from a cyclical (yet converging) adjustment process. Strikingly, this idea that a public institution is able to stabilise the economy on its long-run growth trend echoes the post-war confidence in optimal control devices. The wording 'fine-tuning' has been abandoned. A deep attention is now paid to the private actors' reaction towards policy-makers' decisions and policy regimes are now considered in their ability to anchor nominal expectations. But the fundamental idea remains the same: policy-makers are still considered able to easily design and implement optimal control schemes.

Let us consider the second term of the alternative, namely stabilisation. During the 1950s and 1960s, stabilisation meant *anti-cyclical* policies, i.e. schemes designed and calibrated 'once for all', such as the constant growth rate of some monetary aggregate advocated by Friedman. Regarding fiscal 'automatic stabilisers', a progressive tax rate or social security schemes might also be viewed as being part of the same type of stabilisation policies.

If the debate is framed this way, it is striking that neither 'optimal control' nor obviously 'anti-cyclical devices' corresponds to the position Keynes holds or the position of the opponents he battles with. On the one hand, we have argued that Keynes' policy guidelines means neither focusing on the short run, let alone the dismissal of private actors' expectations – quite the contrary. In this respect, the example of Keynes' 'buffer stocks' scheme proposal is worth highlighting. Indeed, this short-term device designed to dampen the trade cycle is embedded in a long-term matter of concern, which is to provide more knowledge to private actors on the long-term economic price as given by the 'fundamentals' of those commodities. Besides, the Classical economists Keynes targets in his pamphlets, the proponents of the 'Treasury View' and the liquidationists of the 1930s who simply advocate the 'purge to go on' do not resemble the proponents of anti-cyclical devices by aim of long-term policy guidelines but rather the New Classical economists, those who belong to the "Monetarism mark II" as Tobin (1981) calls them, for whom "Keynesian policies do Evil as they do Nothing" (Tobin 1981, p. 35).

Regarding Friedman, his overall policy guidelines are easily located if the debate is stated in terms of 'fine-tuning versus stabilisation'. While the early Friedman called for both monetary *and* fiscal counter-cyclical schemes, especially via money financed by government expenditures in an 'automatic stabilisers' fashion, he later changed his mind. From the early 1960s, Friedman sticks to a strictly monetary stabilisation policy and fully dismisses fiscal policy even in its automatic stabiliser version. When for whatever reason, the economy endures a fall in aggregate demand the provision of purchasing power to private actors would automatically induce them to spend more while restoring the level of the real balances they wish to hold. Stabilisation in Friedman's meaning of the word means devices that are designed 'once for all' (or at least implemented for a very long time, let say at least for five years) and that correspond to mechanical prescriptions, with no discretionary interpretation and no leeway left to policy-makers in the implementation of the anti-cyclical policy.

It comes as no surprise that the 'fine-tuning versus stabilisation' alternative, or rather the 'fine-tuning versus anti-cyclical programmes' to mark the difference with the contemporary framing of the debate, are alternatives that reflect fairly accurately the positions held by Friedman as well as the ones of his opponents. After all, Friedman is one of a very small number of economists who imposed their own way of setting the terms of the debate at that time. Regarding Keynes, what is striking is that the debate as it was not only accepted but also framed by his major heirs, the leading Keynesians of the 'neo-classical synthesis', is wide of the mark from his initial policy guidelines. This is all the more surprising if one remembers the short period of time between the 'macro-economic revolution' held by Keynes and the first Keynesian policies launched in the post-war era.

'Rules versus authorities'

If we go back even further to the 1930s, it might be fruitful to remind ourselves that the debate at that time was framed in terms of 'rules versus authorities'.[8] When he advocates rules instead of authorities in monetary policy, Simons (1936) aims to provide a competitive framework thanks to which economic agents would be confident in the self-adjusting capacity of the economy. In his own words: "The liberal creed demands the organization of our economic life largely through individual participation in a game with definite rules" (Simons 1936, p. 1). Thanks to simple rules, uncertainty related to the day-to-day actions of monetary authorities but also to private banks' behaviour would be erased. The point is that "an enterprise system cannot function effectively in the face of extreme uncertainty as to the action of monetary authorities, or ... as to monetary legislation" (Simons 1936, p. 3). Hence, Simons calls for a 100 per cent reserve basis for demand deposits and the fixity of money (currency plus demand deposits). The peculiar rule he advocates is justified by the following basic concern: "To put our problem as a paradox – we need to design and establish with the greatest intelligence a monetary system good enough so that, hereafter, we may hold to it unrationally – on faith – as a religion if you please" (Simons 1936, p. 14).

To put it in a nutshell: if the debate is framed in terms of 'rules versus authorities' as these two terms were understood in the 1930s, it can be shown that Keynes takes a stand for authorities whereas Simons and Friedman take sides for rules, although the latter part company on the precise rule to follow. Hence, coming back to Simons' plea sheds a new light on Keynes' and Friedman's respective advocacies, but it also calls into question contemporary quarrels.

Let us start with Keynes. According to Friedman (1967b) himself, Keynes shares with Simons a common interpretation of the 1929 episode – an interpretation utterly rejected by Friedman. In short, for both of Simons and Keynes the Great Depression rose in spite of monetary authorities' intervention and not because of it. The common lesson they draw from this dramatic episode is that the financial side of the economy threatens the stability of the system. Yet, Simons and Keynes part company on the issue of the proper reform to implement, and in particular on the ability of public authorities to behave efficiently. While Simons calls for a large financial reform, which means coming back to the competitive order of the ancient times,[9] Keynes' Middle Way doctrine relies on the ability of public authorities to dampen market failures. While Simons is a radical liberal who calls for a return to the old laissez-faire system, Keynes stands as a liberal reformer who prefers to adapt our institutional system to modern times. Ultimately, while the type of 'rules' Simons calls for can be defined as "a legally, even constitutionally, binding constraint on the conduct of monetary policy" (Laidler 2010c, p. 124) Keynes definitely takes sides with 'authorities', understood as public authorities endowed with superior knowledge that are accordingly able both to escape harmful conventions with regard to the remote future and to convince accordingly private actors to follow suit.

Let us turn to Friedman. Above all, Friedman shares with Simons a basic distrust towards collective rationality. For both of them a public body, namely an authority, is in no way able to solve market failures. That is the reason why for both of them monetary rule "requires little or no judgment in its administration; it defines a policy in terms of means, not merely in terms of ends" (Simons 1936, p. 5). On this issue of collective body efficiency, both Simons and Friedman take sides against Keynes. Undoubtedly, the type of rules Friedman calls for corresponds to Simons' overall advocacy.

It is on the issue of the proper reform to implement that Simons and Friedman part company. More precisely, Friedman's position turns out to be symmetrical to Simons'. In particular, according to Simons the price-level rule is easier to implement in the short run while constant money supply is considered more easily achievable in a long-run perspective. The financial reform Simons calls for is merely considered by Friedman as false and irrelevant. Decades after Simons' epoch, Friedman views Smith's doctrine as relevant as ever, especially because of the tendency of the day toward an 'overgoverned society': "as Smith stressed, improvements have come in spite, not because, of governmental intrusion into the market place" (Friedman 1977b, p. 8). In particular, the variety and the diversity offered by financial markets are essential for a market economy to function well. In short, in Friedman's framework the financial and the monetary sides of the economy should be treated as disconnected.

Regarding the theoretical underpinnings of their respective standpoints, it is noticeable that in a way none of the three authors would consider expectations as exogenous and that none of them would have ignored the consequences of such or such a policy scheme on private actors' expectations. The three of them are concerned with uncertainty, yet they deal with it to different degrees and in different manners. Simons aims to forestall problems inherent to the day-day decisions of authorities that do nothing but muddy the waters. The uncertainty he is concerned with is the uncertainty about public bodies' interferences within a laissez-faire economy. As for Keynes, his policy guidelines aim to dampen the uncertainty faced by private individuals with regard to the 'states of the world'; he proves highly confident in the ability of public bodies to achieve this fundamental goal. Finally Friedman shares Simons' concern for the stabilisation of short-term nominal expectations. But he goes further and also relies on an uncertainty-model argument: civil servants and bureaucrats do not know the structure of the economy better than private agents. Friedman would not deny market failures as a matter of principle; rather, what he claims is that state failures are likely to make matters worse.

Ultimately, what is at stake between these three authors in the 'rules versus authorities' debate is the confidence that economic agents can place in the ability of collective bodies to behave efficiently. Framed that way, the issue remains as unsettled as ever.

The economic policy in times of crisis

In the final analysis, few crucial lessons are to be learnt from Keynes and Friedman regarding the critical issue set today of the economic policy in times of crisis. First and foremost, the main lesson to be drawn from them is that an abstentionist viewpoint is untenable and that *something* has to be done. Besides, relying on mere nominal rigidities and in particular on staggered prices might not be a very promising avenue of research to understand what is happening now. Regarding the theoretical principles on which our appraisal of the functioning of a monetary economy is based, both authors would compel us to take the issue of the expectations formation seriously: can we really conflate long-term expectations with the short-term ones? Can we safely assume that private actors possess full knowledge regarding the structure of the economy in a remote future? And even in the short run, can we consider that individuals adapt instantaneously their inflationary expectations to a new policy regime?

The main lessons that we should learn from Keynes for the economic policy in times of crisis are twofold. First and foremost, in the case of a protracted slump it is an imperative that public authorities take measures with the view to falsify private actors' pessimistic long-term expectations. A progressive and gradual wage-cuts policy that is each time accompanied by further cuts would not help, quite the contrary because it sets into motion deflationary spirals. Keynes even speaks of "the unemployment inflicted by deflation" (Keynes 1935, CW 21, p. 360). With regard to the safety and soundness of public finance, this means that "the boom, not the slump, is the right time for austerity at the Treasury" (Keynes 1937, CW 21, p. 390). Undoubtedly, restrictive public budgets, which do nothing but exacerbate the deflationary pressures, are the opposite of what has to be done: how can private actors be encouraged to reverse their long-term real pessimistic expectations while policy-makers' forecasts are based precisely on a similar pessimistic scenario? The provocative tone of Keynes' claim set aside, this may be the perfect time to consider the following quotation:

> Unfortunately the more pessimistic the Chancellor's policy, the more likely it is that pessimistic anticipations will be realised and *vice versa*. Whatever the Chancellor dreams, will come true! We must begin by resuscitating the national income and the national output.
>
> (Keynes 1933, CW 21, p. 184)[10]

Crucially, such a statement applies even more at the international level. We know well that free-rider options activated by governments during the 1930s, such as the huge rise in trade tariffs, seriously aggravated the recession at work at that time. In our view, the accuracy of Keynes' following claim is all the more striking with regard to our contemporary debates, especially in the European Union: "Competitive wage reductions, competitive tariffs, competitive liquidation of foreign assets, competitive currency deflations, competitive economy campaigns, competitive contractions of new developments – all are of this beggar-my-neighbour description" (Keynes 1933, CW 21, p. 53).

In times of deep recession, when it is acknowledged that "we suffered shocks larger than what almost anyone thought was within the realm of reasonable possibility" (Romer 2011, p. 2), it is all the more probable that monetary loosening will not help. The huge amount of 'liquidities' stockpiled by both private wealth owners and banks is evidence for such a diagnosis. Regarding fiscal policy, Keynes' 'pump-priming' option suggests at the practical policy level that we should be much more concerned with the type of fiscal devices that consist in investment-boosting programmes (i.e. the stimulation of the demand for long-lived goods) rather than devices that target consumption (which are short-lived).

Taking a longer-term perspective, the second lesson we may learn from Keynes is that a deep crisis of capitalism is an opportunity to reshape our current institutional setting, to establish new coordination bodies and to provide new stabilisation mechanisms for our decentralised market economies, which have become at the same time financialised and deeply embedded in global exchanges. Keynes 'new liberalism' means the dissemination of knowledge, a growing responsibility in the implementation of long-term capital schemes (as well as in their funding), and above all continuity and steadfastness in the commitments made. Besides, this means also the playing against market convention, the urge to help private agents escape conventions that prove harmful at the collective level and the attempt to take 'unconventional' positions in the markets. Regarding the monetary and financial sides of the economies we currently live in, this may mean a far-reaching reform in our financial arrangements to preserve the functioning of the real side of the economies, thanks to the regulation of the banking system (and especially of what is called 'shadow banking'), the fight against speculation (in the property market, the commodities market as well as the sovereign debt market, to take a few examples) and more generally the forestalling of harmful conventions through a growing responsibility of public but also semi-public bodies (such as semi-private investment funds) in those markets. Regarding the real side of the economy, Keynes' 'new liberalism' invites us for example to design new forms of cooperation between centralised authorities and private actors through public-private partnerships concerned with the implementation of big infrastructure projects, which have the crucial advantage to boost competitiveness while being highly profitable in the long run, even if such schemes imply in the short run an increasing of both private and public indebtedness.

As is the case for Keynes, the lessons we may remember from Friedman's writings apply too to the issue of institutions and information. But in sharp contrast with Keynes, Friedman's bequest is a plea for lowliness. While Keynes insists on the inescapable inter-temporal market failures that a monetary economy endures, Friedman is first and foremost concerned with the coordination troubles that might rise between public authorities and the private sector. Friedman reminds us that we know rather little regarding the 'true' structure of the economy and how precisely an external shock spreads in the economic system through the complex interactions it raises between the real and the monetary sides of the system. For him, better no public institutions at all than collective bodies that behave erratically, take ill-timed measures and that finally come to unfortunately mix up the free adjustment responses to a disturbance (usually small and not so harmful) of the economic system, a system which is supposed to possess inherently strong but not necessarily monotonic spring forces, with the initial shock itself. For those economists who in our turbulent times wish to design a new institutional setting able to cope with uncertainty and for those policy-makers who come to believe that they should be able to overcome market failures, the reminder is ruthless.

6.3 Where to draw the line?

Ultimately, where to draw the line between laissez-faire and planning? Hayek sets the issue in his bestselling *Road to Serfdom* (1944). The commonly accepted lesson that remained from Hayek's pamphlet is this: "the guiding principle that the policy of freedom for the individual is the only truly progressive policy, remains as true to-day as it was in the nineteenth century" (Hayek 1944, p. 178). It appears that the socialisation of a liberal society, the rise of the 'welfare state' and the growing interferences of State intervention in markets has undermined this "guiding principle". And Hayek considers that "if we are to build a better world we must have the courage to make a new start – even if that means some *reculer pour mieux sauter*" (Hayek 1944, p. 177). Indeed, if this proves true, this means the unravelling of the whole 'Middle Way' doctrine erected by Keynes.

Yet, a careful reading of the *Road to Serfdom* shows that Hayek himself takes a nuanced view on the 'laissez-faire versus planning' issue. Let us see how Hayek grasps this alternative. On the one hand, regarding the principles of liberalism Hayek acknowledges that there is no "hard-and-fast rules fixed once and for all" (Hayek 1944, p. 13) but rather "a fundamental principle that in the ordering of our affairs we should make as much use as possible of the spontaneous forces of society, and resort as little as possible to coercion (Hayek 1944, p. 13). It immediately ensues that:

> There is, in particular, all the difference between deliberately *creating* a system within which competition will work as beneficially as possible, and *passively accepting* institutions as they are. Probably nothing has done so much harm to the liberal cause as the wooden insistence of some liberals on certain rough rules of thumb, above all the principle of *laissez-faire*.
>
> (Hayek 1944, p. 13; emphasis added)

Noticeably, Keynes would not argue otherwise. On the other hand, Hayek defines planning as the "central direction and organisation of all our activities according to some consciously constructed 'blueprint'" (Hayek 1944, p. 26). And he adds: "it is important not to confuse opposition against this kind of planning with a dogmatic laissez-faire attitude" (Hayek 1944, p. 27).

As a matter of fact, the concessions made in the direction of planning, i.e. the departures from laissez-faire made by Hayek leads him too to support a 'middle course' option. The "control of prices, the limitation of working hours as well as an extensive system of social services" (Hayek 1944, p. 28) would not impede the general principles of competition so dear to Hayek. Even on the issue of unemployment, the position he holds is not clear-cut. Let us quote his claim extensively, which is quite subtle:

> There is, finally, *the supremely important problem of combatting general fluctuations of economic activity* and the recurrent waves of large-scale unemployment which accompany them. This is, of course, one of the gravest and most pressing problems of our times. But, though *its solution will require much planning in the good sense*, it does not – or at least need not – require that special kind of planning which according to its advocates is to replace the market. Many economists hope indeed that the ultimate remedy may be found in the field of monetary policy, which would involve nothing incompatible even with nineteenth-century liberalism. Others, it is true, believe that real success can be expected only from the skilful timing of public works undertaken on a very large scale. This might lead to much more serious restrictions of the competitive sphere, and *in experimenting in this direction we shall have carefully to watch our step* if we are to avoid making all economic activity progressively more dependent on the direction and volume of government expenditures.
>
> (Hayek 1944, pp. 90–1; emphasis added)

Again, what Hayek denounces here is the abuse from those who would stick to the *extreme* position of planning.[11] He appears as conceding that the line between laissez-faire and planning has to be drawn somewhere. Most strikingly, the type of concessions he acknowledges significatively echoes Keynes' plea.

In summary terms, what the young Hayek denounces in 1944 with the use of the term 'planning' is collectivism and centralism while he readily acknowledges that his liberalism does not amount to an uncritical adherence to the laissez-faire doctrine.

On his journey to Bretton Woods, Keynes came to comment on Hayek's pamphlet. Keynes argued that "morally and philosophically, I find myself in agreement with virtually the whole of it" (Keynes 1944, CW 27, p. 385). If it is kept in mind that for Keynes planning means "not planning in the sense of fully centralised activity, but in the looser sense of central supervision and control of otherwise freely interacting units" (O'Donnell 1989, p. 311), such an appraisal on the part of Keynes is actually no surprise. But the letter continues:

> I come finally to my only serious criticism. You admit here that it is a question of knowing where to draw the line. You agree that the line has to be

drawn somewhere, and that *the logical extreme is not possible.* But you give us no guidance whatever as to where to draw it. In a sense this is shirking the practical issue. It is true that you and I would probably draw it in different places. I should guess that according to my ideas *you greatly under-estimate the practicability of the middle course.* But as soon as you admit that the extreme is not possible, and that a line has to be drawn, you are, on your own argument, done for, since you are trying to persuade us that so soon as one moves an inch in the planned direction you are necessarily launched on the slippery path which leads you in due course over the precipice.

(Keynes 1944, CW 7, pp. 386–7; emphasis added)

As a matter of principle, but only from the perspective of abstract principles, "it is game, set and match to Keynes" (Skidelsky 2000, p. 285): the line has to be drawn somewhere. But Keynes's position too is a moral position. In a very practical sense Keynes, either, is not able to draw the line 'here' rather than 'there'. Indeed, his letter concludes with the following sentences:

I accuse you of perhaps confusing a little bit the moral and the material issues. Dangerous acts can be done safely in a community which thinks and feel rightly, which would be the way to hell if they were executed by those who think and feel wrongly.

(Keynes 1944, CW 27, p. 386)

Ultimately, here is to be found the moral position at the root of Keynes' 'Middle Way' doctrine as well as his confidence towards collective bodies to behave wisely, namely his elitism (Carabelli and De Vecchi 1999). From Keynes' perspective, "the reformer is not he who would impose his own values on society, but he who understands better than others the potential for change in the moral conventions of society itself, and acts in order to effect such change" (Carabelli and De Vecchi 1999, p. 291). As for Hayek, he would never have accepted such an assumption of a well-oriented community endowed with superior knowledge.

Friedman makes no mistake when he evaluates Keynes' political legacy in his 1997 paper simply entitled "John Maynard Keynes". While explicit quotations of Keynes' texts are rather rare on his part, Friedman explicitly refers in this paper to the letter Keynes addressed to Hayek in 1944 about the *Road to Serfdom* and comments on his lengthy quotation:

Keynes was exceedingly effective in persuading a broad group – economists, policymakers, government officials, and interested citizens – of the two concepts implicit in his letter to Hayek: first, the public interest concept of government; second, the benevolent dictatorship concept that all will be well if only good men are in power.

(Friedman 1997, p. 20)

From Friedman's standpoint, Keynes' position is barely acceptable: in the political market as well as in the economic market, power should be as dispersed as materially feasible: "the task, that is, is to do for the political market what Adam Smith so largely did for the economic market" (Friedman 1997, p. 97).

What about Friedman's own way of dealing with the 'laissez-faire versus planning' issue? Aside from a fundamental exception, Friedman's position is rather doctrinaire: he is a tireless advocate for the old principles of laissez-faire and he would not concede as much as Hayek did to Keynes in 1944 regarding social security, for example. But things are different regarding monetary affairs. Contrary to the late Hayek, Friedman does not call for free banking. Money is the very serious affair where State interference in the free functioning of a market economy is an absolute necessity and about which Friedman consistently urges for a reform of our institutional setting:

> Friedman's original attitude to this question was that a stable monetary framework is simply a necessary condition for the market system to function (and hence to gain the benefits of free markets in other areas), but that it is unlikely that the market itself would generate such a framework.
>
> (Smithin 2003, p. 54)

Here is to be found the only yielding Friedman concedes in the direction of planning. This being said, even in the field of monetary policy Friedman readily acknowledges that the reform he calls for is a radical one (Friedman [1984] 1987). Here again, he can hardly be considered as a partisan of the middle course and he seldom accepts adapting his programme to circumstances. Does this mean that Friedman's policy guidelines turn out to be a *petitio principii*? Precisely, his 1984 paper dedicated to the "Monetary Policy for the 80s" seems to offer us a clue to understand the radicalism that permeates Friedman's overall policy philosophy:

> ... it is worth discussing radical changes, not in the expectation that they will be adopted promptly but for two other reasons. One is to construct an ideal goal, so that incremental changes can be judged by whether they move the institutional structure towards or away from that ideal.
>
> The other reason is very different. It is so that if a crisis requiring or facilitating radical changes does arise, alternatives will be available that have been carefully developed and fully explored.
>
> (Friedman [1984] 1987, p. 424)

The second reason advanced for offering radical schemes prevents Friedman from the basic defect involved in a *petitio principii* whereas the first one reveals the true nature of his policy guidelines: to provide at the abstract level a single design reference point from which our present departure can be assessed. In sharp contrast with Keynes, Friedman is barely interested in the "practicality of the middle course" (Keynes 1944, CW 27, p. 386). He is much more concerned with the evolution of our society: are we following the right path? After all, the attempt to draw the line is not that simple.

Notes

2 Keeping the Keynesians off-stage

1 During World War II, Friedman was involved in debates within the US Congress and the Treasury. In his 1942 statement before the House Ways and Means Committee, he argues that "inflation ... must be neutralised by measures that restrict consumer spending. Taxation is the most important of those measures". Looking back on this episode of his career, Friedman points out: "The most striking feature of this statement is thoroughly Keynesian ... Until I reread my statement to Congress in preparing this account, I had completely forgotten how thoroughly Keynesian I then was. I was apparently cured, some would say corrupted shortly after the end of the war" (Friedman and Friedman 1998, pp. 112–13).

2 Hirsch and de Marchi's (1990) study is complementary to ours, in that their study of Friedman's views toward Keynes and the Keynesians focuses on this issue but from a methodological standpoint.

3 The full statement is: "inflation is always and everywhere a monetary phenomenon in the sense that it is and can be produced only by a more rapid increase in the quantity of money than in output" (Friedman 1970a, p. 16).

4 Again, we do not aim here at an exhaustive review of Friedman's paper during the 1940s and 1950s. On this issue, see Chapter 9 of Hirsch and de Marchi (1990).

5 For Friedman, functional finance is defined as "the principle of ... judging fiscal measures only by their effects or the way they function in society" (Lerner 1944, p. 302 n.; quoted in Friedman [1947] 1953a, p. 313). That is,

> under the rules of functional finance, decisions about the deficit and the money supply would be made with regard to their functionality – their effect on the economy – and not with regard to some abstract moralistic premise that deficits, debt and expansionary monetary policy are inherently bad
>
> (Colander 2008, p. 515)

As we will see in Chapter 4, Friedman's latter critiques towards fiscal policy go beyond an 'internal' critique (i.e. in terms of delays, lack of information and pro-cyclicity of fiscal measures) and involve moral principles.

6 Here Keynes has a particular concern for the available statistics on the level of profits.

7 Instead, as we will see in Chapter 4, Keynes favours long-term plans.

8 To take but one example, in a book called *The Legacy of Keynes and Friedman* Frazer (1994) didn't hesitate to present the crudest version of the 45-degree diagram as Keynes' basic model. Without a careful reading of Keynes' writings, such an exercise proves futile.

9 This is also the view held by Hirsch and de Marchi (1990).

10 In Keynes' own words:

> Economics is a science of thinking in terms of models joined to the art of choosing models which are relevant to the contemporary world. It is compelled to be this, because, unlike the typical natural science, the material to which it is applied is, in too many respects, not homogenous through time.... In the second place, as against Robbins, economics is essentially a moral science and not a natural science. That is to say, it employs introspection and judgements of value.
>
> (Keynes 1938, CW 14, pp. 296–7)

11 On this issue, see Leijonhufvud (1998).
12 On Keynes' and Friedman's similar critical views on econometrics, see Leeson (1998a).
13

> The curve was asserted by many Keynesians to be stable over time and to specify a menu of combination of inflation and unemployment, any of which was attainable by the appropriate monetary and fiscal policy.
>
> (Friedman 1997, p. 4).

14 This unfortunate interpretation is due to Leijonhufvud (1968a), a claim that this commentator would deny later on in his 1974 paper.
15 Phelps (1967) is well known to have formulated the 'expectations critique' of the Phillips curve in a way similar to Friedman's. Here, Phelps' contribution is left aside.
16 It should be already noticed that "two mutually inconsistent sketches of the theoretical underpinnings of the curve in question [i.e. the Phillips curve] were in fact present in Friedman's (1968) paper" (Laidler 2012, p. 20). The first interpretation is in terms of *disequilibrium* in that wages prices react to actual quantity disequilibrium in both the labour and the good markets. The second interpretation combines an *equilibrium* approach with the hypothesis of less-than-perfect information: the labour force reacts to the misperceived increase in real wage and increases its supply of labour. Friedman will later disregard the first line of interpretation as he will stick to the second one, as he does in his Nobel lecture (1977a). As we will see in chapters 4 and 5, this rationale of the Phillips curve reflects a highly contrasted dynamics between wages and employment with regard to Keynes'.
17 These possible complications are the following:

> (1) Effective demand will not change in exact proportion to the quantity of money. (2) Since resources are not homogenous, there will be diminishing, and not constant, returns as employment gradually increases. (3) Since resources are not interchangeable, some commodities will reach a condition of inelastic supply whilst there are still unemployed resources available for the production of other commodities. (4) The wage-unit will tend to rise, before full employment has been reached. (5) The remunerations of the factors entering into marginal cost will not all change in the same proportion.
>
> (Keynes 1936, CW 7, p. 296).

18 As shown by Carabelli and Cedrini (2011a), here is to be found a critical application of Keynes' general attempt to cope with the complexity of the material faced by the economist:

> Keynes has accustomed his readers to interpret the ensemble of the 'simplifying assumptions' introduced from time to time in the course of the analysis as the first logical step of a more complicated work, requiring the economist to remove them and allow for probable repercussions.
>
> (Carabelli and Cedrini 2011a, p. 24)

That is: in a preliminary step, the researcher makes use of Marshall's *ceteris paribus* condition; he considers causal analyses as well as independence relations in a highly classical fashion. But in a second and critical step, one will remove those simplifying assumptions: one will take into account complicating factors, roundabout repercussions or discontinuities.

19 However, as we will see the stability of money wages, their rigidity, is for Keynes a critical condition for the stability of the economic system:

> If competition between unemployed workers always led to a very great reduction of the money-wage, there would be a violent instability in the price-level. Moreover, there might be no position of stable equilibrium except in conditions consistent with full employment; since the wage-unit might have to fall without limit until it reached a point where the effect of the abundance of money in terms of the wage-unit on the rate of interest was sufficient to restore a level of full employment. At no other point could there be a resting place.
>
> (Keynes 1936, CW 7, p. 253)

20

> Except in a socialised community where wage-policy is settled by decree, there is no means of securing uniform wage reductions for every class of labour. The result can only be brought about by a series of gradual, irregular changes, justifiable on no criterion of social justice or economic expedience.
>
> (Keynes 1936, CW 7, p. 267)

21 Or, again in 1939 in *How to Pay for the War*:

> But I repeat that this does not mean we are still in the age of plenty. It means that the age of scarcity has arrived *before* the whole of the available labour has been absorbed. I am not saying that our output cannot be increased beyond its present level. Surely it can and must be so increased as our organisation improves. But we are already making all we know how. We have to learn how to make more; and that takes time.
>
> (Keynes 1940, CW 9, p. 385)

22 For an overall review of those debates until the end of the 1970s, see Santomero and Seater (1978).
23 Leeson (1997a) draws anew Phillips' diagram from his data. For the period 1913–48 the data are dispersed, so that the data hardly fit in the curve. For the 1948–57 period, the curve is vertical, implying almost no relationship.
24 Leeson (1997a) helps us to take this reasoning one step further in that he shows that, as a "profound irony" (Leeson 1997a, p. 166), Friedman was deeply influenced by Phillips in his achievement of his own 'expectations critique'. In a private letter to Leeson, Friedman remembers:

> I recall sitting on a bench somewhere in London ... and talking with him [Phillips] about the problem of hyperinflation ... The reason I remember that meeting so clearly is that I recall discussing with Phillips the question of how to approximate expectations about future inflation and his writings on the back of an envelope the basic equation underlying adaptive expectations, i.e. what is equation (5) on page 37 of *Studies in the Quantity Theory of Money*, or, in more general form, equation (1) on page 316 of Phillips' 1954 article in the *Economic Journal*.
>
> (Correspondence dated 25 August 1993, quoted in Leeson 1997a, p. 166)

25 Even Solow (1968, 1969), whose econometrics contradicts Friedman in showing that the inflation-unemployment trade-off does not evaporate in the long run, drew no lesson from his results as a basis of policy. References are made to Lerner's (1960), Haberler's (1960) and Bronfenbrenner's (1963), the three of them being highly concerned with inflation. Forder (2010a, p. 338) also notices that Reuber's (1964) work was not quite influential at that time, so that the sophisticated indifference curves apparatus offering choice set to policy-makers should not be taken too seriously.
26 Yet, Dimand's (1988) investigation shows that the transition between Keynes I and Keynes II at the beginning of the 1930s should not be viewed as a clean break but rather as an evolution.

3 Private, public and semi-public institutions

1 As acknowledged by O'Donnell (1989), as early as his 1904 paper Keynes strongly criticised Burke for his support of laissez-faire and minimum State intervention:

> This is a line of argument of which Burke is overfond and which leads him into more than a fallacious position. Without being very clear what he meant by 'natural', he believed, as others have believed that any process to which that adjective was applicable must be the best and the most desirable.
>
> (Keynes 1904, quoted by O'Donnell 1989, p. 279)

2 This is not to deny, however, the 'shift of paradigm' – to borrow Kuhnian terminology – that was necessary to explain the Great Depression.

3 As an outcome of the discussion above, one might consider that imperfect competition should be embedded from the outset in any analysis of market functioning. This will have dramatic consequences for our inquiry on Keynes' and Friedman's views on the functioning of a monetary economy, and especially of what Friedman calls the 'transmission mechanism'. On this issue, see section 3 of Chapter 5.

4 To say it quite plainly, Keynes is not the forerunner of the Akerlof and Shiller (2009) bestseller dedicated to animal spirits.

5 This is one of the most fundamental issues that we will deal with in Chapter 5.

6 The issue of the confidence we can place in our expectations in case of uncertainty is twofold: there is first the distrust in our own capacity to formulate probable judgements in the case of the precautionary motive, and much more importantly distrust in the conventional valuation operated by the market in the case of the speculative motive. On this issue, see Rivot (2013).

7 As shown by Carabelli and Cendrini, this issue is closely connected to Keynes' anti-utilitarian approach to the concept of happiness, the latter being far from reducible to pleasure in Keynes' vision both of the society and of the individual. In their words:

> Keynes regards sound economic thinking as the necessary condition to produce that era of abundance which will promote the moral renaissance of men, but believes that laissez-faire must be abandoned when it causes men to sacrifice other values unnecessarily, despite the possibilities offered by economic progress, and rejects utilitarianism on this same basis.
>
> (Carabelli and Cedrini 2011b, p. 343)

8 The Marxian terminology disentangles 'formal freedom' from 'real freedom'. In a world of scarcity within which efficiency (i.e. full employment of all the factors of production) is not guaranteed, the matter at hand does not merely consist in restoring individuals in their freedom 'to do something' but more fundamentally to enforce their capability 'to do something'. As we will see below, such a 'Marxian bias', so to say, in Keynes' line of reasoning is unacceptable for Friedman.

9 Friedman's starting point is the crucial roles played by prices in a free society organised through voluntary exchange: "they transmit information, they provide an incentive to users of resources to be guided by this information, and they provide an incentive to owners of resources to follow this information" (Friedman [1962b] 2007, p. 10). The two last functions can be easily lumped together; what actually Friedman later did after his textbook *Price Theory* (1962b). Because of their ignorance of tastes, resources availability, and so on, State authorities would never be able to replace this fundamental role played by prices. Closely examined, the second role of prices as incentives to buyers and sellers, to employers and employees, and so on acknowledged by Friedman is puzzling. As noticed by Gordon (1982) in his comment on *Free to Choose* (Friedman and Friedman 1979), one should properly speak of *profit* here – a term not so used by the Friedmans in their book. More generally, it is the opportunity to get a *surplus* obtained through voluntary exchange

and not prices that led individuals to act according to the information they get thanks to price devices.

10 Again, here one should properly speak of the sharing of the surplus instead of prices.

11 His detestation for redistributive policies, which appear in a direct conflict with these two fundamental goals in a free society, must be understood with regard to his concern for 'equality'. In *Free to Choose* (1979), three types of equality are discussed: first the equality before God considered by the founding fathers of the USA that was understood as 'personal equality'; second the equality of opportunity considered as a strict equivalent for 'free market capitalism'; and last our contemporary understanding of income equality. Friedman unambiguously takes the side of the first type of equality, which refers to 'formal freedom' in the sense of Marx's terminology. Friedman claims that our concern for equality of outcome, in other words our concern for an egalitarian society, was alien for Jefferson and the first liberals in the USA at that time. But Friedman's call for a return to equality as the latter was understood by the founding fathers of the USA is quite controversial. Rosanvallon (2011) for example would reject such a contention. Indeed, Rosanvallon holds on the contrary that, at Jefferson's time, equality was precisely conceived first and foremost as an equality of income: "most of the Americans were thus living in a 'society of confidence', roughly homogenous, under strong social pressure, and in such a context the idea of freedom was not disconnected from a vigorous egalitarian feeling" (Rosanvallon 2011, p. 53). Jefferson himself was a strong advocator for high fossilisation of inheritance to prevent reproduction of inequalities and the gradual creation of a cast system (Rosanvallon 2011, p. 243).

12 For example, while using the Marshallian supply and demand framework Friedman and Kuznets (1945) show that the occupational choice can be explained through market mechanisms: the income differences between occupations are the results of interactions between free optimising individuals. As another example, Friedman and Savage (1948) reconcile gambling with the traditional expected-utility hypothesis by considering a utility-function that is alternatively convex and concave. Combining these two developments, Friedman (1953b) argues in his paper entitled "Choice, Chance, and the Personal Distribution of Income" that "one cannot rule out the possibility that a large part of the existing inequality of wealth can be regarded as produced by men to satisfy their tastes and preferences" (Friedman [1953b] 1962b, p. 277).

13 The first metaphor is about the leaves of a tree growing 'as if' they were maximising the quantity of light received and the second one is about the billiard player who "made his shots *as if* he knew the complicated mathematical formulas that could give the optimum directions of travel, could estimate accurately by eye the angles, etc." (Friedman 1953c, p. 21).

14 In this study, Keynes' views on the role of the State in the fields of the arts as well as of international arrangements are left aside. For an overview on these subjects, see Skidelsky (2000) and Dostaler (2005).

15 See also Keynes, "A Programme for Unemployment" (1933), CW 21, pp. 154–61.

16 A long time before Keynes argued that "in many cases the ideal size for the unit of control and organisation is between the individual and the modern State" (Keynes 1926, CW 9, p. 288).

17 At the end of his career, Keynes takes sides with the Labour Party to call for the nationalisation of the Bank of England. And he will become the first director of the nationalised institution.

18 For example in 1981 he argued about externalities that "*In principle, nonetheless, we cannot deny that there is a case for that kind of intervention*" (Friedman [1981] 1987, p. 32; emphasis added). But this kind of statement is very rare on the part of Friedman.

19 In his manner of dealing with externalities, Friedman's empirical stance strikingly

echoes Coase's way of answering the interventionist wing of economists. While Coase (1974) takes pains to carry out an empirical study of lighthouses in the Great Britain of the nineteenth century to show that the so-called public goods were actually dealt with privately, the Friedman of *Capitalism and Freedom* (1962a) gives both the examples of roads and national parks to make his point. To support his denial of State intervention to mitigate externalities, Friedman could have easily relied on the Coase theorem as formulated by Stigler (1966) in reference to Coase (1960). To put it in a nutshell: if transaction costs (that is, costs of coordination between agents) are nil and if property rights are well defined, the economic allocation obtained through voluntary bargaining will be efficient even if at first sight externalities exist. But if one follows Friedman's own complain that "one should either compare the real with the real or the ideal with the ideal" (Friedman 1977b, p. 10), what is the relevance of the zero transaction hypothesis in our real world? Actually, Friedman is well aware of Coase's work even though he never refers explicitly to it. About the famous dinner when Coase was invited by Director (Friedman's brother-in-law) to discuss his paper on radio frequency, Stigler remembered:

> Friedman did most of the talking, as usual. He did also most of the thinking, as usual. In the course of two hours of argument, the vote went for twenty against and one for Coase to twenty-one for Coase. What an exhilarating event! I lamented afterward that we had not had the clairvoyance to tape it.
>
> (Stigler 1988, p. 76)

To the best of our knowledge, the only occasion on which Friedman indirectly refers to Coase is in his "Adam Smith's Relevance for Today" (1977b) in which he refers to "external effects (equivalent, as the recent literature has made clear, to transaction costs)" (Friedman 1977b, p. 10). But this comes as no surprise. Indeed, Coase's line of reasoning (i.e. to internalise those externalities through the setting of markets instead of Pigou's case for taxes and subsidies) would be far too dangerous for Friedman's standpoint since it opens the door for State invasiveness in the free play of unfettered markets. Friedman cannot accept this new duty for the State in our modern economies through the set-up of new markets. To preserve the internal consistency of his overall policy guidelines, it might be less risky to remind us that trying to solve externalities raises new externalities. On the 'Coasian syllogism' (i.e. if transaction costs were zero, we wouldn't need institutions, contracts as well as firms) and for an interpretation of Coase theorem as an impossibility theorem, see Ferey (2008), Chapter 1.

20 That is why it can be rightly stated that "Smith's conception [of the role of the government] often went beyond modern views" (Backhouse and Medema 2008, p. 850). Backhouse and Medema remind us of Smith's "support for education", "a standing army rather than a militia", "the stultifying effects of the division of labour", "regulations dealing with public hygiene, legal ceilings on interest rates", "light duties on imports of manufactured goods, the mandating of quality certifications on linen and plate, certain banking and currency regulations", "the discouragement of the spread of drinking establishments through taxes on liquor", and last but not least "regulations that restricted wages in the interests of the labourer ... on the ground that these redressed the imbalance between worker and employer" (Backhouse and Medema 2008, p. 850).

21 Regarding sympathy, "the principle of sympathy dominated all other human passions; this is the ability of men to share in some degree the sentiments of other people, a fellow-feeling, which provides the cement for every society" (Vaggi and Groenewegen 2003, p. 105). And regarding the second concept, "the impartial spectator is a metaphor Smith used to enlighten what he saw as an ideal rule in the behaviour of the individual in society" (Vaggi and Groenewegen 2003, p. 105).

22 See "The Case for the Negative Income Tax" (1968b).

23 By the way, it can be noticed that a way found by companies to escape this tax is precisely to undertake 'social responsibility' activities that allow for deductibility.

> The direction in which policy is now moving, of permitting corporations to make contributions for charitable purposes and allow for deduction for income tax, is a step in the direction of creating a true divorce between ownership and control and of undermining the basic nature and character of our society. It is a step from an individualistic society and toward the corporate state.
>
> (Friedman 1962a, pp. 135–6)

24

> Our own conclusion – like that of Walter Bagehot and Vera Smith – is that leaving monetary and banking arrangements to the market would have produced a more satisfactory outcome than was actually achieved through governmental involvement. Nevertheless, we also believe that the same forces that prevented that outcome in the past will continue to prevent it in the future.
>
> (Friedman and Schwartz 1986, p. 59)

25 In his vitriolic "The Business Community's Suicidal Impulse" (1999) paper, Friedman argued:

> When I started in this business, as a believer of competition, I was a great supporter of antitrust laws; I thought enforcing them was one of the few desirable things that the government could do to promote more competition. But as I watched what actually happened, I saw that, instead of promoting competition, antitrust laws tended to do exactly the opposite, because they tended, like so many government activities, to be taken over by the people they were supposed to regulate and control. And so over time I have gradually come to the conclusion that we would be better off if we didn't have them at all, if we could get rid of them. But we *do* have them.
>
> (Friedman 1999, p. 7)

26 See for example Cole and Ohanian (1999) for detailed figures.
27 As underlined by Gazier, it is now considered as worthwhile to compare the 1929–39 depression with the 'Other Depression' – to borrow the expression of Breton *et al.* (1997) – that occurred in 1873–95. Yet, "more than twenty years of persistent sluggishness in the economy, punctuated with bankruptcies and crashes in Europe and in the United States, did not however question the existence of the Gold Standard" (Gazier 2011, pp. 92–3).
28 In the interview given to Snowdon and Vane, Friedman acknowledged that the Great Depression left a strong impression on him, leading him to study economics: "What was the important problem [in 1932]? It was obviously economics and so there was never any hesitation on my part to study economics" (Friedman's interview in Snowdon and Vane 1999, p. 125).
29 Actually, the Fed was not so much influenced by Hayek and Robbins but by the 'liquidationists' such as Miller, an explicit holder of the 'real bills' doctrine. On this issue, see White (2008).
30 In particular, Hayek's (1929) monetary norm means a constant monetary income. In short, the monetary side of the economy should not disturb the real side. This means that money supply should fall in pace with the growth trend of the economy. Hayek's diagnosis of the 1929 crisis directly ensues from this. During the 1920s the United States benefited from a constant growth of the real economy yet with almost constant prices and a rise of the money supply. For him, this means 'monetary instability': the general level of prices should have fallen. The changes in the market interest rates are directly attributable to the central bank (here the Fed) behaviour. For Hayek (1925) the 1920s in the United States were characterised by a money-induced boom that entailed misallocation of resources. The precise meaning of 'relative inflation' is this:

a stable price level despite growing real output. The larger the gap between the natural and the market interest rate, the longer the misalignment is endured, the more violent the downturn in the business cycle will be because of the large amounts of resources misallocated. That is, busts necessarily follow booms because of inter-temporal coordination problems *within* the investment sector.

31 "The Great Contraction" is the title of Friedman and Schwartz (1963) Chapter 7.

32 However, through a careful examination of leading bankers' analyses held at that time Wicker (2002) makes the following point: "The evidence is quite clear that the Fed did successfully offset the increase in hoarding by the increase in Federal Reserve credit, which it understood, and did not offset the increase in the currency-deposit ratio, which it did not!" (Wicker 2002, p. 50). If the Fed was lacking a comprehensive theory of the money supply determination, because of its lack of understanding of the influence of the currency-deposit ratio on the total supply stock, it can hardly be argued that the Fed did *with full background knowledge* let the monetary supply fall. Worse, it can then be shown that the Fed *did* take the impact of variation of the reserve-deposit ratio into account. The rise in the monetary base from 1929 to 1933 precisely corresponds to the attempt to counteract the rise in the reserve-demand deposit ratio. In the same line of argument, Dominguez *et al.* (1988) show that neither Harvard nor Yale economic forecasting services were able to predict the severe depression that would follow the 1929 crash. Worse, contemporary econometric methods that are in use today, such as VAR models, would still even now be unable to predict the Great Depression. If so, the case for the Fed's *refusal* – and even the case for its inability – to undertake monetary loosening would be severely undermined.

33 It might be true that the reading of Strong's testimony before the Committee on Banking and Currency of the US Congress shows him as not so influential. As argued by Wicker, "Strong's testimony was tantalizingly brief and relatively inaccessible except to the few who made a point of following closely what was said in congressional hearings" (Wicker 2002, p. 51). Yet, such a claim does not severely undermine Friedman's point against institutions.

34 In his 1997 interview with Snowdon and Vane, Friedman does not seem highly concerned with this issue of rigidities. See for example the following statement:

> I don't have any doubt that there are wage rigidities because obviously there are, it's a fact of life, it's hard to deny it. The question is whether they are important or not, in what ways they are important and in what kind of phenomena are they important.
>
> (Friedman's interview, Snowdon and Vane 1999, p. 136)

Actually, Friedman keeps this issue open.

35 Another way to formulate the overall issue regarding Friedman's interpretation of the Great Depression, and of business fluctuations in general, is with reference to the identification problem: what remains of Friedman and Schwartz's investigation if the creation of money appears to be driven by demand for loans? This is precisely the case made by Tobin in his famous paper "Money and Income: Post Hoc Ergo Propter Hoc?" (1970). As shown by Hammond (1996), causality is the basic issue underpinning the whole debate. Indeed, "Friedman seems to have become aware of the possible futility of giving empirical evidence a primary role in demonstrating causation to his fellow economists soon after he and Schwartz began presenting their results" (Hammond 1996, p. 210). As Friedman admits: "I have always regarded 'cause' as a very tricky concept. In my technical scientific writings I have to my best of my ability tried to avoid using the word" (letter to Hammond, June 13, 1985, quoted in Hammond 1996, p. 3 and pp. 211–12). At the empirical level, Friedman (1964) elaborates a more general case, showing that the amplitude of an expansion in GDP (in both nominal and real terms) is usually not correlated with the succeeding contraction but

that the reverse is true, which provides a generalised explanation of cyclical patterns (see also Friedman 1993b). Regarding monetary shocks, this explains why Friedman later develops explicitly an analytical argument to explain cyclical patterns in both money supply and output in his "Theoretical Framework for Monetary Analysis" (1970c) when he comes to accept that theoretical underpinnings were needed to address the 'measurement without theory' argument held by his opponents. Even if one considers that the causality goes in the right sense (i.e. from the exogenous money supply to the aggregate nominal income) there is a critical gap to be filled here, namely the issue of the 'transmission mechanism'. That is, what are the mechanisms at work that transmit a variation in the money supply to the aggregate nominal income? And how to disentangle the effects on prices from the effects on output?

36

> For in the middle of a deep depression just when we want Reserve policy to be most effective, the Member Banks are likely to be timid about buying new investments or making loans. If the Reserve authorities buy government bonds in the open market and thereby swell bank reserves, the banks will not put these funds to work but will simply hold reserves. Result: no 5 for 1, 'no nothing,' simply a substitution on the bank's balance sheet of idle cash for old government bonds.
>
> (Samuelson 1948, pp. 353–4)

37 On both these issues of liquidity preference faced by second-tier banks and coordination failures in the relationships between central banks and second-tier banks, see Bibow (2000, 2009).

38 In his review of the *Monetary History*, Tobin (1965) puts his argument in a similar way when he states that

> banks were by the mid-thirties moving along a fairly flat liquidity preference curve. Having invested in short-term Treasury and commercial paper until the rates were virtually zero, they would hold in cash any further accretions of reserves. The more high-powered money, the lower the deposit-reserve ratio-and these two proximate determinants certainly do show strong negative correlation in this period.
>
> (Tobin 1965, p. 471)

Tobin's argument rests on the 'zero-lower bond' hypothesis that reflects the very low profitability of loans for second-tier banks at that time. But as a matter of principle the banking sector can be trapped in a liquidity trap whatever the level of interest rates. All it requires is a general lack of confidence on the part of banks.

39 Keynes clearly targeted Hayek when he claimed:

> Some austere and puritanical souls regard it both as an inevitable and a desirable nemesis on so much over-expansion, as they call it; a nemesis on man's speculative spirit. It would, they feel, be a victory for the mammon of unrighteousness if so much prosperity was not subsequently balanced by universal bankruptcy. We need, they say, what they politely call a 'prolonged liquidation' to put us right.
>
> (Keynes 1931, CW 13, p. 349)

40 See also "An Economic Analysis of Unemployment" (1931, CW 13, especially p. 350).

41 The key concept here is the marginal efficiency of capital. In the language of the *General Theory*, "a collapse in the price of equities, which has had disastrous reactions in the marginal efficiency of capital, may have been due to the weakening either of speculative confidence or of the state of credit" (Keynes 1936, CW 7, p. 158).

42 It is true that the problem is put in a quite different manner in Britain where banks have more discretion in choosing the form of their lending rather than its amount. In

this case, banks would escape the duty of monetary ease in refusing to take long-term involvements that will be translated into long-term interest rates sharply above short-term rates.

43 On this issue of wage rigidity and money-wage cuts, see Rivot (2011a).

44 Taylor's overall thesis, which is shared by Blinder (2009) or Hutton (2009) to take but a few examples, runs as follows. First, the 'Great Moderation' of the previous 20 years was permitted by a monetary policy based on rules. The 'Great Deviation' of 2003–05 happened when interest rates were targeted at too low levels and monetary policy became more interventionist and less based on rules. Should the Fed policy not have been so interventionist, the financial collapse of 2008 would simply not have existed. As we will see in Chapter 4, expectations play here a crucial role. Indeed, Bernanke (2010), well known to be a careful scholar of the 1929 crisis, denies that monetary policy carried out during the 2000s was too lax. For him, there was no 'deviation' from the Taylor rule as soon as anticipations were – hopefully – incorporated into it. So the very cause of the 2008 crisis should lie elsewhere.

45 Things are rendered even more complicated once a more long-run perspective is adopted. Don't the dot.com crisis and the liquidity boom echo Schumpeter's structural interpretation of the 1929 crisis (Perez 2009)?

46 The Hayekian flavour of this diagnosis is noticeable. Indeed, Hayek too would insist on global imbalances, maladjustments between planned savings and investment, and above all maladjustments *within* the investment sector.

47 Closely related to this analysis, Wray (2009) convincingly argues that what we now living through is more consistent with what Minsky (1996) characterises as a money manager crisis. As showed by Minsky (1986), finance capitalism is subject to endogenous crisis. Stability necessarily contains the seeds of instability. To this extent, finance is the very cause of instability. That is the reason why, beyond its Minskian characteristics, the current crisis is a balance-sheet crisis due to a leverage dynamics (Leijonhufvud 2009).

48 Of course, this is not to say that until 2008 the landscape was uniform. For example, in 2005 Krugman asked "Is Fiscal Policy Poised for a Comeback?" The Japanese deflationary experience in the 1990s or more recently the United States' experience in the early 2000s, which was characterised by "a disturbingly close brush with the zero bound on monetary policy after the technology bubble burst" (Krugman 2005, p. 522), provided strong cases for discretionary fiscal policy when the economy faces the zero-bound rate. Arestis and Sawyer (2004) made a similar point: in case of large shocks (to be interpreted in terms of shifts in parameters of the model such as business confidence instead of random shocks), discretionary fiscal policy would still be more potent than monetary policy. Yet, until 2008 most of the economists concerned with economic policy shared a consensual view on the issue, the consensus consisting in a rather distrustful position towards discretion in general, and towards fiscal discretionary policy in particular. In short, this consensus was that under normal circumstances a fiscal stimulus package should be left aside.

49 It might happen that one retrospectively changes his mind at least partially, as is the case for Hayek. Hayek reconsiders his initial views in a talk he gave in 1975: to Keynes he concedes first the possibility of secondary deflation due to a fall in aggregate demand and second the downward-rigidity of wages as an institutional fact; to Friedman he also concedes that in that case of general deflation monetary expansion should be conducted. Ultimately, this is consistent with the monetary policy norm he stated in the 1930s. Hayek's reconsideration of the view he held in the 1930s is thus a good example of recurrent history.

4 Keynes and Friedman on the employment policy: structure and conduct

1 More precisely,

> the consensus model incorporates classical features such as inter-temporal optimization, rational expectations and a real business cycle core, together with Keynesian features such as monopolistically competitive firms, staggered sticky nominal price setting, and a central role for monetary stabilization policy.
>
> (Goodfriend 2007, p. 59)

2 This distinction between involuntary and voluntary unemployment has been considered as dubious on the theoretical ground. See De Vroey (2004) for a thorough exposition of this thesis. In Rivot (2011a), we argue the opposite. In our view, the following quotation shows how fundamental this distinction is on the practical ground:
> Unemployment is due to:

a the hard core of the virtually unemployable (100,000);
b seasonal factors (200,000);
c men moving between jobs (300,000);
d misfits of trade or locality due to lack of mobility (200,000); and
e a deficiency in the aggregative effective demand for labour.
> (Keynes 1942, CW 27, p. 305)

3 De Vroey (2001) points out that the narrative that explicitly discusses unemployment contrasts with the model behind this narrative (to be found in Friedman's *Price Theory* (1962b)) that actually features full employment. Garrison (1984) and Laidler (2012) also emphasise the evolution between Friedman's definition of the natural rate of unemployment between 1968 and, say, 1977.
4 In Tobin's (1972b) words, the essential explanation of this inflationary bias is that "it is an essential feature of the theory that economic-wide relations among employment, wages and prices are aggregations of diverse outcomes in heterogeneous markets" (Tobin 1972b, p. 8).
5 Following the work of Dunlop (1938) and Tarshis (1939), Keynes (1939) admitted that after a protracted slump, the marginal productivity of labour might be increasing during the recovery so that real wages might be pro-cyclical. See Keynes (1939), "Relative Movements of Real Wages and Output", reproduced in CW 7, pp. 394–412. As we will see, this does not undermine Keynes' argument – quite the contrary – since in his theoretical framework real wages are determined by the employment level, and not the other way round.
6 On the role played by nominal wages, see Brenner (1980). On the relative wage argument, see Hoover (1995). And on the effect of a money-wage cut on the employment level, see Dos Santos Ferreira (1999).
7 See also:

> Too much emphasis on the remedial value of a higher price level as an object in itself may lead to serious misapprehension of the part price can play in the technique to recovery. The stimulation of output by increasing aggregate purchasing power is the right way to get prices up; *and not the other way round.*
>
> (Keynes 1933, CW 21, pp. 292–3; emphasis added)

8 Garrison (1984) already pointed out that the analysis carried out in the 1968 paper was flawed in the sense that there was no reason to restrict the perception errors of prices to workers: employers should know that real wages would later rise. Friedman later applied his argument in terms of misperceptions to both workers and employers. But Laidler (2012) shows that the modification operated by Friedman goes much beyond this correction.

9 As is well known, Lucas (1972, 1973) explains departures from the natural rate of employment as the result of 'monetary surprises' on price expectations. Accordingly, his interpretation of the Great Depression sticks to Friedman's point that monetary disorders directly caused the fall in output and in employment. In his review of Friedman and Schwartz's *Monetary History*, one can see Lucas arguing:

> Viewed as positive theory, real business cycle models do not offer a serious alternative to Friedman and Schwartz's monetary account of the early 1930s.... There is no real business cycle model that can map these shocks into anything like the 40% decline in real output and employment that occurred between 1929 and 1933 (nor, indeed, does anyone claim that there is). Even if there were, imagine trying to rewrite the Great Contraction chapter of *A Monetary History* with shocks of this kind playing the role Friedman and Schwartz assign to monetary contractions. What technological or psychological events could have induced such behavior in a large, diversified economy? How could such events have gone unremarked at the time, and remain invisible even to hindsight?
>
> (Lucas 1994, p. 13)

10 This conceding severely undermines the claim for generality of the real business cycle approach. Before the 2008 episode it could be easily argued that the Great Depression was a 'highly unique event', a black swan. Lucas himself restricts the validity of the paradigm he contributed to launch. Indeed:

> The problem is that the new theories, the theories embedded in general equilibrium dynamics of the sort that we know how to use pretty well now – there's a residue of things they don't let us think about. They don't let us think about the US experience in the 1930s or about financial crises and their real consequences in Asia or Latin America. They don't let us think, I don't think, very well about Japan in the 1990s.
>
> (Lucas 2004, p. 23)

11 This is not to say that fiscal policy is rendered unnecessary in the long run: "I should regard state intervention to encourage investment as probably a more important factor than low rates of interest taken in isolation" (Keynes 1943, CW 27, p. 350).

12 See Keynes' CW 22, p. 393.

13 In Keynes' words: "the technique of tap issues, by which the preferences of the public rather than of the Treasury determine the distribution of the debt between different terms and maturities, should be continued in peace-time" (Keynes 1945, CW 27, p. 396).

14 The case made by Carabelli and De Vecchi (2000) regarding Keynes and Friedman easily applies to the dividing line between Keynes and Friedman:

> Keynes' public institutions are collective agents endowed with partial knowledge and reason: what Hayek called 'fatal conceit' was, for Keynes, a positive aspect. As well as individual agents, social bodies have a 'mind' or a 'system or rules of decision'. But, unlike the minds of individuals, the collective mind is necessarily an 'artificial mind'. Hayek thought the idea of a collective and artificial mind totally unacceptable. Keynes, on the contrary, maintained that the collective mind is an autonomous conceptual entity and that public institutions know more than individuals.
>
> (Carabelli and De Vecchi 2000, p. 237)

15

> Changes in the complex of interest rates, with a view to controlling the trade cycle and to offset inflationary or deflationary trends, should not be precluded, but should affect the shorter, rather than the longer-term, issues, and should, as a rule,

be regarded as secondary to the technique of rationing the volume, rather altering the terms of credit.

(Keynes 1945, CW 27, p. 397)

16 This point has been dealt with in Chapter 2. On this issue of Keynes' views on inflation, see for example Trevithick (1975) or Leeson (1999). Besides, there are better remedies to dampen the boom and to achieve this fundamental goal: the alternatives to dear money include income policy and especially wage policy in cooperation with trade unions, taxation and buffer stock schemes to deal with 'cost inflation', planning of public investment and the control of private investment for 'demand inflation'.

17 More precisely, strategy corresponds to "the ideal monetary institutions and arrangements for the conduct of monetary policy that should be adopted" (Friedman [1984] 1987, p. 404).

18 More precisely, "three issues are involved in the tactics of monetary policy: adopting a variable target or targets; choosing the desired path of the targeted variables; devising procedures for achieving that path as closely as possible" (Friedman [1984] 1987, p. 409).

19 Put differently, Friedman's argument relies on "our present inability to predict at all accurately this same relation over short periods, from month to month, quarter to quarter, even year to year" (Friedman 1969b, p. 144).

20 In his "Monetary and Fiscal Framework for Economic Stability" (1948), Friedman argued:

Deficits or surpluses in the government budget would be reflected dollar for dollar in changes in the quantity of money; and, conversely, the quantity of money would change only as a consequence of deficits or surpluses. A deficit means an increase in the quantity of money; a surplus, a decrease.

(Friedman 1948, p. 251)

21 In Friedman's words: "the elimination of discounting and of variable reserve requirements would leave open market operations as *the* instrument of monetary policy proper" (Friedman 1960a, p. 50).

22 What is more, in his pamphlet *Why Government is the Problem* (1993a) Friedman stated: "You are all fully aware of the weakness of our financial system. Is there any doubt that that weakness owes much to Washington?" (Friedman 1993a, p. 5).

23 In Friedman's words:

There is no way to make precise numerical estimates, but there is every reason to anticipate that for decades after the introduction of a freeze on high-powered money, both the money multiplier and velocity would tend to rise at rates in the range of historical experience. Under these circumstances, a zero rate of growth of high-powered money would imply roughly stable prices, though ultimately, perhaps, slightly declining prices.

(Friedman [1984] 1987, p. 423)

As is often the case with Friedman, the causal relationship between some magnitudes and others is carefully set aside here.

24 See Cagan (2008).

25 Precisely:

Unless changes in velocity can be understood and measured accurately in real time as they occur, then changes in velocity may cause grave difficulties for a monetary policy based on monetary aggregates, regardless of whether the shift in velocity later seems to be understandable, with the benefit of hindsight.

(De Long 2000b, p. 227)

26 For other similar references, see Nelson (2007). There are two main exceptions to this general denial of instability in velocity of money. In his answer to De Long (2000a), Friedman (2000) clearly distinguishes changes in velocity of M1, M2 and M3, the break of M1 velocity being with no influence on M2 and M3 until the early 1990s. This does not lead him to revise his general advocacy. There is also his interview with Taylor in which he acknowledges change in stability in 1992 and recognises to be "baffled" (in Taylor 2001, p. 105) by the efficiency of monetary policy at that time: "What I'm puzzled about is whether, and if so how, they suddenly learned how to regulate the economy. Does Alan Greenspan have an insight into the movements in the economy and the shocks that other people don't have?" (in Taylor 2001, p. 105). Yet in his 2010 paper, Friedman has got over his astonishment and emphasises once more long-term correlation between money supply and output.

27 This statement is also found in Friedman (1982a).

28 For a thorough overview on 'planning' and the socialisation of investment advocated by Keynes, see Rivot (2011b).

29 The capital budget is defined as "a compilation of and budgetary forecast of *all* capital expenditure under *public* control, including local authorities and public boards" (Keynes 1945, CW 27, p. 405).

30 See also for example: "The main task should be to *prevent large fluctuations by a stable long-term programme*. If this is successful it should not be too difficult to offset small fluctuations by expediting or retarding some items in this long-term programme" (Keynes 1943, CW 27, p. 322; emphasis added).

31 Recall that

> under the rules of functional finance, decisions about the deficit and the money supply would be made with regard to their functionality – their effect on the economy – and not with regard to some moralistic premise that deficits, debt and expansionary monetary policy are inherently bad.
>
> (Colander 2008, p. 515)

32 See for example in the booklet co-written with Heller: "I am delighted to attest to the correctness of Walter's [Heller] statement that many of our views have not changed over time" (Friedman and Heller 1969, p. 47).

5 The functioning of a monetary economy

1 See also Roncaglia (2009).

2 In Keynes' own words:

> Probability is not related to the balance between favorable and unfavorable evidence but to the balance between the *absolute* amount of relevant knowledge and of relevant ignorance.[... An accession to new evidence increases the *weight* of an argument. New evidence will sometimes decrease the probability of an argument, but it will always increase its 'weight'.
>
> (Keynes 1921, CW 8, p. 77)

3 For a rationale of liquidity understood as a distinct concept from 'marketability' or 'easy convertibility' in money, see Rivot (2013). See also Leijonhufvud (1968a) and more recently Hayes (2006, 2012).

4 See Hayes (2006), and especially Chapter 4.

5 "Hicks' theorem states that the separate quantities of a group of goods, the prices of which always vary in proportion, can be aggregated without loss of information or introduction of predictive error" (Leijonhufvud 1968a, p. 118). See also Hicks quoted by Leijonhufvud: "if the prices of a group of goods change in the same proportion, that group of goods behaves just as if it were a single commodity" (Hicks 1946, p. 313).

6 Miller (1985) convincingly shows that Keynes includes 'savings deposits' in his 'money' aggregate.
7 For example, Clarida *et al.* (1999) consider a single aggregative good, where consumption goods – by definition short-lived – are lumped together with newly produced capital goods – that are long-lived.
8 On this issue of knowledge and expectations in Keynes' system of thought, see Carabelli (2003). As Carabelli and Cedrini (2012) make clear, this concern for knowledge and speculation comes from afar in Keynes' writings. In his 1910 lectures dedicated to speculation, Keynes establishes a sharp distinction between speculation and gambling, the former requiring "the possession of superior knowledge" (Keynes MSS 1910, UA/6/3, p. 93; quoted in Carabelli and Cedrini 2012, p. 22), while the latter does not. Strikingly, "what would be gambling for one man would be sound speculation for another" (Keynes MSS 1910, UA/6/3, p. 93; quoted in Carabelli and Cedrini 2012, p. 23). Going a little further, it can be stated that the 'speculator' in Keynes' language is the one who uses his superior knowledge to 'beat the gun' with the view to anticipate the market valuation while the 'entrepreneur' is the one who uses too a kind of superior knowledge (together with the information provided by State authorities), but yet with the purpose to escape harmful conventions and to develop accordingly long-term views.
9 Indeed, "holding assets that have a greater term to maturity involves a greater degree of uncertainty because the predictability of future events decreases as the term to maturity increases" (Koutsobinas 2011, p. 753).
10 This allows him to escape most of the logical difficulties encountered by the loanable funds idea, among which the integration of the stock-flows dimensions of the analysis and the circular reasoning involved, the loanable funds being used to derive a theory of the interest rate while the value of capital cannot be determined until the rate of interest is obtained (see Smithin 2003, especially p. 114).
11 Here, I draw on Leijonhufvud (1974) and Smithin (2012).
12 New Keynesians too consider a non-vertical aggregate supply curve, i.e. a non-vertical expectations-augmented Phillips curve. For them, because of monopolistic competition (Akerlof and Yellen 1985) or staggered contracts (Taylor 1980, Calvo 1983), there are delays in the adjustment process. Here, forward-looking expectations apply to the old Keynesian framework, in which the aggregate supply curve was not vertical because prices took time to adapt (in this *disequilibrium* interpretation of the Phillips curve prices reacted to excess demand). In the theoretical framework built for example by Clarida *et al.* (1999) or Woodford (2003) there is now a trade-off between variations in the output gap and variations in the inflation rate prevailing in the short run (instead of the old trade-off between inflation and unemployment). This new trade-off guides government's action to stabilise the economy.
13 Reasonableness must be understood with regard to Keynes' *Treatise on Probability*; it means "'having some reason' to believe or to act. It is a kind of cogent rationality, which varies according to circumstances" (Carabelli 2013, p. 17). Accordingly,

> to Keynes reasonableness does not depend on the fulfilment of expectations, for mere luck does not turn foolish judgments into reasonable judgements (a point against Friedman's instrumentalism or positivism). Reasonableness is based on a non-demonstrative logic and on intuition versus psychology and behaviourism. But reasonableness must not be confused with following habits, rules and market conventions: Keynes defends partial knowledge against mere experience.
> (Carabelli 2013, p. 18)

14 As we have seen in the previous chapter, Laidler (2012) shows that in Friedman's 1967 AER lecture "The Role of Monetary Policy" (Friedman 1968a) there is a tension between two hardly reconcilable market foundations of the expectations-augmented Phillips curve: the first one in terms of disequilibrium in line with the general framework

considered at that time by Keynesians (prices react to disequilibrium between supply and demand); the second one in terms of equilibrium but imperfect information (which prefigures Lucas' interpretation of Phillips curve as an aggregate supply function). Consideration of Laidler's line of argument should lead us to pass over this 1968a paper and to restrict the scope of our analysis to Friedman's definitive argument. But in the 1977a paper "Inflation and Unemployment", Friedman considers a rise in aggregate nominal demand but without making explicit the initial cause of this unexpected rise in aggregate demand. Accordingly, we will focus here on the 1968a paper despite the local amendments that were later made.

15 It could be argued that through Tobin's q one might have a more reliable transmission mechanism than 'mere' interest rates. But if one remembers that in Keynes' system, the interest rate plays the role of an (inverse) index of the market valuation of the existing stock of capital (Leijonhufvud 1968a), Tobin's analysis appears as strongly echoing Keynes' original one. Actually, Tobin's (1978) paper should be interpreted rather as a reformulation of Keynes' ideas than a straightforward extension of the arguments put forward in the *General Theory*.

16 The parable of the buried bottles with banknotes runs as follows:

> If the Treasury were to fill old bottles with banknotes, bury them at suitable depth in disused coalmines which are then filled up to the surface with town rubbish, and leave it to private enterprise on well-tried principles of laissez-faire to dig the notes again (the right to do so being obtained, of course, by tendering for leases of the note-bearing territory), there need be no more unemployment and, with the help of the repercussions, the real income of the community, and its capital wealth also, would probably become a good deal greater than it actually is. It would, indeed, be more sensible to build houses and the like; but if there are political and practical difficulties in the way of this, the above would be better than nothing.
>
> (Keynes 1936, CW 7, p. 129)

17 Besides, the reference Tobin makes to his own Tobin's q severely undermines the consistency of a predetermined rate of investment in the short run once open-market monetary policy is under consideration (Tobin 1972a, p. 83).

18 See Friedman and Savage (1952) for their reconciliation of 'gambling' with the maximising-utility hypothesis.

19 There is a particular exception where Friedman explicitly deals with financial markets. During the 1980s Friedman takes stock of the development of financial markets, which entails in particular a porous or tenuous frontier between 'money' and near-money assets. At that time, this loosening of the link between M0 (i.e. the high-powered money) and M2 ('money' and closed substitutes for money) is used as an argument by policy-makers to shift attention from monetary rules in terms of monetary aggregates to the control of interest rates. Indeed, since the late 1970s M2 appeared much more difficult to control. There seems to have been a shift away in the velocity of money so that central bankers have lost control over the money supply. Friedman reacts to this new 'monetary regime' as follows: while he previously advocated for years a constant monetary growth rule applying to M2, he shifts to a rule consisting in the freezing of the monetary base (i.e. M0). As a counterpart to this very strict and unambiguous monetary rule that applies to M0, Friedman recommends that the deregulation of the financial sector follows its natural course. Far from Keynes' 'beauty contest' parable, no doubt that in Friedman's eyes financial markets function well, just like 'any other' markets. Noticeably, Friedman was already asking in the late 1960s: "why should we not have variety and diversity in the market for borrowing and lending as in other markets?" (Friedman [1967b] 1969a, p. 83).

6 Conclusion: where to draw the line between laissez-faire and planning?

1 In Keynes' own words: "we should not conclude from this that everything depends on irrational psychology. On the contrary, the state of the long-term expectation is often steady, and, even when it is not, the other factors exert their compensating effects" (Keynes 1936, CW 7, p. 162).

2 As stated by Blinder (1986), "matching subjective probability distribution to an objective one is no trivial matter when the objective distribution may not be stationary, nor even exist, because the events being forecast are not repetitive" (Blinder 1986, pp. 213–14).

3 By the way, it can be noticed that this idea of continuous market clearing renders the New Classicals economists much better qualified as 'neo-Austrians' than as a 'Monetarism mark II' brand, as Tobin (1981) calls them (Hoover 1984, Laidler 1982, 2006).

4 As mentioned by Cherrier (2011), Friedman acknowledges in a letter written to Hayek in 1975 to have been much influenced by Savage, who "claimed that probability judgements are judgements held by individuals separately, that there is nothing objective about any of these, and that the only way to define objective probability is in terms of agreement among different persons' subjective probabilities" (Friedman to Hayek, 11/09/75 Box 20 folder 19, Hayek papers, quoted in Cherrier 2011, p. 341). Yet, in Keynes' philosophy probability is not subjective but logical.

5 A simple rule for monetary policy able to encompass the *Lucas critique* (Lucas 1976) can be written as in Taylor (1993):

$$r = r* + \pi + 0.5(\pi - \pi*) + 0.5(y - y*) \qquad (1)$$

where r is the Federal Funds rate and $r*$ is the equilibrium *real* Federal Funds rate, i.e. the estimated natural interest rate. According to its initiator, this classic Taylor rule can be qualified as a 'policy rule' insofar as it relies on a predetermined plan and implements a strategy fixed in advance. Actually, Taylor himself moved from "optimal monetary control rules" (Taylor 1979, p. 1268) to a simpler feedback rule in Taylor (1993). Yet, this classic Taylor rule has been criticised as being 'backward-looking'. More precisely, it rests on the assumption that the future is likely to be like the past.

Hence the appearance of 'forward-looking' rules – also called generalised or broader Taylor rules. Thanks to its forecasts, the central bank is now able not only to correct output and inflation deviations from their targets but also and above all to pre-empt these deviations. As stated by Clarida *et al.* (2000), a broader Taylor rule can be written as follows:

$$r_t^* = r* + \beta \left[E\left(\frac{\pi_{t,k}}{\Omega_t} - \pi* \right) \right] + \gamma E\left[\frac{y_{t,k}}{\Omega_t} \right] \qquad (2)$$

where r_t^* is the target for the nominal Federal Funds rate, $r*$ and $\pi*$ the desired nominal interest rate and inflation rate, $\pi_{t,k}$ the rate of inflation and $y_{t,k}$ the output gap between periods t and $t + k$, and Ω_t the information set available at time t. By definition, $r*$ is equal to the desired nominal interest rate when output and inflation are at their target level. The underlying real interest rate is, as in equation (1), determined by non-monetary factors and considered as a first approximation as given. The point is that the dose of leeway available to policy-makers has significantly increased since they now react to anticipated inflation deviations and output gaps rather than to lagged values. To the extent that forecasts made by the central banks include upside and downside risks, this 'broader' Taylor rule is properly labelled a discretionary rule. Indeed, the broader interpretation of Taylor's policy framework places its emphasis on the identification of the System's operational objectives regarding price stability and economic growth and *asks that policymakers apply their collective judgment* to adjust interest rates so as to balance the perceived risks with regard to the outlook for the two objectives.

(Orphanides 2003, p. 989; emphasis added)

For an overview of the classic Taylor rule and other generalised rules, see Snowdon and Vane (2002) and Orphanides (2008).

6 Worse, a medium-term positive relation might appear, especially because higher inflation is likely to be accompanied by higher volatility in inflation with "distorting effects on uncertainty" and will accordingly "render market prices a less efficient system for coordinating economic activities" (Friedman [1977a] 1987, p. 363).

7 Friedman's (2010) paper was written in 2006, as a contribution to a conference in honour of David Laidler in August 2006.

8 This is not to say that Simons was the first in the twentieth century to advocate monetary rule. Indeed, as shown by Laidler (1999), "in the 1920s, Fisher was the main proponent of legally mandating the Federal Reserve System to pursue a price-stabilization" (Laidler 1999, p. 18). On this issue, see in particular Fisher (1934). One can also go back even further and mention the debate between the Banking School and the Currency School on this issue of monetary rules.

9 In order to circumscribe the financial side of the economy, Simons holds that public debt should be financed either by zero-interest bonds or by long-term bonds, ideally perpetuities.

10 It cannot be excluded that the enlargement of 'fiscal space', which means fiscal consolidation in chronic deficit countries (i.e. reduction of structural government deficits) in the middle of a recession, might have positive effects on GDP thanks to the reversal of private expectations. Yet, what has been observed so far is that austerity is currently detrimental even for public budgets.

11 In this respect, the statement made regarding unemployment is worth highlighting:

there can be no doubt that this must be the goal of our greatest endeavour; even so, it does not mean that such an aim should be allowed to dominate us *to the exclusion of everything else*, that, as the glib phrase runs, it must be accomplished 'at any price'.

(Hayek 1944, p. 153; emphasis added)

Bibliography

References for Friedman

Friedman, M. (1942), "Discussion of the Inflationary Gap", *American Economic Review*, 32(2), pp. 314–20. Reprinted in Friedman (1953a), pp. 251–62.

Friedman, M. (1943a), "The Spendings Tax as a Wartime Fiscal Measure", *American Economic Review*, 33(1), pp. 50–62.

Friedman, M. (1943b), "Predicting the Outset", in C. Shoup, M. Friedman and R.P. Mack, *Taxing to Prevent Inflation*, New York, Columbia University Press, pp. 111–53.

Friedman, M. (1947), "Lerner on the Economics of Control", *Journal of Political Economy*, 55(5), pp. 405–16. Reprinted in Friedman (1953a), pp. 301–19.

Friedman, M. (1948), "A Monetary and Fiscal Framework for Economic Stability", *American Economic Review*, 38(3), pp. 245–64. Reprinted in Friedman (1953a), pp. 133–56.

Friedman, M. (1949), "The Marshallian Demand Curve", *Journal of Political Economy*, 57(6), pp. 463–9. Reprinted in Friedman (1953a), pp. 47–99.

Friedman, M. (1953a), *Essays in Positive Economics*, Chicago, University of Chicago Press.

Friedman, M. (1953b), "Choice, Chance, and the Personal Distribution of Income", *Journal of Political Economy*, 61(4), pp. 277–90. Reprinted in Friedman (1962b), pp. 262–78.

Friedman, M. (1953c), "Methodology of Positive Economics", in Friedman (1953a), pp. 3–43. Reprinted in U. Mäki (ed.) (2009), *The Methodology of Positive Economics, Reflections of the Milton Friedman Legacy*, Cambridge, Cambridge University Press, pp. 1–43.

Friedman, M. (1957), *A Theory of The Consumption Function*, Princeton, Princeton University Press.

Friedman, M. (1959), "Statements on Monetary Theory and Policy", in *Employment, Growth and Price Levels*, U.S. Government Printing Office, pp. 605–12. Reprinted in R.J. Ball and P. Doyle (eds) (1969), *Inflation: Selected Readings*, Harmondsworth, Middlesex, Penguin Books, pp. 136–45.

Friedman, M. (1960a), *A Program for Monetary Stability*, New York, Fordham University Press.

Friedman, M. (1960b), "In Defense of Destabilizing Speculation", in R.W. Pfouts (ed.), *Essays in Economics and Econometrics*, Chapel Hill, University of North Carolina Press. Reprinted in Friedman (1969a), pp. 285–91.

Friedman, M. (1962a) [2002], *Capitalism and Freedom*, Chicago, University of Chicago Press.

Friedman, M. (1962b) [2007], *Price Theory*, New Brunswick, NJ, Transaction Publishers.

Friedman, M. (1962c), "Should There Be an Independent Monetary Authority?", in L.B. Yeager (ed.), *Search of a Monetary Constitution*, Cambridge, MA, Harvard University Press, pp. 219–43. Reprinted in Friedman (1968c), pp. 173–94.

Friedman, M. (1963), *Inflation, Causes and Consequences*, Bombay, Asia Publishing House. Reprinted in Friedman (1968c), pp. 17–71.

Friedman, M. (1964), "Monetary Studies of the National Bureau", The National Bureau Enters Its 45th Year, 44th Annual Report, pp. 7–25. Reprinted in Friedman (1969a), pp. 261–84.

Friedman, M. (1966a), "An Inflationary Recession", *Newsweek*, 17 October.

Friedman, M. (1966b), "What Price Guideposts?", in G.P. Shultz and R.Z. Aliber (eds), *Guidelines: Informal Contracts and the Market Place*, Chicago, Chicago University Press. Reprinted in Friedman (1968c), pp. 97–121.

Friedman, M. (1967a), "An All-Volunteer Army", *The New York Times Magazine*, 14 May. Reprinted in K.R. Leube (ed.) (1987), *The Essence of Friedman*, Stanford, Hoover Institute Press, pp. 69–78.

Friedman, M. (1967b), "The Monetary Theory and Policy of Henry Simons", *The Journal of Law and Economics*, 10, pp. 1–13. Reprinted in Friedman (1969a), pp. 81–93.

Friedman, M. (1968a), "The Role of Monetary Policy", *The American Economic Review*, 58(1), pp. 1–17. Reprinted in Friedman (1969a), pp. 95–110.

Friedman, M. (1968b), "The Case for the Negative Income Tax", in M.R. Laird (ed.), *Republican Papers*, Garden City, NY, Doubleday & Co. Reprinted in K.R. Leube (ed.) (1987), *The Essence of Friedman*, Stanford, Hoover Institute Press, pp. 57–68.

Friedman, M. (1968c), *Dollars and Deficits. Inflation, Monetary Policy and the Balance of Payments*, Englewood Cliffs, NJ, Prentice-Hall International.

Friedman, M. (1969a), *The Optimum Quantity of Money and Other Essays*, Chicago, Aldine Publishing Company.

Friedman, M. (1969b), "Monetary Theory and Policy", in R.J. Ball and P. Doyle (eds), *Inflation, Selected Readings*, Harmondsworth, Middlesex, Penguin Books, pp. 136–45.

Friedman, M. (1970a), *The Counter-Revolution in Monetary Theory*, Occasional Paper 33, London, Institute of Economic Affairs, for the Wincott Foundation.

Friedman, M. (1970b), "The Social Responsibility of Business Is to Increase Profits", *The New York Times Magazine*, 13 September. Reprinted in K.R. Leube (ed.) (1987), *The Essence of Friedman*, Stanford, Hoover Institute Press, pp. 36–42.

Friedman, M. (1970c), "A Theoretical Framework for Monetary Analysis", *Journal of Political Economy*, 78(2), pp. 193–238. Reprinted in R.J. Gordon (ed.) (1974), *Milton Friedman's Monetary Framework, A Debate with his Critics*, Chicago, University of Chicago Press, pp. 1–62.

Friedman, M. (1972), "Comments on the Critics", *Journal of Political Economy*, 80(5), pp. 906–50. Reprinted in R.J. Gordon (ed.) (1974), *Milton Friedman's Monetary Framework, A Debate with his Critics*, Chicago, University of Chicago Press, pp. 132–77.

Friedman, M. (1977a), "Nobel Lecture: Inflation and Unemployment", *Journal of Political Economy*, 85(3), pp. 451–72. Reprinted in K.R. Leube (ed.) (1987), *The Essence of Friedman*, Stanford, Hoover Institute Press, pp. 347–69.

Friedman, M. (1977b), "Adam Smith's Relevance for Today", *Challenge*, March–April, pp. 6–12.

Friedman, M. (1981), "Market Mechanisms and Central Economic Planning", American Institute for Public Policy Research, Washington, D.C. Reprinted in K.R. Leube (ed.) (1987), *The Essence of Friedman*, Stanford, Hoover Institute Press, pp. 18–35.

Friedman, M. (1982a), "Monetary Policy, Theory and Practice", *Journal of Money, Credit and Banking*, 14(1), pp. 98–118.

Friedman, M. (1982b), "Letter to Roger W. Jensen, Vice-Chairman Economic Committee. In Joint Economic Committee", *Monetarism and the Federal Reserve's Conduct of Monetary Policy: Compendium of Views Prepared for the Use of the Subcommittee on Monetary and Fiscal Policy*, Washington DC: Government Printing Office, pp. 73–4.

Friedman, M. (1984), "Monetary Policy for the 80s", in J.H. Moore (ed.) *To Promote Prosperity: U.S. Domestic Policy in the Mid-1980s*, Stanford, Hoover Institution Press. Reprinted in Leube (ed.) (1987), *The Essence of Friedman*, Stanford, Hoover Institute Press, pp. 404–26.

Friedman, M. (1992), *Monetary Mischiefs, Episodes in Monetary History*, Orlando, Harcourt Brace & Company.

Friedman, M. (1993a), *Why Government Is the Problem*, Hoover Institution, Stanford University.

Friedman, M. (1993b), "The 'Plucking Model' of Business Fluctuations Revised", *Economic Inquiry*, 31, April, pp. 171–7.

Friedman, M. (1995), "Public Schools: Make Them Private", Cato Briefing Paper No. 23, 23 June.

Friedman, M. (1996), "Fed and the Natural Rate", *Wall Street Journal*, 25 September.

Friedman, M. (1997), "John Maynard Keynes", Federal Reserve Bank *Economic Quarterly*, 83(2), pp. 1–23.

Friedman, M. (1999), "The Business Community's Suicidal Impulse", *Cato Policy Report*, March/April, pp. 6–7.

Friedman, M. (2000), "Monetarist Thoughts", *Journal of Economic Perspective*, 14, p. 225.

Friedman, M. (2005), "A Natural Experiment in Monetary Policy Covering Three Episodes of Growth and Decline in the Economy and the Stock Market", *Journal of Economic Perspectives*, 19(4), pp. 145–50.

Friedman, M. (2010), "Tradeoffs in Monetary Policy", in R. Leeson (ed.), *David Laidler's Contributions to Economics*, Houndmills, Basingstoke, Palgrave Macmillan, pp. 114–18.

References for Friedman in collaboration

Friedman, M. and Becker, G.S. (1957), "A Statistical Illusion in Judging Keynesian Models", *Journal of Political Economy*, 65(1), pp. 64–75.

Friedman, M. and Friedman, R. [1979] (1990), *Free to Choose, A Personal Statement*, Orlando, Harcourt Books.

Friedman, M. and Friedman, R. (1998), *Two Lucky People*, Chicago, University of Chicago Press.

Friedman, M. and Heller, W.W. (1969), *Monetary vs. Fiscal Policy*, New York, W.W. Norton & Company Inc.

Friedman, M. and Kuznets, S. (1945), *Income from Independent Professional Practice*, New York, National Bureau of Economic Research.

Friedman, M. and Savage, L.J. (1952), "The Expected-Utility Hypothesis and the Measurability of Utility", *Journal of Political Economy*, 60(6), pp. 463–74. Reprinted in

K.R. Leube (ed.) (1987), *The Essence of Friedman*, Stanford, Hoover Institute Press, pp. 206–21.

Friedman, M. and Schwartz, A. (1963), *A Monetary History of the United-States 1867–1960*, Princeton, Princeton University Press.

Friedman, M. and Schwartz, A. (1982), *Monetary Trends in the United States and the United Kingdom. Their Relation to Income, Prices, and Interest Rates, 1867–1975*, Chicago, University of Chicago Press.

Friedman, M. and Schwartz, A. (1986), "Has Government Any Role in Money?", *Journal of Monetary Economics*, 17(1), pp. 37–62.

Friedman, M. and Schwartz, A. [1963] (2008), *The Great Contraction 1929–1933. With a New Preface by Anna Jacobson Schwartz and a New Introduction by Peter L. Bernstein*, Princeton, Princeton University Press.

References for Keynes

Keynes, J.M. (1971–89) *The Collected Writings of John Maynard Keynes*, 30 vols, London, Macmillan for the Royal Economic Society.

CW 2, *The Economic Consequences of the Peace*, 1919.

CW 5, *The Treatise on Money, Part 1: The Pure Theory of Money*, 1930.

CW 6, *The Treatise on Money, Part 2: The Applied Theory of Money*, 1930.

CW 7, *The General Theory of Employment, Interest and Money*, 1936.

CW 8, *A Treatise on Probability*, 1921.

CW 9, *Essays in Persuasion*, 1972.

CW 11, *Economic Articles and Correspondence: Academic*.

CW 13, *The General Theory and After, Part I Preparation*.

CW 14, *The General Theory and After, Part II Defence and Development*.

CW 19, *Activities 1922–1929: The Return to Gold and Industrial Policy*, 2 volumes.

CW 20, *Activities 1929–1931: Rethinking Employment and Unemployment Policies*.

CW 21, *Activities 1931–1939: World Crises and Policies in Britain and America*.

CW 22, *Activities 1939–1945: Internal War Finance*.

CW 27, *Activities 1940–1946: Shaping the Post-War World: Employment and Commodities*.

CW 29. *The General Theory and After. A supplement*.

Other references

Akerlof, G.A. and Shiller, R.J. (2009), *Animal Spirits, How Human Psychology Drives the Economy, and Why It Matters for Global Capitalism*, Princeton, Princeton University Press.

Akerlof, G.A. and Yellen, J.L. (1985), "A Near-Rational Model of the Business Cycle with Wage and Price Inertia", *Quarterly Journal of Economics*, 100(supplement), pp. 823–38.

Arestis, Ph. and Sawyer, M. (2004), "On the Effectiveness of Monetary Policy and of Fiscal Policy", *Review of Social Economy*, 62(4), pp. 441–63.

Auerbach, A.J., Gale, W.G. and Harris, B.H. (2010), "Activist Fiscal Policy", *Journal of Economic Perspectives*, 24(4), pp. 141–64.

Backhouse, R.E and Bateman, B.W. (2009), "Keynes and Capitalism", *History of Political Economy*, 41(4), pp. 645–71.

Backhouse, R.E and Medema, S.G. (2008), "Laissez-faire, Economists and", in S. Durlauf and L.E. Blume (eds), *New Palgrave Dictionary of Economics*, 2nd edition, Vol. 4, London, Macmillan, pp. 848–56.

Bainar, W. and Tobin, J. (1968), "Pitfalls in Financial-Model Building", *American Economic Review*, 58(2), pp. 99–122.

Ball, R.J. and Doyle, P. (eds) (1969), *Inflation: Selected Readings*, Harmondsworth, Middlesex, Penguin Books.

Bernanke, B.S. (1983), "Nonmonetary Effects of the Financial Crisis in the Propagation of the Great Depression", *American Economic Review*, 73(3), pp. 257–76.

Bernanke, B.S. (1995), "The Macroeconomics of the Great Depression: A Comparative Approach", *Journal of Money, Credit and Banking*, 27(1), pp. 1–28.

Bernanke, B.S. (2003), " 'Constrained Discretion' and Monetary Policy", *Remarks to the Monetary Marketeers of New York University*, 3 February, www.federalreserve.gov.

Bernanke, B.S. (2004), *Essays on the Great Depression*, Princeton, Princeton University Press.

Bernanke, B.S. (2010), "Monetary Policy and the Housing Bubble", Speech at the Annual Meeting of the American Economic Association, Atlanta, GA, 3 January.

Bibow, J. (2000), "On Exogenous Money and Bank Behaviour: The Pandora's Box Kept Shut in Keynes' Theory of Liquidity Preference", *European Journal for the History of Economic Thought*, 7(4), pp. 532–68.

Bibow, J. (2009), *Keynes on Monetary Policy, Finance and Uncertainty. Liquidity Preference Theory and the Global Financial Crisis*, London, Routledge.

Blanchard, O., Dell'Ariccia, G. and Mauro, P. (2010), "Rethinking Macroeconomic Policy", *Journal of Money, Credit and Banking*, 42 (Issue Supplement s1), pp. 199–215.

Blinder, A. (1986), "Keynes After Lucas", *Eastern Economic Journal*, 12(3), pp. 209–16.

Blinder, A. (2009) "6 Bad Moves that Led US into Crisis", *International Herald Tribune*, 26 January.

Brechling, F. (1968), "The Trade-Off between Inflation and Unemployment", *Journal of Political Economy*, 76(4), pp. 712–37.

Brenner, R. (1980), "The Role of Nominal Wage Contracts in Keynes' *General Theory*", *History of Political Economy*, 12(4), pp. 582–7.

Breton, Y., Broder, A. and Lutfalla, M. (1997), *La Longue Stagnation en France. L'Autre Grande Dépression, 1873–1895*, Paris, Economica.

Bronfenbrenner, M. (1963), "A Sample Survey of Commission on Money and Credit Research Papers", *Review of Economics and Statistics*, 45(February), pp. 115–19.

Brunner, K. and Meltzer, A.H. (1972), "Friedman's Monetary Theory", *Journal of Political Economy*, 78(2), pp. 837–51. Reprinted in R.J. Gordon (ed.) (1974), *Milton Friedman's Monetary Framework, A Debate with his Critics*, Chicago, University of Chicago Press, pp. 63–76.

Buchanan, J.M. and Tullock, G. (1962), *The Calculus of Consent, Logical Foundations of Constitutional Democracy*, Ann Arbor, University of Michigan Press.

Burstein, M.L. (1995), "Classical Macroeconomics for the Next Century", Unpublished Manuscript, York University, Toronto.

Cagan, Ph. (2008), "Monetarism", in S. Durlauf and L.E. Blume (eds), *New Palgrave Dictionary of Economics*, 2nd edition, London, Macmillan, Vol. 5, pp. 677–83.

Calvo, G. (1983), "Staggered Prices in a Utility-Maximizing Framework", *Journal of Monetary Economics*, 12(3), pp. 383–98.

Carabelli, A. (2003), "Keynes: Economics as a Branch of Probable Logic", in J. Runde and S. Mizuhara (eds), *Keynes's Economics. Probability, Uncertainty and Conventions*, London, Routledge, pp. 216–26.

Carabelli, A. (2013), "A New Methodological Approach to Economic Theory: What I Have Learnt from 30 Years of Research on Keynes", in J. Jespersen and M.O. Madsen (eds), *Keynes's General Theory for Today*, Cheltenham, Edward Elgar.

Carabelli, A. and Cedrini, M. (2011a), "Chapter 18 of the General Theory 'Further Analysed': The Theory of Economics as a Method", SEMeQ Working Paper 128/2011 (Paper presented at the 5th 'Dijon' Post-Keynesian Conference, University of Roskilde, Denmark, 14 May 2011).

Carabelli, A. and Cedrini, M. (2011b), "The Economic Problem of Happiness: Keynes on Happiness and Economics", *Forum for Social Economics*, 40, pp. 335–59.

Carabelli, A. and Cedrini, M. (2012), "On the New Appeal of Chapter 12 of the General Theory. Complicating Remarks on the Keynes-Hume Connection and the Presumed Novelty of the Analysis of Financial Markets in the *General Theory*", mimeo.

Carabelli, A. and De Vecchi, N. (1999), "'Where to Draw the Line'? Keynes versus Hayek on Knowledge, Ethics and Economics", *European Journal of the History of Economic Thought*, 6(2), pp. 271–96.

Carabelli, A. and De Vecchi, N. (2000), "Individuals, Public Institutions and Knowledge: Hayek and Keynes", in P.L. Porta, R. Scazzieri and A. Skinner (eds), *Division of Labour and Institutions*, Aldershot, Edward Elgar, pp. 229–48.

Carabelli, A. and De Vecchi, N. (2001), "Hayek and Keynes: From a Common Critique of Economic Method to Different Theories of Expectations", *Review of Political Economy*, 13(3), pp. 269–85.

Cherrier, B. (2011), "The Lucky Consistency of Milton Friedman's Science and Politics", in Ph. Mirowski, T. Stapleford and R. Van Horn (eds), *Building Chicago Economics: New Perspectives on the History of America's Most Powerful Economic Programme*, Cambridge, Cambridge University Press.

Clarida, R., Gali, J. and Gertler, M. (1999), "The Science of Monetary Policy: A New Keynesian Perspective", *Journal of Economic Literature*, 37(4), pp. 1661–1707.

Clarida, R., Gali, J. and Gertler, M. (2000), "Monetary Policy Rules and Macroeconomic Stability: Some Evidence and Some Theory", *Quarterly Journal of Economics*, 115, pp. 147–80.

Coase, R.H. (1960), "The Problem of Social Cost", *Journal of Law and Economics*, 3(1), pp. 1–44.

Coase, R.H. (1974), "The Lighthouses in Economics", *Journal of Law and Economics*, 17(2), pp. 357–76.

Coddington, A. (1976), "Keynesian Economics: The Search for First Principles", *Journal of Economic Literature*, 14(4), pp. 1258–73.

Colander, D. (2008), "Functional Finance", in S. Durlauf and L.E. Blume (eds), *New Palgrave Dictionary of Economics*, 2nd edition, Vol. 3, London, Macmillan, pp. 515–17.

Cole, H.L. and Ohanian, L.E. (1999), "The Great Depression in the United States from a Neoclassical Perspective", *Federal Reserve Bank of Minneapolis Quarterly Review*, 23(1), pp. 2–24.

Davidson, P. (1972), "A Keynesian View of Friedman's Theoretical Framework for Monetary Analysis", *Journal of Political Economy*, 78(2), pp. 193–238. Reprinted in R.J. Gordon (ed.) (1974), *Milton Friedman's Monetary Framework, A Debate with his Critics*, Chicago, University of Chicago Press, pp. 90–110.

De Long, J.B. (2000a), "The Triumph of Monetarism", *Journal of Economic Perspectives*, 14(1), pp. 83–94.

De Long, J.B. (2000b), "Response from J. Bradford De Long", *Journal of Economic Perspective*, 14(1), p. 227.

De Vroey, M. (2001), "Friedman and Lucas on the Phillips Curve: From a Disequilibrium to an Equilibrium Approach", *Eastern Economic Journal*, 27(2), pp. 127–48.

De Vroey, M. (2004), *Involuntary Unemployment, the Elusive Quest for a Theory*, London, Routledge.

De Vroey, M. (2009), "On the Right Side for the Wrong Reasons: Friedman on the Marshall-Walras Divide", in U. Mäki (ed.), *The Methodology of Positive Economics, Reflections of the Milton Friedman Legacy*, Cambridge, Cambridge University Press, pp. 321–46.

Dimand, R.W. (1988), *The Origins of the Keynesian Revolution, the Development of Keynes's Theory of Employment and Output*, Aldershot, Edward Elgar.

Dimand, R.W. and Dimand, M.A. (1990), "J.M. Keynes on Buffer Stocks and Commodity Price Stabilization", *History of Political Economy*, 22(1), pp. 113–23.

Dimand, R.W., Mundell, R.A. and Vercelli, A. (eds) (2010), *Keynes's General Theory after Seventy Years*, London, Palgrave Macmillan.

Dixon, H.D. (2008), "New Keynesian Macroeconomics", in S. Durlauf and L.E. Blume (eds), *New Palgrave Dictionary of Economics*, 2nd edition, Vol. 6, London, Macmillan, pp. 40–4.

Dominguez, K.M., Fair, R.C. and Shapiro, M.D. (1988), "Forecasting the Depression: Harvard versus Yale", *American Economic Review*, 78(4), pp. 595–612.

Dos Santos Ferreira, R. (1999), "La Relation Salaires-Emploi sous l'Eclairage de la Concurrence Imparfaite", *Cahiers d'Economie Politique*, 34, pp. 15–40.

Dos Santos Ferreira, R. (2000), "Keynes et le Développement de la Théorie de l'Emploi dans une Economie Monétaire", in A. Beraud and G. Faccarello (eds), *Nouvelle Histoire de la Pensée Economique*, Vol. 3, Paris, La Découverte, pp. 236–93.

Dostaler, G. (1998), "Friedman and Keynes: Divergences and Convergences", *European Journal of the History of Economic Thought*, 5(2), pp. 317–47.

Dostaler, G. (2005), *Keynes et ses combats*, Paris, Albin Michel.

Dunlop, J. (1938), "The Movement of Real and Money Wages", *Economic Journal*, 48(191), pp. 413–34.

Epstein, G. (1999), "Mr Market [An Interview with Milton Friedman]", *Hoover Digest*, 1. Available at www.hooverdigest.org/991/epstein.html.

Feldman, G. (2007), "Putting Uncle Milton to Bed, Reexamining Milton Friedman's Essay on the Social Responsibility of Business", *Labor Studies Journal*, 32(2), pp. 125–41.

Ferey, S. (2008), *Une Histoire Economique du Droit*, Bruxelles, Bruylant.

Fisher, I. (1926), "A Statistical Relation between Unemployment and Price Changes", *International Labour Review*, 13(6), pp. 785–92.

Fisher, I. (1934), *Stable Money: A History of the Movement*, New York, Adelphi Company.

Forder, J. (2010a), "Friedman's Nobel Lecture and the Phillips Curve Myth", *Journal of the History of Economic Thought*, 32(3), pp. 329–48.

Forder, J. (2010b), "The Historical Place of the 'Friedman-Phelps' Expectations Critique", *European Journal of the History of Economic Thought*, 17(3), pp. 493–511.

Frazer, W. (1994), *The Legacy of Keynes and Friedman*, Westport, CT, Praeger.

Friedman, D. (2008), "Libertarianism", in S. Durlauf and L.E. Blume (eds), *New Palgrave Dictionary of Economics*, 2nd edition, Vol. 5, London, Macmillan, pp. 103–11.

Gamble, A. (1991), "The Decline of Corporatism", in D. Crabtree and A.P. Thirlwall (eds), *Keynes and the Role of the State, The Tenth Keynes Seminar Held at the University of Kent at Canterbury*, London, Macmillan, pp. 41–68.

Garrison, R.W. (1984), "Time and Money: The Universals of Macroeconomic Theorizing", *Journal of Macroeconomics*, 6(2), pp. 197–213.

Garrison, R.W. (2006), "Natural and Neutral Rates of Interest in Theory and Policy Formulation", *Quarterly Journal of Austrian Economics*, 9(4), pp. 57–68.

Gazier, B. (2011), *La crise de 1929*, Paris, Presses Universitaires de France, collection Que Sais-Je?, 7th edition.

Goodfriend, M. (2007), "How the World Achieved Consensus on Monetary Policy", *Journal of Economic Perspectives*, 21(4), pp. 47–68.

Gordon, R.J. (ed.) (1974), *Milton Friedman's Monetary Framework, A Debate with his Critics*, Chicago, University of Chicago Press.

Gordon, W. (1982), "What of the Friedmans' *Free to Choose?*", *Journal of Economic Literature*, 16(1), pp. 301–8.

Greenspan, A. (2008), "Testimony before a US House Overnight and Government Reform Committee", 23 October.

Haberler, G. (1937), *Prosperity and Depression, A Theoretical Analysis of Cyclical Movements*, New York, Leagues of Nation edition.

Haberler, G. (1960), *Inflation – Its Causes and Cure*, Washington DC, American Enterprise Institute.

Hammond, J.D. (1996), *Theory and Measurement, Causality Issues in Milton Friedman's Monetary Economics*, Cambridge, Cambridge University Press.

Hayek, F.A. (1925). In German. "The Monetary Policy of the United States after the Recovery from the 1920 Crisis". Reprinted in F.A. Hayek (1984), *Money, Capital, and Fluctuations: Early Essays*, R. McCloughry (ed.), Chicago, University of Chicago Press.

Hayek, F.A. [1929] (1933a). In German. *Monetary Theory and the Trade Cycle*, London and Toronto, Jonathan Cape.

Hayek, F.A. (1933b), "The Present State and Immediate Prospects of the Study of Industrial Fluctuations". Reprinted in F.A. Hayek (1939), *Profits, Interest and Investment*, London, Routledge.

Hayek, F.A. (1944), *The Road to Serfdom*, London, Routledge.

Hayek, F.A. (1975), *A Discussion with Friedrich A. von Hayek*, Washington, DC, American Enterprise Institute.

Hayes, M.G. (2006), *The Economics of Keynes, A New Guide to The General Theory*, Cheltenham, Edward Elgar.

Hayes, M.G. (2012), "Keynes, the Neglected Theorist", in T. Cate (ed.), *Keynes's General Theory Seventy-Five Years Later*, Cheltenham, Edward Elgar, pp. 35–57.

Heller, W.W. (1967), *New Dimension of Political Economy*, New York, Norton.

Hetzel, R.L. (2007), "The Contributions of Milton Friedman to Economics", *Economic Quarterly*, 93(1), pp. 1–30.

Hicks, J.R. (1946), *Value and Capital, An Inquiry into Some Principles of Economic Theory*, Oxford, Clarendon Press.

Hirsch, A. and de Marchi, N. (1990), *Milton Friedman, Economics and Theory and Practice*, Ann Arbor, University of Michigan Press.

Hood, J. (1998), "Do Corporations Have Social Responsibilities?", *The Freeman*, 48(November), pp. 680–4.

Hoover, K.D. (1984), "Two Types of Monetarism", *Journal of Economic Literature*, 22(1), pp. 58–76.

Hoover, K.D. (1995), "Relative Wages, Rationality, and Involuntary Unemployment in Keynes's Labor Market", *History of Political Economy*, 27(4), pp. 653–85.

Hutton, W. (2009) "High Stakes, Low Finance," *Guardian*, 2 May.

Kahn, R. (1976), "Unemployment as Seen by the Keynesians", in G.D. Worswick (ed.), *The Concept and Measurement of Involuntary Unemployment*, Boulder, CO, Westview Press, pp. 19–34.

Knight, F.H. (1921), *Risk, Uncertainty and Profit*, Boston, Houghton Mifflin.

Kocherlakota, N.R. (2008), "Monetary and Fiscal Overview", *New Palgrave Dictionary of Economics*, 2nd edition, Vol. 5, London, Macmillan, pp. 708–13.

Koutsobinas, T.T. (2011), "Liquidity Preference in a Portfolio Framework and the Monetary Theory of Kahn", *Cambridge Journal of Economics*, 35(2), pp. 751–69.

Krugman, P. (2005), "Is Fiscal Policy Poised for a Comeback?", *Oxford Review of Economic Policy*, 21(4), pp. 515–23.

Kydland, F.E. and Prescott, E.C. (1982), "Time to Build and Aggregate Fluctuations", *Econometrica*, 50(6), pp. 1345–70.

Laidler, D. (1982), *Monetarist Perspectives*, Cambridge, MA, Harvard University Press.

Laidler, D. (1999), *Fabricating the Keynesian Revolution. Studies in the Inter-war Literature on Money, the Cycle, and Unemployment*, Cambridge, Cambridge University Press.

Laidler, D. (2006), "Keynes and the Birth of Modern Macroeconomics", in R.E. Backhouse and B.W. Bateman (eds), *The Cambridge Companion to Keynes*, Cambridge, Cambridge University Press, pp. 39–57.

Laidler, D. (2010a), "Lucas, Keynes, and the Crisis", *Journal of the History of Economic Thought*, 32(1), pp. 39–62.

Laidler, D. (2010b), "The Monetary Economy and the Economic Crisis", Western Economic Policy Research Institute, EPRI Working Paper Series, Working Paper No. 2010–1.

Laidler, D. (2010c), "Discussion", in R. Leeson (ed.), *David Laidler's Contributions to Economics*, Houndmills, Basingstoke, Palgrave Macmillan, pp. 121–7.

Laidler, D. (2012), "Milton Friedman and the Evolution of Macro-economics", Introductory Essay for Milton Friedman's collected writings, revised January 2012. Available at http://economics.uwo.ca/centres/epri/workingpapers.asp#2012.

Leeson, R. (1997a), "The Trade-Off Interpretation of Phillips's Dynamic Exercise", *Economica*, 64(February), pp. 155–71.

Leeson, R. (1997b), "The Political Economy of the Inflation-Unemployment Trade-Off", *History of Political Economy*, 29(1), pp. 117–56.

Leeson, R. (1998a), "'The Ghosts I Called I Can't Get Rid of Now': The Keynes-Tinbergen-Friedman-Phillips Critique of Keynesian Macroeconometrics", *History of Political Economy*, 30(1), pp. 51–94.

Leeson, R. (1998b), "The Origins of the Keynesian Discomfiture", *Journal of Post-Keynesian Economics*, 20(4), pp. 597–619.

Leeson, R. (1999), "Keynes and the Keynesian Phillips Curve", *History of Political Economy*, 31(3), pp. 493–509.

Leijonhufvud, A. (1968a), *On Keynesian Economics and the Economics of Keynes*, Oxford, Oxford University Press.

Leijonhufvud, A. (1968b), "Comment: Is There a Meaningful Trade-Off between Inflation and Unemployment", *Journal of Political Economy*, 76(4), pp. 738–43.

Leijonhufvud, A. (1974), "Keynes' Employment Function: Comment", *History of Political Economy*, 6(2), pp. 164–70.

Leijonhufvud, A. (1981), *Information and Coordination: Essays in Macroeconomic Theory*, Oxford, Oxford University Press.

Leijonhufvud, A. (1994), "Hicks, Keynes and Marshall", in H. Hagemann and O.F. Hamounda (eds), *The Legacy of Hicks*, London, Routledge, pp. 147–60.

Leijonhufvud, A. (1998), "Mr Keynes and the Moderns", *European Journal of the History of Economic Thought*, 5(1), pp. 189–220.

Leijonhufvud, A. (2000), *Macroeconomic Instability and Coordination, Selected Essays of Axel Leijonhufvud*, Cheltenham, Edward Elgar.

Leijonhufvud, A. (2006), "Keynes as a Marshallian", in R.E. Backhouse and B.W. Bateman (eds), *The Cambridge Companion to Keynes*, Cambridge, Cambridge University Press, pp. 58–77.

Leijonhufvud, A. (2009), "Out of the Corridor", *Cambridge Journal of Economics*, 33(4), pp. 741–57.

Leijonhufvud, A. (2010), "Nature of an Economy", CEPR Policy Insight No. 53, January.

Lerner, A.P. (1941), "The Economic Steering Wheel", *University Review*, June, pp. 2–8.

Lerner, A.P. (1944), *The Economics of Control*, New York, Macmillan.

Lerner, A.P. (1960), "Discussion", *American Economic Review*, 50(2), pp. 215–18.

Leube, K.R. (ed.) (1987), *The Essence of Friedman*, Stanford University, Stanford, CA, Hoover Institute Press.

Lipsey, R.G. (1960), "The Relation Between Unemployment and the Rate of Change of Money Wage Rates in the UK 1862–1857: A Further Analysis", *Economica*, 27(February), pp. 1–31.

Lucas, R.J. (1972), "Expectations and the Neutrality of Money", *Journal of Economic Theory*, 4(2), pp. 103–24.

Lucas, R.J. (1973), "Some International Evidences on Output-Inflation Tradeoffs", *American Economic Review*, 63(3), pp. 326–34.

Lucas, R.J. (1976), "Econometric Policy Evaluation", in K. Brunner and A. Meltzer (eds), *Theory, Policy, Institutions, Papers from the Carnegie-Rochester Conference Series on Public Policy*, Elsevier Science Publishers B.V., Amsterdam, North-Holland, pp. 19–46.

Lucas, R.J. (1980), "Problems and Methods in Business Cycle Theory", *Journal of Money, Credit and Banking*, 12(4), pp. 696–715.

Lucas, R.J. (1994), "Review of Milton Friedman and Anna J. Schwartz's *A Monetary History of the United States, 1867-1960*", *Journal of Monetary Economics*, 34(1), pp. 5–16.

Lucas, R.J. (2004), "Keynote Address to the 2003 HOPE Conference: My Keynesian Education", *History of Political Economy*, 36(supplement), pp. 13–24.

Lucas, R.E. and Rapping, L.A. (1969), "Real Wage, Employment, and Inflation", *Journal of Political Economy*, 77(5), pp. 721–54.

Lucas, R.E. and Rapping, L.A. (1972), "Unemployment in the Great Depression: Is There a Full Explanation", *Journal of Political Economy*, 80(1), pp. 186–91.

Mäki, U. (ed.) (2009), *The Methodology of Positive Economics, Reflections of the Milton Friedman Legacy*, Cambridge, Cambridge University Press.

Meccheri, N. (2007), "Wage Behaviour and Unemployment in Keynes' and New Keynesians' Views: A Comparison", *European Journal of the History of Economic Thought*, 14(4), pp. 701–24.

Meltzer, A.H. (1981), "Keynes' General Theory: A Different Perspective", *Journal of Economics Literature*, 19(1), pp. 34–64. Reprinted in J.C. Wood (ed.) (1983), *John Maynard Keynes, Critical Assessments*, London, Croom Helm, Vol. 2, pp. 418–55.

Meltzer, A.H. (1996), "The General Theory after Sixty Years", *Journal of Post Keynesian Economics*, 19(1), pp. 35–45.

Miller, E. (1985), "Keynesian Economics as a Translation Error: An Essay on Keynes' Financial Theory", *History of Political Economy*, 17(2), pp. 265–85.

Minsky, H.P. (1986), *Stabilizing an Unstable Economy*, New Haven, CT, Yale University Press.

Minsky, H.P. (1996), "Uncertainty and the Institutional Structure of Capitalist Economies", Working Paper No. 155, Jerome Levy Economics Institute, April.

Mishkin, F.S. (2009), "Is Monetary Policy Effective during Financial Crisis?", Working Paper No. 14678, National Bureau of Economic Research.

Modigliani, F. (1977), "The Monetarist Controversy or, Should We Forsake Stabilization Policies?", *American Economic Review*, 67(2), pp. 1–19.

Moggridge, D.E. and Howson, S. (1974), "Keynes on Monetary Policy, 1910–1946", *Oxford Economic Papers*, 26(2), pp. 226–47. Reproduced in J.C. Wood (ed.) (1983), *John Maynard Keynes, Critical Assessments*, London, Croom Helm, vol. 1, pp. 451–71.

Nelson, E. (2007), "Milton Friedman and U.S. Monetary History: 1961–2006", Federal Reserve Bank of St Louis *Review*, 89, pp. 153–82.

North, D.C. (1991), "Institutions", *Journal of Economic Perspectives*, 5(1), pp. 97–112.

O'Donnell, R.M. (1989), *Keynes: Philosophy, Economics and Politics. The Philosophical Foundations of Keynes's Thought and their Influence on his Economics and Politics*, Houndmills, Basingstoke, Hampshire and London, Macmillan.

Orphanides, A. (2003), "Historical Monetary Policy Analysis and the Taylor Rule", *Journal of Monetary Economics*, 50(5), pp. 983–1022.

Orphanides, A. (2008), "Taylor Rules", in S. Durlauf and L.E. Blume (eds), *New Palgrave Dictionary of Economics*, 2nd edition, Houndmills, Basingstoke, Vol. 8, pp. 200–4.

Perez, C. (2009), "The Double Bubble at the Turn of the Century: Technological Roots and Structural Implications", *Cambridge Journal of Economics*, 33(4), pp. 779–805.

Phelps, E.S. (1967), "Phillips Curve, Expectations of Inflation and Optimal Unemployment Over Time", *Economica*, 34(August), pp. 254–81.

Phelps, E.S. (2010), "Corporatism and Keynes: His Views on Growth", in R.W. Dimand, R.A. Mundell and A. Vercelli (eds), *Keynes's General Theory after Seventy Years*, London, Palgrave Macmillan, pp. 91–100.

Phillips, A.W. (1954), "Stabilisation Policy in a Closed Economy", *Economic Journal*, 64(254), pp. 290–323.

Phillips, A.W. (1958), "The Relation Between Unemployment and the Rate of Change of Money Wage Rates in the United Kingdom, 1861–1857", *Economica*, 25(November), pp. 283–99.

Pigou, A.C. (1932), *The Economics of Welfare*, London, Macmillan.

Rees, A. (1970), "On Equilibrium in Labor Markets", *Journal of Political Economy*, 78(2), pp. 306–10.

Reuber, G.L. (1964), "The Objectives of Canadian Monetary Policy 1949–61: Empirical Trade-Off and the Reaction Function of the Authorities", *Journal of Political Economy*, 72, pp. 109–32.

Rivot, S. (2011a), "Special Cures for Special Remedies: Involuntary Unemployment in Keynes' Political Writings", *Cambridge Journal of Economics*, 35(4), pp. 785–803.

Rivot, S. (2011b), "Where to Draw the Line Between *Laissez-Faire* and Planning? Keynes and Friedman on Public and Semi-Public Institutions", *History of Economic Ideas*, 2, pp. 69–96.

Rivot, S. (2012),"The Great Divide? Keynes and Friedman on Employment Policy", *Cahiers d'Economie Politique*, 62, pp. 223–51.

Rivot, S. (2013), "Gentlemen Prefer Liquidity: Evidence from Keynes", *Journal of the History of Economic Thought*, forthcoming.

Robertson, D. (1934), "Industrial Fluctuations and the Natural Rate of Interest", *Economic Journal*, 44, pp. 650–6.

Romer, D. (2011), "What Have We Learned about Fiscal Policy fro the Crisis?", IMF Conference on Macro and Growth Policies in the Wake of the Crisis.

Roncaglia, A. (2009), "Keynes and Probability: An Assessment", *European Journal of the History of Economic Thought*, 16, pp. 489–510.

Rosanvallon, P. (2011), *La Société des Egaux*, Paris, Seuil.

Runde, J. (1994), "Keynesian Uncertainty and Liquidity Preference", *Cambridge Journal of Economics*, 18, pp. 129–44.

Samuelson, P.A. (1948), *Economics*, New York, McGraw-Hill.

Samuelson, P.A. and Solow, R.M. (1960), "Problem of Achieving and Maintaining a Stable Price Level, Analytical Aspects of Anti-Inflation Policy", *American Economic Review*, 50(2), pp. 177–94.

Santomero, A.M. and Seater, J.J. (1978), "The Inflation-Unemployment Trade-Off: A Critique of the Literature", *Journal of Economic Literature*, 16(2), pp. 499–544.

Say, J.B. [1803] (1841), *Traité d'Economie Politique, ou, Simple Exposition de la Manière Dont se Forment, se Distribuent et se Consomment les Richesses*, 6th edition, Paris, Slatkine.

Sen, A. (2008), "Rational Behaviour", in S. Durlauf and L.E. Blume (eds), *New Palgrave Dictionary of Economics*, 2nd edition, Vol. 6, London, Macmillan, pp. 856–66.

Simons, H.C. (1936), "Rules versus Discretion in Monetary Policy", *Journal of Political Economy*, 44(1), pp. 1–30.

Skidelsky, R. (2000), *John Maynard Keynes, Fighting for Britain (1937–1946)*, London, Macmillan.

Skidelsky, R. (2011), "The Relevance of Keynes", *Cambridge Journal of Economics*, 35(1), pp. 1–13.

Smith, A. [1759] (1984), *The Theory of Moral Sentiments*, Indianapolis, Liberty Classics.

Smith, A. [1776] (1930), *An Inquiry into the Nature and Causes of the Wealth of Nations*, London, Methuen & Co., Ltd.

Smithin, J. (2003), *Controversies in Monetary Economics*, Revised Edition, Cheltenham, Edward Elgar.

Smithin, J. (2012), "A Rehabilitation of the Model of Effective Demand from Chapter 3 of Keynes's *General Theory* (1936)", *History of Economics Society Conference*, Sainte Catherines (Ontario), Canada, June, pp. 22–5.

Snowdon, B. and Vane, H.R. (1999), *Conversations with Leading Economists, Interpreting Modern Macroeconomics*, Cheltenham, Edward Elgar.

Snowdon, B. and Vane, H.R. (2002), "Rules versus Discretion", in B. Snowdon and H.R. Vane (eds), *An Encyclopedia of Macroeconomics*, Cheltenham, Edward Elgar, pp. 634–43.

Solow, R.M. (1968), "Recent Controversies in Theory of Inflation: An Eclectic View", in S.W. Rousseas (ed.), *Inflation: Its Causes, Consequences, and Control*, New York, New York University, pp. 1–17.

Solow, R.M. (1969), *Price Expectations and the Behavior of the Price Level*, Manchester, Manchester University Press.

Solow, R.M. (2002), "Peut-on Recourir à la Politique Budgétaire? Est-ce Souhaitable?", *Revue de l'OFCE*, 83, pp. 7–24.

Spilimbergo, A., Symansky, S., Blanchard, O. and Cottarelli, C. (2008), *Fiscal Policy for the Crisis, IMF Staff Position Note*, 29 December, SPN/08/01, International Monetary Fund.

Stigler, J.G. (1966), *The Theory of Price*, 3rd edition, New York, Macmillan.

Stigler, J.G. (1988), *Memoirs of an Unregulated Economist*, New York, Basic Books.

Tarshis, L. (1939), "Changes in Real and Money Wages", *Economic Journal*, 49, pp. 150–4.

Taylor, J.B. (1979), "Estimation and Control of a Macroeconomic Model with Rational Expectations", *Econometrica*, 47, pp. 1267–86.

Taylor, J.B. (1980), "Aggregate Dynamics and Staggered Contracts", *Journal of Political Economy*, 88(1), pp. 1–23.

Taylor, J.B. (1993), "Discretion versus Policy Rules in Practice", *Carnegie-Rochester Series on Public Policy*, 39, pp. 195–214.

Taylor, J.B. (2000), "Reassessing Discretionary Fiscal Policy", *Journal of Economic Perspectives*, 14(3), pp. 21–36.

Taylor, J.B. (2001), "An Interview with Milton Friedman", *Macroeconomic Dynamics*, 5(1), pp. 101–31.

Taylor, J.B. (2009), *Getting off Track: How Government Actions and Interventions Caused, Prolonged and Worsened the Financial Crisis*, Stanford, CA, Hoover Press.

Taylor, J.B. (2010), "Macroeconomic Lessons from the Great Deviation", Remarks at the 25th NBER Macro Annual Meeting, May.

Teira, D. (2007), "Milton Friedman, the Statistical Methodologist", *History of Political Economy*, 39(3), pp. 511–27.

Tily, G. (2006), "Keynes's Theory of Liquidity Preference and his Debt Management and Monetary Policies", *Cambridge Journal of Economics*, 30(5), pp. 657–70.

Timberlake, R.H. (2008), "The Federal Reserve's Role in the Great Contraction and the Subprime Crisis", *Cato Journal*, 28(2), pp. 303–12.

Tobin, J. (1965), "The Monetary Interpretation of History", *American Economic Review*, 55(3), pp. 464–85.

Tobin, J. (1969), "A General Equilibrium Approach to Monetary Theory", *Journal of Money, Credit and Banking*, 1(1), pp. 15–29.

Tobin, J. (1970), "Money and Income: Post Hoc Ergo Propter Hoc?", *Quarterly Journal of Economics*, 84(2), pp. 301–17.

Tobin, J. (1972a), "Friedman's Theoretical Framework", *Journal of Political Economy*, 78(2), pp. 853–63. Reprinted in R.J. Gordon (ed.) (1974), *Milton Friedman's Monetary Framework, A Debate with his Critics*, Chicago, University of Chicago Press, pp. 77–89.

Tobin, J. (1972b), "Inflation and Unemployment", *American Economic Review*, 62(1/2), pp. 1–18.

Tobin, J. (1978), "Monetary Policies and the Economy: The Transmission Mechanism", *Southern Economic Journal*, 44(3), pp. 421–33.

Tobin, J. (1981), "The Monetarist Counter-Revolution Today – An Appraisal", *Economic Journal*, 91(361), pp. 29–42.

Trevithick, J.A. (1975), "Keynes, Inflation and Money Illusion", *Economic Journal*, 85, pp. 101–13.

Vaggi, G. and Groenewegen, P. (2003), *A Concise History of Economic Thought, From Mercantilism to Monetarism*, Houndmills, Basingstoke, Macmillan.

Vercelli, A. (2010), "Mr Keynes and the Liberals", in R.W. Dimand, R.A. Mundell and A. Vercelli (eds), *Keynes's General Theory after Seventy Years*, London, Palgrave Macmillan, pp. 63–90.

Wade, R. (2009) "From Global Imbalances to Global Reorganisations", *Cambridge Journal of Economics*, 33(4), pp. 539–64.

White, L.H. (2008), "Did Hayek and Robbins Deepen the Great Depression", *Journal of Money, Credit and Banking*, 40(4), pp. 751–68.

Wicker, E. (2002), "Money Supply Theory and the Great Depression: What Did the Fed Know?", *History of Political Economy*, 34(1), pp. 31–53.

Wicksell, K. (1998), *Interest and Prices*, New York, Augustus M. Kelley.

Wood, J.C. (ed.) (1983), *John Maynard Keynes, Critical Assessments*, London, Croom Helm, 4 volumes.

Woodford, M. (2003), *Interest and Prices*, Princeton, Princeton University Press.

Wray, L.R. (2009), "The Rise and Fall of Money Manager Capitalism: A Minskian Approach", *Cambridge Journal of Economics*, 33(4), pp. 807–28.

Index